BLACK UNEMPLOYMENT

BLACK UNEMPLOYMENT

Part of Unskilled Unemployment

DAVID SCHWARTZMAN

Contributions in Labor Studies,
Number 50

GREENWOOD PRESS
Westport, Connecticut • London

Library of Congress Cataloging-in-Publication Data

Schwartzman, David.
    Black unemployment : part of unskilled unemployment / David
Schwartzman.
        p.   cm.—(Contributions in labor studies, ISSN 0886–8239 ;
no. 50)
    Includes bibliographical references and index.
    ISBN 0–313–30166–2 (alk. paper)
    1. Afro-Americans—Employment.   2. Unemployed—United States.
3. Unskilled labor—United States.   I. Title.   II. Series.
HD8081.A65S38   1997
331.6′396073—dc20   96–42462

British Library Cataloguing in Publication Data is available.

Library of Congress Catalog Card Number: 96–42462
ISBN: 0–313–30166–2
ISSN: 0886–8239

First published in 1997

Greenwood Press, 88 Post Road West, Westport, CT 06881
An imprint of Greenwood Publishing Group, Inc.

Printed in the United States of America

The paper used in this book complies with the
Permanent Paper Standard issued by the National
Information Standards Organization (Z39.48–1984).

10 9 8 7 6 5 4 3 2

*For my grandchildren
Joseph, Adam, and Lianna*

Contents

Tables

Preface

I began thinking about black unemployment in 1988, when it occurred to me that it may have been due to the postwar full-employment policy, which induced a rapid pace of mechanization of production on farms and in the economy generally by reducing the cost of financing investment. The policy cut the nominal interest rate, and by inducing inflation it reduced the real interest rate even more. The mechanization of production displaced more blacks than whites, because blacks were disproportionately unskilled. This was the key idea that set me off on an analysis of the rise of black unemployment. But in this preface I will briefly lay out my main points in the order the book presents them.

Chapter 1 shows that more blacks than whites are unskilled, and that in the postwar period black unemployment grew with unskilled unemployment. I provide a historical explanation of the large proportion of blacks who are unskilled. Blacks came into the urban labor markets from Southern farms beginning in the 1920s, and the movement continued until as late as 1970. They have had much less time to become skilled workers than the European immigrants, who entered in large numbers before World War I. Moreover, in contrast to the European immigrants, who arrived when manufacturing employment was growing, many blacks were still moving into the cities when the demand for unskilled labor in manufacturing was declining. A large proportion of blacks are unskilled because they are historically behind whites. The number of skilled blacks has grown enormously since 1950, but the unskilled continue to represent a large portion.

Chapter 2 discusses the Fed's monetary policy, which was designed to prevent recessions or mitigate their effects when they occurred by reducing the nominal interest rate. The policy thus induced firms to invest in new plant and machinery. By causing inflation the policy resulted in a sharp fall in the real interest rate—the nominal interest rate minus the inflation rate—which lowered the cost of financing the purchase of machinery even more than the policymakers had intended. We must also understand that the Roosevelt administration's wartime policy of raising the wages of low-paid workers increased employers' cost of unskilled labor. The combination of the low real interest rates and the high wages being paid to unskilled workers sharply lessened the cost of machinery relative to the cost of unskilled labor. It was much more economical to substitute machinery for unskilled labor after the war than it had been in prewar decades. The substitution was an important contributor to the growth of unskilled and therefore of black unemployment.

Chapter 3 discusses the wartime policy of raising the wages of low-paid workers. Wages generally were controlled during the war, but the administration's wage-equalization policy exempted low-wage workers from the controls. The wages of unskilled workers rose relative to those of skilled workers, and the skilled-unskilled wage gap did not return to the prewar level until the late 1980s. The minimum-wage policy, which raised the wages of farm laborers, had a particularly strong effect on black unemployment because many blacks worked on Southern farms. The policy induced farm operators to substitute machinery and chemicals for unskilled labor. Over most of the postwar period the relative wages of unskilled workers were high compared to wages paid in earlier decades.

Chapter 3 also shows that the government's postwar policy of subsidizing higher education contributed to the decline in the demand for unskilled labor. The subsidies boosted the supply of skilled labor, which reduced the cost of skilled labor relative to that of unskilled labor. Immediately after the war the GI Bill authorized payments to veterans attending college. Subsidies for higher education continued to increase, especially after the Sputnik-induced scare that the Soviets were ahead in science. The subsidies added to the supply of managers, professionals, technicians, and other skilled workers. The resulting fall in the cost of skilled labor to employers relative to the cost of unskilled labor encouraged employers to substitute skilled for unskilled workers.

The other cause of the decline in the demand for unskilled labor and therefore of black unskilled labor was the growth of manufactured imports from developing countries. The products of low-cost workers in these countries were substituted for those of unskilled U.S. workers. The growth of such imports, which began in the 1970s, was the result of the different administrations' trade liberalization policy. Chapter 4, which examines the case for the policy, argues that it harmed unskilled U.S. workers.

Both black and white unskilled workers suffer from unemployment owing to the postwar industrial revolution brought about by government policies already mentioned. The substitution of capital and skilled labor caused productivity to grow rapidly, which is to say, led to the displacement of unskilled workers. High productivity has been good for skilled workers, but it has inflicted costs on the unskilled. Also, trade liberalization benefited skilled workers by reducing the prices of imports and by raising the output of export industries, which employ large numbers of skilled workers. But it harmed unskilled workers by increasing imports that compete with unskilled labor–intensive domestic industries.

Other theories, including the IQ, the welfare-incentive, and the poverty-culture theories, are examined in Chapter 5, which shows that they do not explain the growth of black unemployment.

Chapter 6 ascribes the failure of poor blacks to receive better treatment from the government to policymakers' lack of understanding of black unemployment, pervasive hostility towards blacks, and the political manipulation of this hostility by both Republicans and Democrats. Moreover, black organizations have not represented poor blacks. Utilizing the problems of the inner cities to advance the interests of their middle-class members, they have fought for affirmative action and other racially oriented policies, which do nothing to remedy the condition of poor blacks.

Chapter 7 examines current public policies, which stress welfare reform and training. Welfare reformers erroneously ascribe black unemployment to the destructive effect of welfare on work incentives. Moreover, since the demand for unskilled labor is falling, programs which train the unemployed for unskilled jobs will not raise employment. The government will not spend the funds necessary to train unskilled workers for skilled jobs, and, in any case, it is too late for most unskilled adults to acquire the necessary training.

Chapter 8 ends the book with policy proposals. The long-range goal must be to reduce the number of unskilled workers by improving the education of disadvantaged children. In disadvantaged areas the public-school systems perform poorly; because these school systems resist change, improvement will require the spur of competition. The federal government should give disadvantaged parents education vouchers usable in private as well as in public schools. The resulting increase in the number of private schools will force the public schools to improve the quality of their services. In addition, more funds should be made available for higher education for disadvantaged youths.

Because the demand for unskilled workers continues to fall, the government needs to fill the gap. To deal with the immediate problem the government should undertake a public employment program for unskilled workers.

In addition, the government should abandon its policy of encouraging imports of manufactured products from developing countries. It should restrict the markets for textile, apparel, electronic, and other products of unskilled labor to domestic producers. The primary goal should be to employ U.S. workers.

Acknowledgments

Francisco Grullon, Togu Oppusunggu, and Persefoni Tsaliki have been capable, hard-working research assistants. Samiha Matin, Julie Barnes, and Karin Ray have provided excellent secretarial assistance. I am grateful to Edward Nell, June O'Neill, Robert Cohen, Anwar Shaikh, Richard Freeman, Jacob Mincer, Edmund Phelps, Sidney Morgenbesser, Nilufer Catay, John Eatwell, Roger Alcaly, David Howell, David Krit, Myron Lieberman, and the late David Gordon for helpful discussions. As always, my wife Gertrude has been a loyal supporter.

1

Black Unemployment

THE RISE OF BLACK UNEMPLOYMENT

In the midst of the current boom, black unemployment persists at a discouragingly high rate. In 1995 the black male unemployment rate—10.6 percent—was nearly twice as great as the overall unemployment rate—5.6 percent.[1] When the boom ends jobs will be fewer, and the rate may return to the average for the 1980s of 15.3 percent.[2] I emphasize joblessness among males rather than total unemployment, since this is the source of many inner-city problems. The large number of single-mother households, which is blamed for many of the ills, is due to men not having jobs, not to joblessness among women. The high rate of incarceration among young men is also due to male unemployment.

More upsetting than the black male unemployment level is the upward trend. The current high unemployment level did not happen all at once; and unless we know the causes of the trend, we cannot explain the high level. Yet efforts to explain highlight the relationships between unemployment and other variables at one time. Even academics ignore the growth and ascribe the high level to blacks' relatively low educational attainment and IQ scores.[3] They try to show the causes of the difference in unemployment rates between whites and blacks rather than analyze the rise of black unemployment. But such an analysis is necessary for an understanding of the high level of black unemployment. Because educational attainment among blacks has improved relative to that of whites, and blacks' IQ scores have not dropped, the fault lies with neither. Without a historical explanation, the causes of the high level of black unemployment will remain unknown. Education and IQ may be blamed for part of the white-black difference at any one time, but not the whole of the current high level. What is more, an analysis linking high black unemployment to low educational attainment is incomplete and therefore misleading.

Without an analysis of the rise, policymakers will continue to drift. Not having made much of an effort to solve the problem, the Clinton administration cannot be said to have failed. But the lack of effort stems from the hopelessness resulting from a lack of understanding. The easiest course for policymakers to take is to follow popular prejudices and blame welfare.

The rise of black unemployment is readily seen. In the early 1950s the unemployment rate for black males was only 5.4 percent—about half the current rate.[4] Black unemployment was higher than white unemployment, but the early 1950s were a golden age for blacks compared to today. Things have gotten even worse for black youths. The unemployment rate among young men and women 16 to 19 years of age in 1995 was 37.1 percent,[5] compared to 16 percent in the early 1950s.[6] Moreover, these numbers understate the magnitude of the problem. Since the U.S. Bureau of the Census defines as unemployed only those who are actively looking for a job, the count of the unemployed excludes the incarcerated and the discouraged jobless who have given up and are no longer in the market. The Bureau of Labor Statistics (BLS) estimates that in 1995 the black male unemployment rate (including the discouraged jobless) was 11.6 percent—one percentage point higher than the official unemployment rate. Employment data give us a truer picture. The fall in the average black male employment rate from 76.0 percent in 1954–1959 to 61.7 percent in 1995 is both more revealing and more impressive.[7] The progeny of this decline are the tragic crime and drug problems.

That inner-city blacks are worse off now than in the 1950s should not be news. The evidence of the unemployment data is supported by graphic descriptions of the worsening life of poor blacks. In the early postwar years children did not give birth, they did not enter schools through metal detectors, they did not buy drugs at the corner; the homeless were fewer, and five-year-olds were not shot in the streets. Because the men had jobs, the big cities were not the crime centers they are today. Senator Daniel Patrick Moynihan, speaking on April 15, 1993, described New York in the 1940s and 1950s:

We were a city that already had a social structure . . . the best urban school system in the world and in many ways, the best behaved citizens. . . . Over on the west side we made a business about Hell's Kitchen and a street warrior caste, but in truth the neighborhood was in a way idyllic. In 1943 there were exactly 44 homicides by gunshot in the City of New York. Last year there were 1,499. . . . In 1943 the illegitimacy rate in New York City was 3%. Last year it was 45%.

This is not evenly distributed across the city. It is 80% in some health districts. There are parts of the city overwhelmed by the social chaos that comes in the aftermath of the inability to socialize young males. It grows worse by the year. . . . The slaughter of the innocent marches unabated: subway riders, bodega owners, cab drivers, babies; in laundromats, at cash machines, on elevators, in hallways. . . . It was a much poorer city 50 years ago; but a much more stable one. One that prepared you better for the uses of prosperity when it came. . . .There is an expectation of crime in our lives. We are becoming captive to that expectation and to the new tolerance to criminal behavior, not only in regard to violent crime.[8]

Then-Mayor of New York David Dinkins responded aptly that conditions in the 1940s and 1950s were hardly ideal. Blacks were excluded from certain neighborhoods, they were the last hired and the first fired, and they were poorer than whites. However, while joblessness was no easier then than now, the unemployed were not numerous enough yet for crime and drugs to disrupt urban black communities. Discrimination was worse in the early postwar years than now, but this comparison does not deny the deteriorating economic and social conditions of the inner cities. Dinkins's comment notwithstanding, conditions have worsened.

While many agree that poor blacks are worse off, we still have no explanation. One reason is that attention has been fixed on blacks' immediate conditions and characteristics blocking their economic success. A true analysis must view unemployment in a wider context. I have emphasized the need for an analysis of the trend. Merely observing the rising trend is of no value unless it is linked to underlying economic forces. The misfortune of poor blacks has its origins in changes affecting the economy as a whole. Analyses restricted to the weaknesses and immediate condition of poor blacks are incomplete and therefore misleading. By itself the information that blacks' average IQ score is relatively low does not explain the rise of black unemployment. Black-deficiency theories dwelling on low IQs, the refusal of poor blacks to abide by whites' work values, and other black characteristics are particularly suspect. At the heart of black unemployment are wide economic changes, not blacks' values.

The road to understanding begins with two facts: many blacks are unskilled and unskilled unemployment has grown. More blacks are jobless now than in the 1950s because they are unskilled, and the number of unskilled jobs has dwindled. Many more blacks than whites are unskilled. Including service workers, laborers, operatives, and farm workers, the unskilled comprise 46 percent of blacks compared to 27 percent of whites.[9] Many blacks being unskilled, the drop in the number of unskilled jobs inflicted losses on more blacks than whites. Joblessness affects black laborers and factory operatives—not black professionals and managers—and black laborers are jobless for the same reason that white laborers are jobless. A larger problem affecting all unskilled workers underlies the growth of black unemployment. The forces propelling unskilled unemployment from 5.4 percent in the 1950s to 10.0 percent in the 1980s pushed up black unemployment. The current boom brought the unskilled unemployment rate down to 7.9 percent in 1995, which was still high.[10] The fact that the black unemployment rate exceeds the unskilled unemployment rate does not deny that much of the story is lack of skill.

In 1950 many more workers were unskilled than now, but as many as nearly one-third continue to belong to that category. Postponing a discussion of the decline in the number of unskilled workers, I emphasize here that many workers still are unskilled. The problems of the unskilled are not confined to the inner cities. The ranks of the unskilled include machine operators, assemblers, checkers, handlers, helpers, laborers, farm workers, cleaners, guards, waiters, food counter workers, and nursing aides. The number of people who are unemployed or threatened by unemployment is large enough to deserve more attention from policymakers.

As much as the losses of jobs by executives due to downsizing of corporations have been lamented by the media, the unemployment rate among executives, administrators, and managers is low. In December 1995 this group's unemployment rate was 2.1 percent, compared to 8.2 percent for operators, fabricators, and laborers.[11] Nor are there many more unemployed executives now than in 1958, when the rate was 1.7 percent.[12] The difference between 1.7 and 2.1 is proportionally large, but the absolute difference is what matters—and it is small. It may not be surprising enough to attract much media attention, but unskilled workers have a severe problem.

The principal causes of the postwar decline in the demand for unskilled labor are three forms of substitution. First, employers have substituted machinery for unskilled labor. Second, they have substituted skilled labor for unskilled labor. Third, imports have displaced unskilled labor. Chapter 2 shows that employers cut their costs by further mechanizing production. The additional machinery displaced unskilled workers and increased skilled employment. But the rise of skilled employment was not entirely due to greater mechanization. Part of the shift from unskilled to skilled workers was independent of the greater use of machinery. Businesses cut costs by employing more managers, professionals, and technicians to displace unskilled laborers and factory operatives. The substitution of imports for unskilled labor, discussed in Chapter 4, has attracted more attention than the other sources of unskilled unemployment.

Benevolent government policies have been the chief source of the worsening condition of unskilled workers. The federal administration's wage-equalization policies during the war together with the great demand for labor for the production of munitions raised the wages of laborers, factory operatives, and other unskilled workers relative to the wages of professionals, managers, and other skilled workers and therefore the cost to employers of hiring them. Because of the unusual wartime conditions, the deleterious employment effect of the egalitarian policy was postponed until after the war. Only after the war did the high cost of employing unskilled labor result in unemployment. That effect was exacerbated by the minimum-wage law, which raised the wages of low-paid unskilled workers, especially those of farm laborers. The problems of the unskilled were also worsened by monetary and fiscal full-employment policies, which by reducing the cost of capital, accelerated the substitution of machinery for unskilled labor. The educational policies pursued by federal, state, and local governments further added to the harm done to unskilled workers. The subsidies for higher education encouraged employers to substitute skilled for unskilled workers by boosting the supply of skilled workers, which lowered the wages employers had to pay to hire them. Like the long-run harmful effects of wage-equalization, the minimum-wage, and full-employment policies on the unskilled, the similar effect of the education policy remains unrecognized. Exacerbating the problem, the policy of trade liberalization allowed the manufactured products of developing countries to destroy the jobs of many unskilled workers. The jobs of textile, apparel, electronics assembly, and shoe workers fled to the Far East, Mexico, Brazil, and other developing countries. One reason the long-run harmful consequences of the benevolent public policies and the trade liberalization policy have not been recognized lies in their timing. The wartime rise of wages increased unemployment, but the effect was spread out over four decades, and the unemployment rate varied over that time for other reasons. Moreover, more attention has focused on total unemployment than on unskilled unemployment.

Following a long tradition of ascribing major economic changes to technological change, to the extent that unskilled unemployment has attracted attention, other writers have blamed the rise on this source. But the role of technological change is much more limited than is commonly thought because it is confined to new products and production processes emerging from new knowledge. True, technology brought about the Industrial Revolution beginning in the eighteenth century, mass production, and the automobile; the latest major technological change is microelectronics. According to some writers, discussed in Chapter 2, in the 1980s computers displaced many unskilled workers. Most economic writings assign government a peripheral role in economic change—the major player being technology, which is treated as an uncontrollable natural force. Even economists use such phrases as "inexorable march" and "forces of technology." To the extent that humans had any role, the heroes are James Watt, Alexander Graham Bell, and Henry Ford, who rode on the backs of anonymous earlier scientists.

However, the major sources of the problem were the policies identified with John Maynard Keynes and David Ricardo. Keynesian full-employment policies speeded the mechanization of production in the postwar period, and Ricardo's ideas inspired trade liberalization. Not justified by an economic theory, the wartime wage equalization policy was the feat of New Deal policymakers, who believed in the justice of greater equality. While the social benefits of subsidizing higher education were thought to be obvious, Edward Denison's estimate of the growth of productivity due to gains in educational attainment was interpreted as justifying increases in the subsidies.[13]

The industrial revolution brought about by the wartime and postwar public policies shriveled the demand for unskilled workers. This effect was neither intended nor anticipated. The economists and policymakers who fought for full-employment policies had no idea that their long-run effect would be to impoverish the unskilled, desolate what became the inner cities, and create the current drug and crime problems besetting them.

The obverse side of the decline in the demand for unskilled workers was the growth of the demand for skilled workers. Over the postwar period the skilled workers' share of total employment expanded enormously. This growth was generated by the government policies already mentioned and was not the inevitable result of market forces. An interesting but usually forgotten fact is that many blacks became skilled workers. As is usual with good news, the gains in the number of skilled blacks is neglected.

As I will keep repeating, after World War II the policies led manufacturers and other employers to abandon unskilled labor–intensive production methods in favor of capital–intensive and skill–intensive methods. Between 1950 and 1993 the number of unskilled workers dwindled from 50 percent of total employment to 31 percent,[14] which is an enormous change. We keep reading about the benefits to the economy, as measured by the gross domestic product (GDP), of the rise in the skills of the labor force. But only the skilled workers benefited. There were losers, and these were the unskilled.

OTHER THEORIES OF BLACK UNEMPLOYMENT

Other theories highlight racial differences. Discussions of welfare's incentive-destroying effect feature differences between blacks and whites.

Although those who disparage welfare dare not risk the mark of racism by characterizing blacks as especially amenable to its attraction, the illustrations carry this implication. Newspaper articles, politicians' speeches, and even academic articles feature blacks in the inner cities. While champions of "welfare reform," a euphemism for removing beneficiaries from the rolls, avoid referring to blacks, there is a theory—the poverty-culture theory—that says that poor blacks in the inner cities deny the larger society's prevalent work values. Welfare benefits, which shelter poor blacks, perpetuate the culture. Were it not for welfare, the harsh world would enforce the work values of the larger society. The theory does not mention work incentives, but the connection is obvious. The vivid descriptions of inner-city life accompanying the theory imply that poor blacks find welfare more attractive than economically similar whites. Thus, Aid to Families with Dependent Children (AFDC) creates islands of shiftless, black, welfare mothers rearing welfare mothers. But why the rise of black unemployment? Was the culture in place in the early postwar years? If so, why was black unemployment low then? A theory of black unemployment should answer these questions, which the poverty-culture theory fails to do.

Welfare reformers emphasize incentives rather than work values. According to the welfare-incentive theory, the choice of welfare over work is rational because minimum-wage jobs do not pay enough to compensate for the loss of Medicaid and the cost of day care as well as the loss of AFDC benefits. The Clinton administration's former chief welfare expert, David Ellwood, agrees with the Republicans that it would be senseless for welfare recipients to give up their benefits and get a minimum-wage job.[15] Reluctantly, Democrats now concede that Charles Murray was right to blame welfare for the worsening condition of blacks.[16] This concession and polls revealing that blue-collar whites condemn welfare recipients as slothful and exploitative have pushed Democrats into the antiwelfare camp. Neither Ellwood nor Murray appears to be aware that their argument implies that poor blacks are more rational than poor whites, not that they are more slothful or exploitative. This theory justifies poor, single mothers no longer being entitled to AFDC benefits in many states. However, the critical question again is: Why is black unemployment so much higher now than in the early 1950s? Chapter 5 shows that the incentive theory is not the answer.

We also have the single-motherhood theory. Many years before being elected to the Senate, while a member of the Johnson administration, Moynihan argued that welfare assistance encouraged single women to bear children. He described single-mother households as festering nests of successive generations of the poor. Moynihan suggested but did not emphasize that many mothers were single because many black males of marriageable age were jobless. Subsequent discussions treat single moth-

erhood as an independent source of welfare dependency, unemployment, and other ills. This theory too does not answer the question: Why
the rise of black unemployment?

Another theory is Herrnstein and Murray's recently prominent and,
because it invokes biology, apparently fundamental IQ argument that
blacks' genetically endowed and therefore immutably low intelligence
dooms them in the modern economy.[17] The fear of being attacked as
racist blocks welfare reformers from publicly adopting this very hot argument. The genetic case is dubious, but blacks' average low IQ test
score cannot be dismissed. Chapter 5 shows that low IQ scores may
account for part of the racial difference in unemployment rates but not
the rise of black unemployment.

We also have the technology theory, which has the virtue of not focusing on blacks and of analyzing the rise of unskilled unemployment.
Because blacks are disproportionately unskilled, this theory may explain
their high unemployment rate; because technological change takes time,
it may also explain the trend. According to the theory, discussed in
Chapter 2, scientific progress destroys some jobs and creates others.[18] To
avoid being discarded unskilled workers must get appropriate training.
As automation displaces assembly-line workers, they should be trained
for the technical and professional jobs that are in demand. We cannot
block and, indeed, should welcome society's cornucopia.

However, "technological change" has become too wide a net, embrac-
ing increased mechanization due to cost changes occurring independently of scientific advances. The shift from using a laborer pushing a
cart to using a conveyor reflects a new choice not a technological advance. Properly defined, "technological changes" includes only changes
in production methods springing from new knowledge. As we will see,
government policies caused the changes in production methods occurring before the late 1980s. Only then did microelectronics, the great postwar technological advance, add significantly to productivity.

Arguing that labor-saving production methods displace workers only
briefly, many economists deny the technology theory of unemployment.
Similar reasoning would lead them to deny the theory advanced here
that government policy caused unskilled unemployment by accelerating
productivity growth. Mechanization raises output per worker—labor
productivity—but, according to the prevalent view, it does not lower the
demand for labor, for output will grow sufficiently to offset the labor-
saving effect on employment. Postponing an examination of this optimistic argument to a later section, I note only its popularity and that this
book takes the opposite position.

The popularity of the technology theory among economists is due to
the role they assign to technological change as the source of long-lasting
changes in the prices of goods and services. Shortages and surpluses of

goods arising from changes in demand or nontechnological changes in supply conditions cause short-run price changes, which are regarded as small movements around trends brought about by technology. From this perspective the advent of electricity was a fundamental change altering the prices of goods and services. By contrast, the effects of government policy are regarded as temporary. Thus, when price controls are imposed, they prevent prices from responding to demand, but they return to their "natural" level when the controls are removed. Economists, of course recognize that government policies can have persistent effects. A minimum-wage law will raise wages of low-paid workers and may do so over a long period. It may also cause long-lasting unemployment. Nevertheless, the prevalent view among economists is that technology is the dominant force for change.

However, government policies may cause large changes in relative prices, and the new relationships may persist. The combined effects of the wartime wage-equalization policy, the postwar full-employment policy, and the education policy together caused the cost of unskilled labor to rise relative to that of capital and skilled labor. The change brought about persistent unskilled unemployment. As we will see, the eventual fall in the real wages of unskilled labor was insufficient to eliminate the unemployment. Once unskilled labor was displaced by machinery and skilled labor, the fall in the cost of unskilled labor did not induce employers to return to unskilled labor-intensive methods of production.

Then there is the theory that unemployment as a whole, including that of skilled workers, is high. According to this theory, the high unemployment rates of blacks and of unskilled workers are not a special problem. This position reflects the Keynesian view that the slow growth of total output is the fundamental problem, which in turn is due to inadequate investment. A consequence is that total output fails to grow sufficiently to maintain high employment. A study by the Organization for Economic Co-operation and Development (OECD) expresses the view that unemployment has risen in member countries since 1970 because the growth rate of output has slowed.[19] In support, the OECD argues that the unemployment rate of skilled workers has risen as much as that of unskilled workers; the ratio of the unemployment rate of the two groups has remained the same. Denying any adverse employment effects of productivity growth, the OECD urges governments to accelerate growth by encouraging technological advance and higher rates of investment and savings. The study also dismisses as trivial the effects of imports on employment.

The argument is hard to maintain in the face of the low overall U.S. unemployment rate of 5.1 percent in August 1996,[20] but the study makes a brave effort. Let us consider it. The study suggests that the U.S. measure of unemployment understates the true level because many workers are in low-paid service jobs. In Europe, where they have the option of generous unemployment and welfare benefits, workers have not chosen to take low-paid service jobs. Therefore, the measured unemployment rate there is higher than in the United States. In August 1996 the unemployment rate in Germany was 10.2 percent; in France 12.5 percent; and in the United Kingdom 7.5 percent.[21] Moreover, according to the OECD, the demand for skilled labor has declined as much as the demand for unskilled labor. We return to this argument later in the chapter.

GOVERNMENT POLICY AND THE DEMAND FOR UNSKILLED LABOR

This book's theory of black unemployment starts with the proposition that it is a component of unskilled unemployment and that the demand for unskilled labor has fallen. To moderate inflationary pressures during the war the administration controlled wages, but to better the lot of the poor it allowed employers to raise the wages of low-paid workers, producing an enormous increase in the relative wages of unskilled workers. The rise in the cost of unskilled labor relative to the cost of capital and of skilled labor encouraged employers after the war to abandon unskilled labor–intensive production methods and to substitute these inputs for unskilled labor. The huge wartime rise in unskilled workers' wages supplemented the effect of the postwar full-employment policy on the cost of unskilled labor relative to the cost of capital.

The government also raised black unemployment by raising the minimum wage for agricultural workers in 1966. The law accelerated farm mechanization and thus the flow of black farm workers from the farms to the cities, thereby increasing the supply of unskilled labor to manufacturing and other industries.

Black unemployment also rose because of the Fed's and the federal administration's full-employment policy, which stimulated investment. The Fed sought to prevent recessions or hasten their end by reducing the nominal interest rate, which is the rate specified on bond certificates or other loan documents. A lower interest rate increases investment by cutting the cost of financing the purchase of plant and machinery, which adds to the total demand in the economy and therefore to employment. The policy had a greater effect than intended, because it caused inflation, which lowered the real interest rate. The Fed reduced the nominal rate by buying government bonds in the open market. Its payments to the bond sellers increased the supply of money, which raised prices. The real interest rate is the nominal rate minus the inflation rate over the life of the loan. It is called the real interest rate because inflation reduces the cost of the loan to the borrower in terms of the dollar's purchasing power at the date of the loan. The Fed's policy had a double effect on the cost of financing—the intended one of lowering the nominal interest rate plus the possibly unintended one of inflation, which lowered the real interest rate more than the nominal rate. Because the cost of financing investment fell, while the cost of unskilled labor did not, businesses increased the rate at which they were mechanizing production. Owing to the wartime wage-equalization policy, the cost of unskilled labor had already risen relative to the cost of capital. The Fed's policy increased the relative cost of unskilled labor even more by reducing the cost of capital. To accelerate the recovery from the recession that began in 1958, the Kennedy administration added to the inflationary pressures by reducing taxes, and President Lyndon Johnson's refusal to increase taxes during the Vietnam War also contributed to the continuing rise in prices.

The full-employment policy made it more economical for businesses to mechanize their production. Owing to the resulting rise in the cost of unskilled labor relative to the cost of machinery, the pace of mechanization quickened after the war. Part of the full-employment policy's effect on investment via the nominal interest rate was intentional, but the part due to the resulting inflation may not have been desired by policymakers. Economists were aware of the risk of inflation entailed by the full-employment policy; however, they minimized the risk. Moreover, the theory underlying the Fed's monetary policy did not take inflation's effect on the real interest rate into account. Indeed, it did not distinguish between the nominal and real interest rates. Furthermore, awareness of the inflationary effect of the policy and the consequences for the real interest rate and investment would not have persuaded the Keynesian economists and policymakers to abandon it. Blind to everything but the immediate effect on employment, they favored increasing total investment.

The long-run displacement effect of the faster mechanization of production was furthest from their minds. The fact that the new machinery once installed displaced workers was of no concern. What mattered was that workers were hired to manufacture the new machinery, and their purchases of consumer goods stimulated production and employment in other industries. Those who raised the question of displacement, if any did, were dismissed as ignorant, unsophisticated Luddites, who were unaware of the long-run effect of productivity growth on total income and therefore on the total number of jobs. Eventually there was no displacement effect. The only problem was the immediate one of unstable demand, whose remedy was an investment-stimulating policy.

The pace of mechanization quickened on farms as well as in manufacturing and other parts of the economy. In the 1950s and 1960s the inflationary policy caused farm workers, including black farm workers in the South, to be displaced by machinery. Thus, the policy was partly responsible for the movement of blacks from the farms into the cities, which added to the unemployment of unskilled workers.

Immediately after the war the federal, state, and local governments also reduced the demand for unskilled labor by subsidizing higher education. The subsidies aggravated the effects of the wage-equalization, minimum-wage, and full-employment policies on black unemployment. The postwar subsidies for higher education added to the inducement to substitute skilled for unskilled labor. By increasing the supply of skilled workers, which reduced the cost to those businesses employing them, the policy encouraged the substitution of skilled for unskilled labor. In the 1940s, as I show in Chapter 3, unskilled workers' wages had risen relative to those of skilled workers. This rise alone tended to increase the demand for skilled labor and to reduce the demand for unskilled labor. The subsidies for higher education kept the relative wages of skilled workers from rising before the 1980s. Too, the resulting increase in schooling together with advances in science improved the skills of skilled workers. Some knowledge of chemistry helped lab technicians perform better. Unskilled workers also achieved higher educational attainment levels, but the skill of laborers, laundry workers, and dishwashers did not benefit. The improvement in skilled workers' skills, however, made them even more attractive to employers.

The education policy was driven by the goal of improving the skill of the labor force and thereby raising productivity, improving U.S. competitiveness in world markets, and enhancing the country's ability to defend itself. In addition, the subsidies were intended to promote equality by enabling many people to attend college and thus lessening the advantages of the rich. It did not occur to policymakers that the resulting expansion of the supply of skilled workers would aggravate the problems of the unskilled.

Finally, government policy promoted a shift from unskilled labor to imports by opening U.S. markets to imports of manufactured goods produced by low-paid workers in developing countries. The policy was justified by the doctrine of free trade, which held that a country benefited from producing the goods in which it had a comparative advantage. Chapter 4 discusses the theory supporting trade liberalization. Policymakers, who were aware that liberalization favored the skilled at the expense of the unskilled, set up programs to train the displaced for skilled jobs. But the training programs did little good.

The government policies had vast economic consequences. The wage-equalization, minimum-wage, full-employment, and education policies brought about an industrial revolution in the postwar period. The productivity growth resulting from increases in the stock of capital per worker and in the proportion of skilled workers affected many markets. The pace of productivity growth was uneven; the more rapid rates occurred in agriculture, manufacturing, and public utilities; and the slower rates took place in the service industries, including retailing, education, medical care, restaurants, and hotels. Because fewer workers were required to produce a given output in sectors in which productivity was advancing rapidly, employment shifted from these sectors into the sectors of slow productivity growth. Indeed, despite its prominence in economic writings, manufacturing now employs no more than retailing. Productivity growth also reduced the prices of television sets, air conditioners, cars, and aircraft. Because the cost of producing these goods fell as less labor was needed, their prices fell. Education, some aspects of medical care, police, and other services became much more expensive relative to manufactured goods. Education did not consume more labor and other resources than before the war, but it now cost more in terms of manufactured goods. Teachers' wages rose along with other workers' wages, as productivity rose in the progressive sectors and therefore as the average productivity level rose. The disparity in productivity growth rates has led to high prices for certain services, thus to some economic problems. The cost of medical care would not have risen as much as it did were it not for the high rate of productivity growth in other economic sectors. This is similar for education.[22]

The other major consequence of the postwar growth in productivity was the entry of married women into the labor force. The higher wages now available made it more expensive for them to stay home. Like the prices of haircuts, restaurant meals, hotel services, and educational services, the price of household service increased. I mention these economic and social changes to show that productivity growth had wide effects. The theory of black unemployment presented here stresses one of the effects of productivity growth. One's confidence in the theory increases with the scope of the phenomena that it explains.

The measure of welfare being the GDP, economists and policymakers have hailed the growth of productivity. As productivity rose, more was produced with the available resources. Currently some economists deplore the Fed's policy of maintaining what they consider to be high interest rates because it tends to reduce the rate of investment, slowing productivity growth. For them the goal of rapid productivity growth is paramount because it increases the GDP. But the postwar policies inducing investment inflicted losses on some. The unskilled lost while the skilled gained. The worsening problems of the inner cities were some of the consequences. Not all blacks were losers, however. The discussion of the tragedy of the inner cities often identifies all blacks with the residents, ignoring the fact that many blacks became skilled workers along with whites.

The black-deficiency theories of black unemployment ignore the context of the postwar period's fundamental economic changes. Their narrow focus on inner-city blacks and on racial comparisons blocks out the underlying economy-wide forces. A correct analysis must take account of the apparently unrelated rapid mechanization of production, of the number and skill of professionals and managers, and of the quantity of imports from developing countries.

PRODUCTIVITY GROWTH AND UNSKILLED UNEMPLOYMENT

Paeans to productivity growth forget the resulting loss of employment. Unless output rises by the same percentage, an increase in output per labor hour will cause employment to fall. If output stays the same and productivity rises by 10 percent, then employment falls by 9 percent. Data for the recovery of 1992 show that productivity growth may in fact reduce employment. That year the output of the private business sector was 2.6 percent higher than in 1991, but productivity was 2.9 percent higher, resulting in a fall in labor hours of 0.3 percent.[23] Moreover, output must increase sufficiently to provide jobs not only for those who are displaced but also for new workers. The rise of output was insufficient to prevent the growth of unemployment among the unskilled.

Because productivity growth was the source of much unskilled unemployment, it merits discussion. It is remarkable that over the postwar period productivity growth has accounted for much more of the increase of total output than the additional number of labor hours. Between 1948 and 1994 the total output of the private nonfarm business sector grew at the average annual rate of 3.4 percent. Inasmuch as the number of labor hours grew at the average annual rate of 1.3 percent, labor productivity increased at the difference—2.1 percent per year.[24]

Capital goods and improved skills were major sources of productivity growth. The quantity of capital goods grew at the average annual rate of 3.8 percent, or nearly three times as much as labor hours. Thus, in 1994 on the average each labor hour was employed with 3.2 times as much plant and machinery as in 1948.[25] Of the total growth in labor productivity, the growth of capital contributed 38 percent. Estimates by the BLS of the gains in skill due to education and work experience indicate that they contributed 10 percent. The rest of the growth of labor productivity—as much as 52 percent—is not explained.

Economists credit a large share of this unexplained part to technological advance. For the present purpose of explaining the fall in the demand for unskilled labor, much of the so-called technological contribution to productivity growth should be credited to the gain in skill. One reason economists put the technological contribution in a separate place is that they conceive of technology as being embodied in new and more productive machines. But knowledge is carried by people, and technological advances are applications of new knowledge. Much of German industry was destroyed during the war, but the economy recovered rapidly because skilled workers retained the knowledge of the production processes. Although the new knowledge adds to the skill of skilled workers, the BLS does not include the resulting skill enhancement in its measure of skill.

Although this book calls attention to the role of government, independent forces were also at work. The capital stock and the number of skilled workers would have grown relative to the number of unskilled workers, the skill of skilled workers would have improved, and science would have advanced without the government's promotion. However, government policies probably made the difference between a low rate of unskilled unemployment and a high rate. Inflation induced by the Fed reduced the real interest rate significantly, the wartime administration's wage-equalization policy raised low-paid workers' wages, as did the minimum-wage policy; and subsidies made higher education affordable for many middle-class families. Moreover, the policy of trade liberalization worsened the problems of the unskilled. Reducing the average tariff rate on dutiable imports from 30 percent to 4 percent over the postwar period had some effect on imports from developing countries.

True, as the number of managers, professionals, and technicians grew, the number of laborers, assembly-line workers, and operators fell. The decline in the demand for unskilled workers was partly absorbed by the increase in the number of skilled workers. The subsidies to higher education enabled some youngsters who would have become factory operatives to become technicians. But the number of skilled jobs did not increase sufficiently to offset the fall in the number of unskilled jobs. Indeed, because the productivity of a skilled worker exceeds that of an unskilled worker, the net effect of the subsidies was to raise unskilled unemployment. If a skilled worker is twice as productive as an unskilled worker, the net displacement caused by an additional skilled worker is one unskilled worker.

This is not to dismiss as unimportant technological advances that displace unskilled workers. Robots can paint cars and tighten screws. Computers and microelectronic controls, the great technological advance of the postwar period, accelerated automation; but, as Chapter 2 shows, the growth of productivity due to such innovations was unimportant before the mid-1980s. Over most of the period machinery and skilled labor displaced unskilled labor because the costs of known capital- and skill-intensive production methods fell relative to the costs of unskill-intensive methods, not because of technological advances. And the fall in the relative cost of capital- and skill-intensive production methods were largely due to government policy. Moreover, even the technological advances did not come out of the blue. Government subsidies for research and development speeded the rate of advance.

In the last few years the fall of manufacturing employment has received much attention, even though it employs only 16 percent of all workers. Those lamenting the performance of manufacturing blame the decline on slow productivity growth. During his first election campaign, President Clinton illustrated the drubbing our manufacturers were getting from foreign competitors with the victory of Japan's VCRs. He linked the Japanese manufacturers' victories to their investments, which raised productivity and their competitive strength. However, it was productivity growth that reduced U.S. manufacturing employment, not imports. The proposed cure for the problem of international competitiveness contributed more to the drop in employment than the alleged problem. What Clinton overlooked was that while employment fell, output did not. If imports were chiefly responsible for the fall in employment, then output would have fallen; this did not happen.

The decline of manufacturing sometimes is seen in the apparent fall of its share of the economy's output. However, the pessimists measure output in current dollars; therefore, measured manufacturing's share fell because manufactured goods' prices fell relative to the prices of services. When output is measured in constant dollars, manufacturing's share is seen to have remained about the same. Manufactured goods' relative prices fell because productivity advanced more rapidly in manufacturing than in services. Compare the changes in prices of television sets, air conditioners, refrigerators, and computers with the changes in the prices of haircuts, a year in college, a day in a hospital, and a restaurant meal. A barber today can cut hair no faster than forty years ago, while the same amount of labor can produce three times as much electrical and electronic equipment.

Displaced unskilled auto workers are worse off not only because jobs are fewer but also because the jobs they get as waiters or retail clerks pay lower wages. Unskilled unemployment has risen, and the wages of unskilled workers have fallen. Retail clerks are no less skilled than assembly-line workers, but they are paid less. Unions have more difficulty organizing waiters and retail clerks than auto workers.

The standard reassurance is that, since productivity growth enables us to buy more, it does not take jobs away. As productivity growth cuts computer prices, buyers do not hoard their gains but spend them on other products. It follows that total employment in the economy does not fall and displaced workers find other jobs. However, the argument that the market works miracles in roundabout ways overlooks a great deal. Since this argument comes up repeatedly in discussions about trade liberalization and other policies, it is important to examine it carefully. The following paragraphs take issue with the usual Panglossian refrain.

First, it treats productivity growth as a momentary change. The argument is that when a technological change raises productivity, the price of the product falls. The use of microelectronic controls enables fewer workers to produce the same number of tires, resulting in a fall in the price of tires. Since consumers spend their gains, real GDP rises. The higher GDP means that, despite the growth of output per worker, there are as many jobs as before.

However, while the theory deals with the effect of a once-and-for-all productivity increase, productivity keeps growing. As the stock of plant and machinery mounts, productivity continues to grow. The installation of new machines does not stop, and persistent productivity growth creates persistent unemployment. True, purchases of machines create jobs: manufacturers of stamping presses hire workers. However, the new investment has been insufficient to offset the loss of unskilled jobs. The continuing expansion of the capital stock has displaced more unskilled workers than the machinery industry has hired to make the new equipment.

Second, the addition to total income resulting from productivity growth may not yield enough jobs of the right kind. The addition to GDP may take the form of higher salaries for skilled workers or more jobs for skilled workers. The growth of total income does not guarantee employment for any particular group of workers. Displaced workers cannot be assured of finding jobs merely because total output has increased.

Third, the argument that productivity growth does not cause unemployment often blames displaced workers or workers threatened by displacement for refusing to accept a wage cut. A shrinking demand for labor should reduce wages, not employment. If workers accept wage cuts, then employers will not fire them. And jobless workers, who accept lower wages, can get jobs. But, because wages do not fall quickly, at least part of the impact of a drop in the demand for labor is on employment. Part of the problem is that workers not threatened by displacement must accept wage cuts to save others' jobs. Employers cannot easily cut the wages of the employees they plan to lay off without cutting those of other employees. Explanations of wage rigidity blame the resistance of workers who have jobs and who will not make sacrifices to save others' jobs. Unions protest wage cuts more vigorously than job losses, and employers are unlikely to invite strikes or to take an action that damages the morale of their workers. In addition, minimum-wage laws prevent cuts in the wages of low-wage workers, and nurses' aides earning low wages may prefer unemployment and welfare benefits to working.

However, the theory errs by ignoring the sequence of changes. Machines displace workers because the cost of labor is high. For wage cuts to save jobs, workers must anticipate being displaced and be prepared to accept lower wages in advance. Accepting lower wages after the machines have been installed will not give them back their jobs. Once machines displace them, there is nothing the workers can do. The machines are in place, and the employers will not get rid of them if wages fall. Indeed, once they are installed, the machines will not be removed, even if sales are insufficient to cover their costs. Stockholders and creditors may take losses, but the machines will keep producing. To keep producing, machines need not yield a net positive return.

Moreover, how much do wages have to fall for wage rigidity not to be included among the causes of unemployment? The problem with the theory is that it blames wage rigidity for any rise of unemployment. This follows simply from the argument that employers will hire additional workers providing the wage is low enough. A more reasonable view is that a fall in the demand for unskilled labor reduces both wages and employment. Furthermore, as Chapter 3 reports, the wages of unskilled workers did fall in the late 1970s and 1980s. And, according to Robert Topel, between 1969 and 1989 real wages of workers at the first decile of the wage distribution fell by more than 30 percent. Thus, the largest declines in wages occurred in groups for which unemployment and nonparticipation rose the most.[26]

Fourth, the argument overlooks the unfortunate effect of unemployment on the opportunities open to unskilled workers. Assuming a homogeneous mass of labor, undifferentiated with respect to skill, simplifies the analysis at the cost of missing the problem. Were unemployment distributed more equally between skilled and unskilled workers and the unskilled could compete on equal footing for any job, the adjustment would be easier. However, the market for unskilled workers is separate from that for skilled workers: they cannot compete for skilled jobs.

THE RISE OF UNSKILLED UNEMPLOYMENT

The increase in the difference between the unemployment rates of unskilled and skilled workers indicates that the demand for unskilled labor fell more than the demand for skilled labor. Unskilled unemployment rose from 5.4 percent in the 1950s to 10.0 percent in the 1980s.[27] Since skilled unemployment rose from 2.6 percent to 4.5 percent, the difference in unemployment rates between the two groups grew from 2.8 percentage points to 5.5 percentage points. These estimates are based on a skill classification of occupations and on estimates in the Census Current Population Survey of unemployment rates by occupation.[28]

One might say that because the ratio of the unskilled unemployment rate to the skilled unemployment rate rose only slightly, the relative demand for unskilled workers did not fall. In the 1950s the unskilled unemployment rate was 2.1 times as large as the skilled unemployment rate. In the 1980s it was 2.2 times as large. Adopting the ratio of the unemployment rates as the criterion of relative demand, rather than as I have done, the difference between the two unemployment rates leads to the conclusion that the demand for unskilled labor fell at approximately the same rate as the demand for skilled labor. Applying this criterion, the OECD concluded that insufficient growth of total output since the early 1970s was the fundamental problem. The OECD study referred to earlier observes that the ratio of the unemployment rates of unskilled and skilled workers has persisted in different countries. However, the inference that the demand for skilled workers fell as much as the demand for unskilled workers does not follow. If the demand for both types of labor had fallen at the same rate, then the unemployment rate among skilled workers would have risen more than the rate for unskilled workers. The same fall in the percentage employed in both groups would have reduced the ratio of the unskilled unemployment rate to the skilled unemployment rate.

Suppose the unskilled labor force at the beginning of the period was 500; the number of unemployed unskilled workers was 27, or 5.4 percent. The skilled labor force at the beginning of the period was 500, and the number of unemployed skilled workers was 13, or 2.6 percent. The assumption that the number of unskilled workers was equal to the number of skilled workers corresponds to the actual numbers in 1950, and the assumed unemployment rates are the actual unemployment rates. If the demand for skilled workers fell by the same percentage as the demand for unskilled workers, then employment in each group would fall by, say, 10 percent. The number of unskilled unemployed would rise to 54, or 10.8 percent. The number of skilled unemployed would rise to 62, or 12.4 percent. Thus, an equal fall in demand for skilled as for unskilled labor over the postwar period should have resulted in a higher unemployment rate at the end of the period.

That the increase in unskilled unemployment exceeded the increase in skilled unemployment is also supported by Topel's estimates of the change between 1967–1968 and 1987–1989 in the total number of jobless weeks due to either unemployment or nonparticipation by adult men in the labor force, classified by wage percentiles. Over this period among men at the first decile the number of jobless weeks increased by 8.5 weeks on the average compared to no change among men above the 60th percentile. Topel also says that unemployment and labor force participation among men above the median of the wage distribution were the same at the end of the 1980s as they had been in the mid-1960s.[29]

That the demand for unskilled labor has shrunk is consistent with findings that the incomes of the poor have fallen. The Congressional Budget Office (CBO) concludes that families with heads of household between the ages of 25 and 34 at the 20th income percentile suffered a loss of real income of 18 percent between 1970 and 1986. Those with heads of household under the age of 25 at the 20th percentile lost 34 percent.[30] Studies of incomes of the poor of all ages show either no change over the whole period or a small gain. Additional evidence is provided by Daniel B. Radner of the Social Security Administration, who reports that between 1967 and 1992 the real incomes of the lowest fifth of family units with family heads under the age of 65 fell at an average annual rate of 0.3 percent. Over the same period the average annual rate of growth for all family units of all ages was 1.1 percent.[31]

While the demand for unskilled labor fell, the demand for skilled labor rose. Those at the bottom are worse off now than early in the postwar period, but the prosperous have gained. Radner reports that between 1967 and 1992 the incomes of those in the top fifth of the income distribution of families with heads of household under the age of 65 rose at the average annual rate of 1.3 percent.

The drop in the incomes of unskilled workers reflects the effect of changes in both employment and wage rates. Studies of changes in wage rates alone also reveal a decline in the demand for unskilled labor. According to Chinhui Juhn, Kevin M. Murphy, and Brooks Pierce, between 1963 and 1989, the average weekly wage climbed by 20 percent. However, wages at the 10th percentile fell by 5 percent, and wages at the 90th percentile rose by 40 percent. Over the same period the variance of the log of wages increased by 72 percent.[32] Income inequality has risen, but wage inequality has increased as well.

WHY ARE SO MANY BLACKS UNSKILLED?

Having heard enough about black problems, many whites ask why their poverty persists. Perhaps this is the important question, rather than why unskilled unemployment has risen. Perhaps the usual answers— welfare, culture, and so on—are correct. After all, European immigrants were unskilled, but their children made it into the professional and managerial classes. Some blacks blame slavery and discrimination, but slavery ended well over a century ago. Although discrimination keeps middle-class blacks out of executive positions, it is not the reason many blacks are laborers, cleaners, and factory operatives—nor is it why black laborers are jobless.

To find out why so many blacks are unskilled, we must go back to 1950 and look at where blacks were then. In that year 80 percent of blacks were unskilled compared to 38 percent of whites.[33] The reason so many blacks were unskilled was that many still were farmworkers, and those in the cities had only recently arrived. The movement was continuing. The migration began only about 1920, when nearly half of black males were employed on farms, many as sharecroppers.[34] They were driven off the farms by changes in production methods. Mechanization of Southern farms reduced the number of black males living in rural areas from 49.0 percent in 1920 to 21.8 percent in 1950.

The mechanization of agriculture continued at a rapid rate. Between 1950 and 1970 in U.S. agriculture as a whole, the capital-labor ratio more than tripled; output per labor hour grew at the average rate of over 11 percent per year, producing an enormous cumulative increase of 238 percent.[35] The output per labor hour more than tripled. Nowhere else in the economy was there nearly as great a rise in productivity. In 1970 on the average, each farmworker was working with nearly three and one-half times as much machinery as in 1950. Farms also made much more use of chemical weed killers and fertilizer. Employment in Southern agriculture was especially hard hit, falling by 65 percent. Mechanization of cotton production was important for blacks; in 1950 cotton accounted for 56 percent of the value of products sold by black farmers. In 1950 less than 1 percent of all cotton was harvested with the mechanical cotton picker, and by 1970 nearly all cotton was mechanically harvested. At the same time productivity was enhanced by the development of mechanical ways to apply chemical herbicides. Between the early 1950s and the early 1970s productivity in cotton farming increased by as much as 365 percent, resulting in no less than an 80 percent drop in the number of labor hours employed in cotton farming.[36] Thus, the continued mechanization of agriculture further shrank the number of rural black males in the 1950s. The proportion fell to 8.2 percent in 1960. More blacks than whites were displaced. In the 1920s the percentage of blacks living in rural areas was higher than that of whites, and by 1970 the percentage was lower.

In the 1950s the demand for unskilled labor by manufacturing industries was beginning to fall.

Black youths worked on the farms, and, as farm employment fell, the black youth unemployment rate rose. According to John Cogan, productivity growth in Southern agriculture accounts for much of the decline in black teenage employment. In 1950 the number of employed black teenagers who were agricultural laborers totalled 46 percent, and over 90 percent of them were in the South. The number of employed black male youths in the United States as a whole fell from 46.6 percent in 1950 to 27.0 percent in 1970.[37]

The proportion of blacks who are unskilled is higher than that of whites because whites have had a huge head start. Invidious comparisons of blacks with European immigrants ignore the history. The last great wave of European immigration preceded World War I, while the black movement from the farms began in the 1920s and came to an end as late as 1970. The Europeans also had the advantage of coming into an economy hungry for unskilled labor. Between 1900 and 1920 the number of jobs in manufacturing doubled. In the 1950s and 1960s, by contrast, employers were replacing unskilled workers with machinery.

Education is another important factor. Black farm children received an outrageously poor education. In the one- or two-room plantation-owned schools all the grades were usually taught together, and schooling ended with the eighth grade. Because the planters shut the schools when they needed more field workers, the children often attended school only four or five frequently interrupted months. The children were barely literate when they came out of the plantation schools. Although the schools in the cities were a vast improvement over the rural system, education remained haphazard. As the rising incidence of out-of-wedlock births indicates, worsening economic conditions exacerbated household instability, and the children suffered.

The concentration of unskilled blacks from rural areas in the inner cities aggravated the problems and made them more conspicuous. As skilled blacks moved to the suburbs, the unemployment rate in the inner cities increased; as the demand for unskilled labor fell, the rate continued to grow, leading to high rates of drug abuse, crime, and single-mother households. Spread out geographically and therefore less vulnerable to the contagious diseases associated with unemployment and poverty, poor whites have less severe problems.

Many more blacks than whites are unskilled today, because they were much further behind at the end of World War II. And, although blacks are still behind, they have come a long way. Many blacks became skilled and left the inner cities. The great expansion of the skilled labor force that was part of the postwar industrial revolution was not confined to whites. For many blacks the transformation of the economy had positive effects; 46 percent of blacks were unskilled in 1990 compared to, as we have just seen, 80 percent in 1950. Astonishing as it may be, the change among blacks was much greater than among whites. The unskilled proportion of whites in 1990 was 27 percent, compared to 38 percent in 1950. The growth in the proportion of blacks who are professionals, technicians, and managers is even more impressive. Between 1950 and 1990 the number increased from 4 percent to 20 percent, while the growth among whites was from 19 percent to 32 percent.[38]

That the skilled proportion of blacks has increased more than the skilled proportion of whites is evidenced by the gains in blacks' relative earnings. June O'Neill reports that the weekly earnings of black men between the ages of 25 and 34 rose from an average in 1940 of 48.9 percent of those of white men in the same age group to 79.4 percent in 1980. Blacks' relative earnings fell by about 5 percentage points in the 1980s,[39] but they were still far ahead of where they had been before the war. David Card and Alan Krueger argue that, because the median black male earns about as much as a white male worker at the 25th percentile in the earnings distribution, the appropriate comparison is between black and white workers at these points in the earnings distributions. Between 1960 and 1990 the ratio of median black male earnings to the earnings of the indicated white male gained 34 percentage points.[40]

Unsurprisingly, the huge change in the labor market left more blacks than whites unemployed. While many blacks became skilled workers, the transformation also increased the unemployment rate among the blacks who remained unskilled.

Because the theory presented here invokes wide economic changes, it explains the rise in the number of black skilled workers as well as the rise of black unemployment. And these are only two of the many changes that the theory explains. The theory assigns an important role to productivity growth, much of which it traces to government policies. There were losers as well as winners, and unskilled blacks were among the losers.

THE GENERAL WELFARE

Policies to promote productivity growth and trade liberalization assume that the United States is a community with shared common interests. The goal is a higher average standard of living, the average performing its usual function of representing the whole. Good policies enhance productivity growth, which adds to the national welfare, as measured by GDP. The economist's credo, which assigns a high priority to productivity growth, carries enormous implications. Unions should not block changes in work methods that raise productivity; subsidies that protect peanut farmers against competition should be eliminated; tariffs that protect inefficient manufacturers should be dropped; and investment, education, and research and development (R&D) should be encouraged. Furthermore, that some people lose should not deter trade liberalizers.

The emphasis on GDP reflects the dominant point of view among economists about the nature of their discipline. Economists emphasize the goal of maximizing output out of given resources. When I first studied economics, my teachers defined the field in these terms. As George Stigler said in 1946 in his textbook *The Theory of Price*, "Economics is the study of the principles governing the allocation of scarce means among competing ends when the objective of the allocation is to maximize the attainment of the ends."[41] Despite equivocations seeking to include within the scope of economics work that does not focus on scarcity and choice, economists commit themselves to this definition. Thus, Paul Samuelson and William Nordhaus list some definitions that do not refer to scarcity, but they ultimately adopt the scarcity-choice definition.[42] Although Gary Becker reports that a well-known economist defines the field as what economists do, he offers the scarcity-choice definition as the more serious one.[43]

In general, economists have adopted the goal of maximizing total output, which is defined to include those goods and services that people demonstrate they want by buying them. Given the implicit assumption that the total resources, including the number of workers, are fixed, maximizing total output implies maximizing productivity. The goal is appealing, inasmuch as a large output makes it easier to attain many ends. Maximizing total output thus is the closest that economists come to defining a general goal. Problems arising from environmental goals not represented by market prices are dealt with by estimating the dollar values of gains in air and water quality. Economic theory argues that a freely functioning competitive market in which many sellers compete for sales and many buyers compete for goods allocates resources efficiently, in the sense that the allocation will maximize total output. Under special conditions efficiency requires large and therefore a few, possibly monopolistic, producers; in general, however, competition among many sellers enhances welfare. Economists are constantly on the lookout for misallocation resulting from government intervention in the market or from monopoly power. As economists, their chief objection to the Soviet economy was that without markets it operated inefficiently. Because the government set prices and outputs, much less was produced than was possible.

However, the welfare of the nation is an elusive abstraction. The GDP measure of welfare is not a completely successful attempt to solve the problems, including those related to the policy issues discussed here. The principle underlying the GDP measure of welfare is that each good and service should be assigned its market value. The GDP is defined as the sum of the values of the goods and services sold plus the costs of government services, which equals the sum of wages, interest, profits, and depreciation allowances. Thus, the measure ignores the problems posed by conflicts of interest. If the incomes of some members increase while those of others fall, then we cannot conclude that an increase in GDP is a gain to the society as a whole. This problem arises in various contexts. When economists advocate the elimination of work rules, they skirt the problem by implicitly assuming that the displaced workers are reemployed and paid the same wages. They assume that productivity growth does not destroy jobs—even those of particular groups—implying that there are no conflicting interests. Were economists to recognize conflicts, this realization would challenge their role as experts in evaluating the desirability of different policies. They could not conclude that policies that raise the GDP benefit society. True, economists sometimes recognize that trade liberalization and the elimination of work rules harm some people, but improving the general welfare, as measured by the GDP, is the overriding consideration.

The fundamental problem is that the GDP measure of welfare ignores the distribution of increments of income. According to the measure, an additional dollar adds the same utility regardless of who gets it. A chief executive gets as much utility from an additional dollar as a floor cleaner. Economists who favor greater equality may doubt that productivity growth that hurts the poor raises the general welfare. In general, productivity growth has harmed unskilled, low-paid workers and benefited skilled, high-paid workers. Were Democrats to acknowledge the distributional effects of policies to promote investment, higher education, and trade liberalization, they might be less enthusiastic.

Economists have decided to ignore the problems relating to distribution. This decision reflects their fear that personal, political preferences would dominate their judgments, robbing them of their claim to scientific objectivity. Conservative (liberal) policymakers would dismiss the recommendations of liberal (conservative) economists as biased. The general acceptance by economists of the rule that market prices measure the value of services avoids this difficulty. Accordingly, in the days of his prosperity Michael Milken was worth 30,000 laborers. The GDP measure of welfare is misleading. The effect of a policy to promote investment on the incomes of unskilled workers should not be ignored, despite general agreement that the policy would raise the GDP.

Economists say that trade liberalization increases the GDP. The economist's ideal world is one in which borders are open to trade, nations produce the goods in which they have a comparative advantage, competition reigns, and productivity growth is rapid. The response to the issue of the harm done to displaced workers is that they should be trained for new jobs and compensated for their temporary losses. This response evades the problem. Judging from the record, few displaced workers will be trained for other jobs, and whatever training they receive is for other unskilled jobs. Because the demand for unskilled labor is declining, the training does not reduce unskilled unemployment as a whole.

Questions relating to scarcity and choice dominate the field. The distributional issue is too conspicuous in debates over trade policy to be ignored. Chapter 4 argues that the major effect of trade expansion in the postwar period has been a shift of income from unskilled to skilled workers, not an increase in efficiency. Most of the so-called gains from trade to the nation as a whole consist of this shift of income. The reluctance to take sides on distributional questions is understandable; but unless economists make judgments on the distributional consequences of policies, their recommendations have a weak foundation. The distributional issue is completely ignored in discussions of fiscal and monetary policy and of education policy, where it is less obvious. However, as Chapters 2 and 3 show, it is important even in these contexts.

A DANGEROUS DREAM

Going beyond loyalty to growth, productivity, and progress, liberals have been carried away by Robert Reich's vision of American engineers, programmers, and systems analysts competing in the global economy. Horatio Alger's symbol of America, the capitalist risen from boyhood rags, has been displaced by Reich's symbol—the engineer flying about the world, talking into a cellular phone and tapping on a laptop at the same time. Today's unskilled workers will become programmers, lab technicians, physicists, and lawyers. So, forward with trade liberalization and an industrial policy in which government-appointed crystal-ball gazers will identify the winners in the global competition among industries. Too bad for unambitious workers who fail to retrain themselves for the new world.

Many economists share the Reich vision. They do not represent it as graphically, but even those who oppose an industrial policy are in favor of the same ends. Conservatives are skeptical about the ability of governments to promote generally beneficial economic policies. They doubt that any policymaking body can pick winners among industries, and they are sure that the dying industries commanding many votes will get the subsidies. Conservatives, also supporting the goals of growth, productivity, and progress, believe that government interference with business does more harm than good. They advocate free trade, low taxes, and the elimination of government regulation of business. Furthermore, to ensure the preservation of a competitive economy, conservative economists continue to support the vigorous enforcement of the antitrust laws by the Department of Justice and the Federal Trade Commission. Here too the goals remain growth, productivity, and progress. Thus even conservatives who have no use for industrial policy agree with liberals on the objectives. In short, they too envision an America of highly skilled workers and highly automated machines.

With one-third of the labor force unskilled, the Reich vision is a dangerous dream. The vision and the great goals of growth, productivity, and progress justify dumping the operatives, assemblers, and helpers into the vast ocean of unskilled workers, forcing them to compete against masses working for what are by American standards abysmally low wages. It also justifies accelerating productivity growth by subsidizing investment, education, and research and development. Vague though the ideas are, they direct policies that harm unskilled workers, who have no place in the vision. Nor do low-tech industries employing hundreds of thousands of laborers, operatives, handlers, cleaners, and helpers and few of Reich's symbolic analysts have a place in it.

NOTES

1. *Economic Indicators*, January 1996, 12.

2. *Employment and Earnings*, January 1996, 160, 162; *Economic Report of the President 1993 (ERP 1993)*, 391, table 38.

3. Richard J. Herrnstein and Charles Murray, *The Bell Curve: Intelligence and Class Structure in American Life* (New York: Free Press, 1994); Andrew Hacker, *Two Nations: Black and White, Separate, Hostile, Unequal* (New York: Scribners, 1992).

4. Bureau of Labor Statistics (BLS), *Handbook of Labor Statistics 1975—Reference Edition*, Bulletin 1865, 146, table 60.

5. *Employment and Earnings*, January 1996, 162.

6. BLS, *Handbook of Labor Statistics 1975*, 63.

7. *Employment and Earnings*, January 1996, 162.

8. Daniel Patrick Moynihan, "Toward a New Intolerance," transcript of remarks to Association for a Better New York, Sheraton New York Hotel, April 15, 1993.

9. Data on employment and unemployment after 1959 by occupations were obtained from *Employment and Earnings*, January issues. Data for 1950 to 1959 were taken from the U.S. Department of Labor, *Manpower Report of the President* (Washington, D.C.: U.S. Government Printing Office, April 1967), 217. The data for the 1950s were for members of the labor force 14 years and over. For later decades, they were for those 16 years and over.

Unemployment rates were estimated by dividing the number of unemployed in each occupational group by the sum of the number employed and the number unemployed. The following occupations were classified as skilled: professionals, managers, salesworkers, clerical workers, and craftworkers. Other occupations were classified as unskilled, including operatives, laborers, service workers, and farm workers.

The Bureau of Labor Statistics changed the occupational classification in 1983. To make the data for 1983 and later years comparable with those for earlier years, they were linked at 1982, for which the BLS supplied data under both classifications. Also, see Chapter 3.

10. Based on *Employment and Earnings*, January 1996, 169, 193, and estimates by BLS, Office of Productivity and Technology, of the growth of total output and of the growth of inputs.

11. *Employment and Earnings*, January 1996, 39.

12. BLS, *Handbook of Labor Statistics 1975*, 157.

13. Edward F. Denison, *The Sources of Economic Growth in the United States and the Alternatives before Us* (New York: Committee for Economic Development, 1962).

14. See note 9.

15. David T. Ellwood, *Poor Support: Poverty in the American Family* (New York: Basic Books, 1988), 138.

16. Charles Murray, *Losing Ground: American Social Policy, 1950–1980* (New York: Basic Books, 1984).

17. Herrnstein and Murray, *The Bell Curve.*

18. Lester Thurow, *Head to Head: The Coming Economic Battle among Japan, Europe, and America* (New York: Warner Books, 1993); Robert B. Reich, *The Work of Nations: Preparing Ourselves for 21st Century Capitalism* (New York: Vintage Books, 1992).

19. *The OECD Jobs Study: Facts, Analysis, Strategy* (Paris: Organization for Economic Co-operation and Development, 1994).

20. As of August 1996.

21. *The Economist* (September 14–20, 1996): 104.

22. For a theoretical exposition, see William J. Baumol, "The Macro Economics of Unbalanced Growth," *American Economic Review*, 57 (1967): 415–26.

23. BLS, *News*, February 14, 1995.

24. Based on BLS, Office of Productivity and Technology, estimates of the growth of total output and of inputs.

25. Ibid.

26. Robert Topel, "What Have We Learned from Empirical Studies of Unemployment and Turnover?" *American Economic Review*, 83 (May 1993): 112.

27. See note 9. Unemployment rates of skilled and unskilled groups and the difference by decades were as follows: 1950–1959 skilled 2.6 percent, unskilled 5.4 percent, difference 2.8; 1960–1969 skilled 2.8 percent, unskilled 6.0 percent, difference 3.2; 1970–1979 skilled 3.9 percent, unskilled 7.8 percent, difference 3.8; 1980–1989 skilled 4.5 percent, unskilled 10.0 percent, difference 5.5; 1990–1995 skilled 4.3 percent, unskilled 8.4 percent, difference 4.1.

28. See note 9.

29. Topel, "What Have We Learned from Empirical Studies of Unemployment and Turnover?", 111, 114.

30. Congressional Budget Office (CBO), *Trends in Family Income: 1970–1986* (Washington, D.C.: CBO, February 1988), 89.

31. Daniel B. Radner, *Incomes of the Elderly and Nonelderly, 1967–92*, Division of Economic Research, Office of Research and Statistics, Social Security Division, Washington, D.C., October 1995, ORS Working Paper Series, no. 68, 38.

32. Chinhui Juhn, Kevin M. Murphy, and Brooks Pierce, "Wage Inequality and the Rise of Returns to Skill," *Journal of Political Economy*, 101 (June 1993): 410–11.

33. See Chapter 3.

34. *Historical Statistics of the United States: Colonial Times to 1970, Bicentennial Edition (HSB)*, 1975, Ser. A76, A78.

35. U.S. Department of Agriculture, Economics, Statistics and Cooperative Service, *Changes in Farm Production and Efficiency, 1977*, Statistical Bulletin No. 612. Cited by John Cogan, "The Decline of Black Teenage Employment: 1950–70," *American Economic Review*, 72 (September 1982): 625.

36. Cogan, "The Decline of Black Teenage Employment," 625–27.

37. Ibid., 624–25.

38. Census of Population, 1950 and 1990. For detailed sources see table 3.7.

39. June O'Neill, "The Role of Human Capital in Earnings Differences Between Black and White Men," *Journal of Economic Perspectives*, 4 (Fall 1990): 30, 36.

40. David Card and Alan B. Krueger, ''Trends in Relative Black-White Earnings Revisited,'' *American Economic Review*, 83 (May 1993): 85–91.

41. George J. Stigler, *The Theory of Price* (New York: Macmillan, 1946), 12.

42. Paul A. Samuelson and William D. Nordhaus, *Economics* (New York: Mc-Graw-Hill, 1985), 4.

43. Gary S. Becker, *Economic Theory* (New York: Alfred A. Knopf, 1971), 1.

2

Capital Goods and Technology

Whenever we read about productivity growth, the automation of production, Japanese competition, or worsening poverty in the Third World, the constant refrain is that technological advance or the lack of such advance is responsible. Indeed, for economists technological change is the fount of social and economic change. Standard histories give railroads, automobiles, and telephones, which are deemed technological changes, credit for laying the basis for the modern age. Within this framework, of course, our well being depends on progress. The underlying theory holds that without continued high productivity growth our children will suffer, and without technological advances productivity growth will stop. The losers, who do not learn the appropriate skills, have only themselves to blame. Our children's prosperity should not be sacrificed to preserve some jobs.

Science does drive on inexorably, forcing industries to shift to new technologies. Historians tell us that the Industrial Revolution began in the eighteenth century with the technological advances in spinning and weaving, the first steam engine, and the all-metal lathe. New machine tools that permitted greater precision in cutting metal were essential for the manufacture of interchangeable parts and thus for mass production. Technology continues to advance, and production is further mechanized—microelectronic controls being the most recent stage. But it is a mistake to equate all mechanization with technological advance.

Because this book argues that in the postwar period it was not technological change that induced businesses to increase their investment in new machines, we must explore the meaning of the concept. A technology consists of the known methods for the production of a good, from which manufacturers can choose. The different processes employ different combinations of unskilled labor, skilled labor, and machines that embody different degrees of automation. Therefore different quantities of capital are involved. Firms choose a particular production technique on the basis of cost. A new technology emerges as new knowledge is applied to develop hitherto unknown production processes. The steam engine, the x-ray machine, and microelectronic controls represented new technologies when they were introduced. A new technology presents a previously unavailable set of alternative production methods. Because it takes time for a new technology to prevail, two technologies for producing a good may exist at the same time. In addition, an old technology may survive because the cost of operating old plants may be low after the fixed cost of the plant and equipment are written down to zero. Also, a primitive, labor-intensive technique may be appropriate for small runs.

Cost decides the choice among production techniques, and technological advances are not the only factors that influence cost. Firms choose highly automated techniques which use much capital and little labor, when the cost of labor rises relative to the cost of capital. Changes in relative costs force businesses to shift from labor-intensive to capital-intensive production methods—to mechanize—and adjustments in wages, interest rates, and the prices of capital goods are critical. The faster pace of automation of production in the postwar period was not the offspring of recent scientific discoveries—most of the relevant ones occurred long before. The great spurt of productivity in the 1950s and 1960s was kicked off by changes in the costs of already known methods of production, which were caused by changes in real interest rates and in wages. Most of the acceleration of automation preceded microelectronics. In the early postwar years, labor-intensive production methods were too expensive, so plants installed faster, heavier, and more automatic versions of old fashioned machinery.

An illustration may be useful. The most labor-intensive method of producing metal screws employs a worker turning them out one at a time with a manually operated lathe. An intermediate stage of labor intensity has an operator of a semi-automatic lathe producing a run by inserting a die designed to cut a particular screw. To produce a run of a different screw the operator replaces the die with another one. At the low extreme of labor intensity, a fully automatic lathe, which needs no operator, continuously produces the same screw. The three methods were known and used during World War II; and as the cost of unskilled labor relative to that of new machinery rose, plants shifted to fully automatic lathes. Not all plants made the shift, and those that did retained manual and semi-automatic processes for small production runs. It was not economical to purchase a fully automatic machine to produce a few hundred screws of a particular design. The three methods of production were part of the same technology, and no advance in knowledge—new technology—triggered the shift. The technology represented a set of production options, and a change in costs forced a new choice. Requiring more capital and less labor per unit of production than the manual and semi-automatic methods of production, the fully automatic production method gained popularity as it became more economical. The great technological change of the postwar period was the introduction of microelectronics, which did not take place until the mid-1980s. The displacement of unskilled workers by machines over most of the postwar period was due to the rise in the cost of unskilled labor–intensive processes relative to that of capital-intensive processes within old technologies.

To distinguish between a technological advance and a choice between known production methods is not nitpicking, for my argument that government policies raised unskilled unemployment depends on the difference. I will argue that the wartime rise in the cost of unskilled labor, partly caused by the Roosevelt administration's wage-equalization policy, and the fall in real interest rates, caused by the Fed's postwar full-employment policy, accelerated the movement toward automation—toward capital-intensive processes—by lowering their relative cost.

Moreover, even technological advances may be spurred by changes in the prices of the various inputs. A new technology is not a haphazard development based on the whims of curious lab scientists; firms encourage research when they expect it to lead to less costly production methods. Depending on what they know about possible production techniques, engineers may anticipate economies from new production processes. The basic knowledge may be around for years before any company recognizes a potentially profitable application and proceeds to develop it. One probably representative company's research laboratory undertakes a project only after an operating division has proposed it and estimated the profitability.[1] This requires that the engineers in the operating division, who are not themselves at the frontier of science, know the basic science. Thus, before the firm develops a new process or product, knowledge of the basic science is widespread.

The applications of new knowledge may go unrealized for a long time. To take an extreme case, the fluorescent lamp was invented 79 years before it was commercially produced. Over the period 1885 to 1964 the average length of time between an invention and the commercial production of a new product for use by industry was as much as 34 years.[2]

Cheap capital promotes automation, killing the jobs of machine operatives, helpers, laborers, and other unskilled workers. Not that the skilled are immune, as technicians learn when their laboratories install automated measuring devices, or as accountants learn when businesses discover financial and accounting computer programs. But machines are more easily designed to do the simple, repetitive tasks of laborers carrying bags of cement and of assembly workers tightening screws than to do complex jobs requiring some training and judgment.

Public policy may change the profitability of different production processes. The postwar movement toward automation resulted from the rise in the relative costs of unskilled labor–intensive production methods brought about by public policy. Technological change contributed only in the late 1980s; most of the displacement took place before that time.

The wage-equalization policy during the war and the postwar full-employment policy raised the cost of unskilled labor relative to that of capital. The Fed's full-employment monetary policy reduced the nominal interest rate, as intended. It also reduced the real interest rate by triggering inflation. Capital goods became a bargain. We have been living in the Age of the Great Inflation. Incredible as it may be, prices in 1940 were no higher than in 1778.[3] After the inflations of the Civil War and World War I prices returned to prewar levels; but after World War II prices kept on climbing, and since 1940 prices have sextupled. So chronic has inflation become that the current inflation rate of about 2.5 percent, as measured by the GDP implicit price deflator, is widely accepted as normal and desirable.

As much as creditors suffered from the inflation, the workers robbed of their jobs by the acceleration of mechanization lost more. Blind to everything but employers' hostility, unions are unaware that increased automation has been due more to the effect of the full-employment policy on the cost of capital goods than to employers' hostility. Economists have been equally blind to the long-run effect of the resulting inflation on unskilled employment. Aware only of the immediate positive employment effect of investment, economists have ignored the long-run negative effect. Moreover, the fear that productivity growth creates problems is dismissed on the ground that the displaced eventually find jobs. The preceding chapter showed that the fear is valid.

Obsessed with preventing or mitigating recessions, the Fed undertook the known inflation risk of implementing easy monetary and fiscal policies, which accelerated inflation. Although the recession of 1960–1961 was long over, Congress reduced taxes in 1964 to stimulate the economy. The justification for these monetary and fiscal policies was the theory that the critical factor in the cyclical fluctuations was unstable investment. To stabilize employment, a fall in investment and therefore in the total demand for goods had to be offset by monetary and fiscal policies. Moreover, the policymakers were unaware of the effect of the wartime wage increase on the demand for unskilled labor. In 1954, 1960, and 1970 unemployment was unacceptably high at least in part because the wartime administration had raised the wages of low-paid workers.

The Keynesian employment theory called attention to the instability of total demand. The victory of the New Economics, as Keynes's followers labeled their theory, exorcised the conventional devils—deficits and inflation. Their thinking was dominated by the memory of the Great Depression, as the Keynesians dismissed the danger of inflation by tagging conservatives' belief in a balanced budget as superstition. With unemployment at a high level in 1960 and 1961, Kennedy's Council of Economic Advisers (CEA) judged the inflation risk to be small.[4] So great was Keynes's influence that, although a quarter of a century had passed since the Great Depression, economists continued to dread its return. Keynes's theory, developed when the Great Depression was at its deepest, argued that severe unemployment would persist without government intervention. Even gloomier was Alvin Hansen's theory of secular stagnation, which said that the investment booms ignited by the coming of the railroads and the automobile were over, and there was no prospect of any comparable opportunity. In the late 1940s and early 1950s economists did not expect the coming surge in construction and in the formation of households. Attributing the end of the depression to war expenditures, many economists expected it to return.

In 1946 Congress passed the Humphrey-Hawkins Employment Act, mandating future administrations to maintain a high level of employment and creating the CEA to advise the president on appropriate policies. Subsequent administrations pursued tax and expenditure policies aimed at full employment, and the Fed took its cue from Congress and the prevailing economic theory that the Act reflected. Throughout the period 1950–1979, the Fed's primary goal was to maintain a high level of business activity. The Fed's and the administration's policies caused inflation. Keynes's legacy was chronic inflation.

THE COST OF CAPITAL GOODS AND OF UNSKILLED LABOR

The Alpha Dress Company does not increase its labor productivity by adding 10 percent more sewing machines and 10 percent more workers. When prosperous, optimistic firms add to their capacity without altering the capital-labor ratio, productivity does not rise, and they do not fire workers. Productivity grows, and workers suffer only when companies use more machinery per employee. Employers will substitute machines for labor when they expect the investment to raise profits.

Profits rule, and even when sales prospects are poor, new machines displace workers when they promise to cut costs. Prospects of sales growth were poor in the recession beginning in 1979. Between 1979 and 1980 manufacturing output fell by 5.4 percent and the number of labor hours fell by 4.7 percent. Nevertheless the capital stock grew by 4.8 percent.[5] Indeed, the growth of the capital stock in manufacturing accelerated that year.

Let us examine the cost of machines. The cost to Reliable Auto of a robot includes the price, which is entered in the profit-and-loss statements as depreciation over the life of the equipment, and the interest cost of financing the purchase. I will suppose that the company borrows the money needed; thus, it must make interest payments. Because it is the real—not the nominal—interest rate that matters, I will be more inclined to buy a car if I expect inflation than if I expect prices not to change. Inflation will lessen the value of the loan that I must repay. If I borrow $10,000 for one year and prices rise by 5 percent, then the $10,000 that I must repay at the end of the year will be worth $9,500 in present purchasing power. Inflation will diminish my cost by $500. An inflation rate of 5 percent decreases the real interest rate by that amount. If the nominal interest rate is 9 percent, then the real interest rate is 4 percent. Because manufacturers expected inflation, and the interest rate did not rise to offset its effect, they borrowed heavily to buy new plants and equipment.

Because firms do not know what the inflation rate will be over the life of the loan, their decisions concerning whether and how much to invest are made according to their expectations. Some economists assume that firms base their expectations on the inflation record of recent years. They estimate the real interest rate in a year as the current nominal rate minus a weighted average of inflation rates in that and preceding years, giving the most recent the greatest weight. Other economists simply subtract the current inflation rate from the nominal interest rate, as in my illustration. Because the current inflation rate may differ substantially from an average of preceding years' inflation rates, the choice of method is important for predicting year-to-year changes in investment. But for the purpose of explaining the change in the rate of growth of the capital stock between the prewar and the postwar periods, either method of correcting the nominal rate for inflation is satisfactory. In contrast to the postwar period, which knew only inflation, the prewar period experienced either no inflation or deflation. The 1920s witnessed little inflation, and the 1930s were a decade of deflation. Either method of estimating the real interest rate would show a large fall in the real interest rate. I have adopted the method of subtracting the change in the price deflator from the nominal interest rate.

After World War II inflation was continuous. The average annual inflation rate between 1950 and 1990 was 4.1 percent. Between 1950 and 1980 the nominal interest rate failed to keep up with inflation, so real interest rates were much lower than before the war (see Table 2.1). Despite inflation, the average nominal interest rate in the 1950s for long-term high-rated corporate bonds was 3.3 percent, which was less than the 3.9 percent of the 1930s and the 5.1 percent of the 1920s. Subtracting the inflation rate left an average real interest rate in the 1950s of 0.8 percent. Between 1950 and 1979 the decade average real interest rates

Table 2.1
Decade Averages of Real Long-Term Interest Rates, 1900–1989, and Average
for 1990–1995

	Percent
1900-1909	2.0
1910-1919	-2.7
1920-1929	5.7
1930-1939	5.3
1940-1949	-3.6
1950-1959	0.8
1960-1969	2.6
1970-1979	1.5
1980-1989	6.4
1990-1995	5.2

Notes and Sources: Moody's Aaa bond rate 1919-1989 from *ERP* 1991, 368 and *HSB*, ser.
X477. Extended by yields of American railroad bonds, *HSB*, ser. X476. Railroad bond
yields were multiplied by 1.04 to bring them up to Moody's bond level. GDP implicit
price deflator was used to measure inflation rate. Real interest rate for each year was
computed by subtracting change in price deflator from nominal interest rate.

were well below the averages for the 1920s and 1930s. The financial markets had not seen such low real interest rates except in wartime. Only in
the 1980s, when the Fed tightened its monetary policy, did real interest
rates reach high levels.

Why did nominal interest rates fail to keep up with inflation? The
theory of interest under inflation, as formulated by Irving Fisher in 1930,
held that the nominal interest rate rises by the anticipated inflation rate.
According to the theory, lenders will insist on being compensated for
inflation. However, Fisher observed that nominal rates do not adjust to
inflation.[6] Even after prices rise, the nominal rate does not rise to compensate for the inflation.

Fisher ascribed the fall in the real interest rate under inflation to savers
who failed to adjust completely to price increases. Savers supply the
funds available for investment. They should reduce their savings when
the real interest rate falls, but they do not. The question arises: Why do
savers neglect to take inflation into account? Economists accept the proposition that the immediate effect of unanticipated inflation is a reduction
of real interest rates.[7] However, when inflation continues over a long
period, such as the one under consideration, it becomes anticipated. Savers' behavior when they anticipate inflation needs to be explained. One
explanation by Robert Mundell argues that inflation reduces real money
balances—wealth—which stimulates increased real savings.[8] People in-

crease their savings to offset the erosion of the value of their balances caused by inflation.

What are the facts? Judging by decade average savings rates, not the annual rates, the percentage of GDP saved by businesses and households has been remarkably stable. If businesses and households are extravagant one year, they are frugal the next year. This observation accords with Milton Friedman's theory of permanent consumption that people's savings are related to their long-term estimates of income, not to current income.[9] An implication of Friedman's theory is that the decade average of the percentage of total income saved will be more stable than the annual percentage. The decade rates of gross private savings between 1950 and 1989 varied between 16.7 percent of the GDP and 17.9 percent.[10] Indeed, as Raymond Goldsmith showed, the decade rates were remarkably stable between 1869 and 1928. Over this period the decade average rates varied between 19.5 percent and 22.7 percent.[11]

Despite this remarkable stability, *net* national savings fell as a percentage of GDP between the decade 1960–1969, and the decade 1980–1989 from 8.0 percent to 3.8 percent. This drop has alarmed some economists.[12] However, the fall was not due to a decline in gross private savings but to the growth of the federal deficit and the growth of depreciation as a percentage of the GDP. Depreciation is subtracted from gross savings to arrive at net savings because net investment is defined as equal to net savings. And net investment is equal to gross investment minus the machinery and buildings that are consumed, which is to say, depreciation. The growth of depreciation, which represents a large part of the fall in the net savings rate, is due to the increased importance of machinery in the capital stock, as opposed to buildings. The rise of depreciation has not caused a fall in the availability of funds for investment. Indeed, those who hope that productivity grows rapidly should welcome the growth in the importance of the machinery stock, which adds more to productivity per dollar spent than buildings.

On the other hand, the rise of the federal deficit, which is the other large part of the fall in the net savings rate, has impinged on the availability of funds, tending to raise the real interest rate. Net national savings is calculated as gross savings minus the federal deficit and depreciation.

The stability of gross private savings demonstrates the insensitivity of savings to the interest rates. For all practical purposes, the sole determinant of the decade average savings rate has been decade average total income.

Another part of the story is that the real wages of unskilled workers rose relative to the cost of financing machinery. Table 2.2 reports an index of the real wages of manufacturing production workers, most of whom are unskilled. Real wages more than doubled between the 1920s and the 1950s. As Chapter 3 reports, the increase was due to the great

Table 2.2
Indexes of Manufacturing Production Workers' Real Wages and Interest
Rates and of the Wage/Interest Rate Ratio (1929 = 100) by Decade, 1900–
1989, and for 1900–1995

		Indexes	
			Wage/
		Interest	Interest
	Wages	Rate	Rate
1900-1909	53	40	134
1910-1919	56	−53	*
1920-1929	92	118	78
1930-1939	113	104	109
1940-1949	149	−70	*
1950-1959	180	15	1222
1960-1969	211	51	413
1970-1979	236	30	781
1980-1989	245	124	197
1990-1995	234	100	236

*Not shown because average real interest rate was negative in this period.

Notes and Sources: Annual price increase: GDP implicit price deflator for 1900-1949 from
   Historical Statistics ser. F1-5, vol. 1, p. 224. Other years from *ERP* 1995, p. 278. Nominal interest rate: Moody's Aaa bond rate 1919-1989 from *ERP* 1995, p. 358 and Historical Statistics ser. X477, vol. 2, p. 1003. Series extended by unadjusted index of
   yields of American railroad bonds, ibid., ser. X476, p. 1003. Railroad bond index was
   consistently lower than the Moody rate for 1919-1930, so it was multiplied by 1.04.
   The real interest rate was computed for each year by subtracting the percentage increase in the price deflator from the nominal interest rate. Indexes were based on
   1929. Source for wages is *ERP* 1995, p. 326.

demand for unskilled labor to manufacture munitions during the war
and President Roosevelt's policy of allowing the wages of low-paid
workers to rise. Effectively, low-paid workers were exempted from the
wartime wage controls.

The index of real wages relative to the real interest rate shown in the
third column tells the story of the rise in the cost of unskilled labor
relative to the cost of financing capital goods. The rise of this index accounts for much of the increase in the employment of machinery per
labor hour. The highest figure, that for the decade of the 1950s—1222—
says that in the 1950s real wages were over 12 times as high relative to
the cost of financing than in 1929. In the 1950s it was enormously more
expensive than in the 1920s to use unskilled workers when machines
could replace them. The indexes for the 1960s and 1970s, 413 and 781
respectively, are not as dramatic, but they also show high multiples. It
had become more profitable to acquire machinery and hire fewer work-

Table 2.3
Indexes of Real Wages, Real Prices of Investment Goods, and of the Wage/
Real Prices of Investment Goods Ratio by Decade, 1930–1989, and for 1990–
1995 (1929 = 100)

	Indexes		
	Investment Goods Prices	Wages	Wages/ Investment Goods Prices
1930-1939	106	113	107
1940-1949	112	149	133
1950-1959	122	180	147
1960-1969	120	211	176
1970-1979	115	236	205
1980-1989	108	245	227
1990-1995	93	234	252

Notes: Index of real prices of investment goods was based on GDP implicit deflator for gross
private domestic nonresidential investment deflated by GDP implicit price deflator
for all goods and services. Index of real wages was based on average hourly earnings
of manufacturing production workers deflated by GDP implicit price deflator for all
goods and services.
Sources: 1930-1959 GDP implicit price deflator for gross private domestic nonresidential
investment from HSB, ser. E1-22. Later years from Survey of Current Business, Janu-
ary/February 1996, 107-15, tables 1-3, and from Bureau of Economic Analysis. Average hourly earnings in manufacturing from ERP 1996, 330 and HSB, ser. D-802.

ers. In the 1980s real interest rates were higher than before the war; but
because real wages were much higher, the index continued to be much
higher than in the first four decades of the century. A 97 percent increase
in the relative cost of labor since the 1920s cannot be dismissed as small.
We also see in the table that the fall in the real interest rate between the
1980s and the early 1990s raised the relative cost of unskilled labor.

The prices of machinery and buildings also declined relative to wages,
adding to the effect of the fall in the cost of financing. Productivity
growth in the investment goods industries allowed the prices of these
industries' products to rise less than wages did. In the 1980s the index
of wages relative to investment goods prices, shown in the third column,
was more than twice as high as in 1929 (see Table 2.3). In the 1990s the
relative cost of unskilled labor continued to increase, resulting in a powerful incentive to substitute capital goods for unskilled labor.

Economic studies have shown that a lower cost of capital goods, including both the cost of financing and their price, will tend to reduce

the demand for unskilled labor. Daniel M. Hamermesh and James Grant report the general conclusion of the related literature that an increase in the use of capital goods will tend to reduce the demand for unskilled labor. Moreover, capital goods are a closer substitute for unskilled labor than for skilled labor. Falling capital goods prices tend to reduce unskilled employment more than skilled employment. In other words, mechanized production methods are more likely to replace laborers than technicians. In skilled occupations ability also increases with experience. Because managers, technicians, and professionals gain experience with age, capital goods are less easily substituted for middle-aged skilled workers than for young skilled workers. One implication, according to Hammermesh and Grant, is that an investment tax credit will reduce employment among those demographic groups having little training and, among those with training, will reduce employment of those with little experience. Another implication is that an employment tax credit subsidizing low-wage workers will reduce investment demand as well as induce the substitution of low- for high-skilled workers.[13]

Reaching a stronger conclusion, studies by Sherwin Rosen and Zvi Griliches show that capital and skill are complements rather than substitutes. In other words, an increase in the quantity of capital goods employed raises the demand for skilled labor.[14] Case studies of the effects of quantity increases of capital on employment in different industries, which are reported later in this chapter, indicate that they tend to displace unskilled workers and to increase the employment of repairers and other skilled workers.

MONETARY AND FISCAL POLICY

It is difficult to exaggerate the Fed's influence on the price level and thus on the real interest rate. When it sought to prevent or mitigate a recession, the Fed attempted to spur the economy by raising the demand for the output of the machinery and construction industries. The Fed hoped that the effect would reverberate throughout the economy. Newly employed workers in the machinery industries would spend more, raising employment in consumer goods industries. The Fed strove to stimulate purchases of plant and equipment by reducing interest rates and thus the cost of financing. By buying government securities in the open market, it raised their prices, which is equivalent to reducing the interest rate. The promised interest payment on any security remained the same; and as the price of the security rose, the yield, which was the promised interest payment divided by the price, dropped, causing the interest rate that businesses had to pay to fall. When banks earn a lower yield on government securities, they demand lower interest rates on loans. Thus, the Fed reduced the rate of interest on commercial and other loans when a recession either threatened to occur or had set in.

The Fed cut not only the nominal interest rate—the rate appearing on loan agreements—but also the real interest rate—the nominal rate minus the inflation rate—even more. When the Fed pays for the securities it purchases, the quantity of money available for bank loans rises. The sellers of the securities deposit their receipts with the commercial banks, adding to their reserves for loans. Rapid increases in the quantity of money resulting from the Fed's purchases inflated the general price level. Tormented by the fear of another Great Depression, the Fed kept swelling the money stock by buying government securities. Because the resulting growth of the quantity of goods sold did not match the growth of the quantity of money, the Fed's actions raised the price level and thus lowered the real interest rate. In other words, the nominal interest rate did not rise enough to compensate for the inflation. The real interest rate fell more than the nominal interest rate, inducing businesses to borrow and buy more machinery and plant. Inasmuch as the Fed did not intend to raise the price level, its policy had a greater stimulative effect on investment than it sought.

That the Fed raised prices is shown by the relationship between increases in the stock of money and increases in the price level. Consider the growth rate of the amount of money in circulation. If the amount of money grows faster than the economy's total output, measured by constant-dollar GDP, then prices go up. If the money in circulation doubles while output remains the same, then prices will double. Thus, according to the quantity theory of money, the difference between the growth rate of the stock of money (say, 6 percent per year) and the growth rate of output (say, 3 percent per year) will equal the rate of inflation (3 percent per year). Controversy arises over the quantity theory because people may keep their money idle or they may run their bank balances down, resulting in a poor explanation of short-term price movements. Moreover, the postulated line of causality from the quantity of money to output and prices may have the direction wrong. As sales pick up, businesses borrow and write checks, increasing the supply of money. However, the theory explains remarkably well changes in the price level over long periods, which are the concern here.

The theory does not work perfectly: the average inflation rate between 1950 and 1990 was higher than predicted, but the difference can be explained. Inasmuch as the money stock, or M2, the sum of currency, checkable deposits, savings deposits, and small time deposits, grew at the average annual rate of 6.8 percent and real GDP grew at the rate of 3.3 percent, the inflation rate should have been the difference, 3.5 percentage points (see Table 2.4). The actual inflation rate was higher—4.1 percent—because the inflation rate of the 1950s was above the expected

Table 2.4
Decade Average Annual Growth Rates of Money, Real GDP, and Prices,
1950–1990 and 1990–1995

	(1) Money	(2) GDP	(3) Prices	(4) (1) – (2)
1950-1960	3.5	3.2	2.5	0.3
1960-1970	7.0	4.0	2.7	2.9
1970-1980	9.5	3.1	6.8	6.4
1980-1990	7.2	2.9	4.4	4.4
1950-1990	6.8	3.3	4.1	3.5
1990-1995	2.4	1.9	2.8	0.5

Notes: Money is M2. Price index is GDP implicit deflator.
Source: Rates of growth were calculated from estimates in *ERP*, various years.

rate. The growth rate of the money stock in that decade—3.5 percent—
exceeded the growth rate of real GDP—3.2 percent—very little. But the
Fed's additions to the money stock were supplemented by excess bank
balances caused by the wartime conditions of the preceding decade,
when the quantity of money almost doubled, price controls were effective, and cars and major appliances were not produced. The table also
shows that the quantity theory does not work well for the period 1990
to 1995, when the average inflation rate exceeded the difference between
the rates of growth of the money stock and GDP. The excess was probably due to the greater use of such money substitutes as credit cards,
certificates of deposit, and deposits with nonbank financial institutions.

The Fed intervened in money markets to reduce the interest rate. The
recession in 1953 and 1954 provoked the Fed to buy government securities. To make doubly sure of inducing banks to raise their lending to
businesses, it reduced banks' reserve requirements, enabling them to expand their lending. The Fed requires member banks to keep reserves
against deposits, including those representing loans. So fearful of a recession was the Fed that it also cut the rate on its loans to banks, reducing
the cost of augmenting their reserves. Member banks keep part of their
reserves on deposit with the Fed. When the banks exhaust their reserves
by adding to their loans, they borrow from the Fed.

The average unemployment rate was as high as 5.5 percent in 1954,
which exceeded the rate in 1951, 1952, and 1953, when the average was
3.1 percent. Part of the problem may have been due to the large increase
in wages during the war. The cost of unskilled labor was much higher
relative to the real interest rate and relative to the cost of skilled labor
than before the war. The Fed had to reduce the real interest rate suffi-

ciently to offset the effect of the high wages as well as the cyclical down-turn in total demand.

With bank balances already high at the beginning of the decade, inflation was inevitable. During the war decade, cars, appliances, and other goods were not available; thus, depositors had accumulated large balances. These balances plus the Fed's additions to the money stock and the expanded lending by commercial banks pushed prices up. By recent standards, the average inflation rate of 2.5 percent in the 1950s was not high. However, because the nominal rate was low, the real interest rate was very low. Thus, as we have seen, in the 1950s the real interest rate on long-term, high-grade commercial bonds was as low as 0.8 percent—lower than in any other decade of this century.

Between 1960 and 1970 the supply of money spurted at the astonishingly high average annual rate of 7.0 percent. Real GDP grew at a higher rate—4.0 percent—than the average for any decade of the century except the first, and this tended to bring prices down. As we have seen, the price level will rise at a rate which is the difference between the growth rate of the money supply and the growth rate of total output. Thus, the predicted inflation rate of 2.9 percent, the difference between the rates of growth of the money supply and real GDP, came close to the actual inflation rate—2.7 percent.

Again, it was the Fed that brought about inflation. Business activity, which had been depressed in 1958 and 1959, was rising in 1960. But, not satisfied with the recovery, the Fed added to the money supply, cut the discount rate, and reduced member banks' reserve requirements.[15] In 1961, still not satisfied with the recovery, the Fed again added to the money supply. The Fed kept expanding the money supply rapidly until 1965.

Over the same period, fiscal policy added to the inflationary spiral. Disregarding the warnings of a recession by CEA Chairman Arthur Burns, the Eisenhower administration stuck to a balanced budget. Despite some recovery, when Kennedy took office the unemployment rate was as high as 6.6 percent. Kennedy appointed three committed Keynesians to the CEA, Walter Heller, James Tobin, and Kermit Gordon, and he consulted with Paul Samuelson, who carried the same banner. Determined to lift the economy, they urged Kennedy to overcome his fear of a budget deficit and reduce taxes.

Calling for action to end the recession, in his first State of the Union Message Kennedy proposed tax incentives for investment, which were enacted in 1962. Companies earned a credit against their taxes by purchasing plant and equipment. The government also reduced the after-tax cost of investment by allowing larger depreciation allowances. To stimulate consumer spending, in 1964 Congress also cut personal income taxes. The tax cuts added to the inflationary pressure by encouraging businesses and consumers to increase their expenditures.

Congress did not need much prodding to enact a large income-tax cut. The legislators now had a respectable theory which taught that, backed as the government was by the economy as a whole, the fear of bankruptcy was inappropriate. The government risked nothing by incurring a deficit. Moreover, as long as the budget was balanced over the business cycle, the public debt would not mount. And the additional government expenditures would add to output by pushing the economy to produce more.

In 1966 investment and consumption expenditures were rapidly climbing, and the Vietnam War and the Great Society programs drove up federal expenditures. Real GDP grew by 5.9 percent, the unemployment rate came down to 3.8 percent, and the inflation rate accelerated to 3.5 percent.

Fearful of inciting more opposition to an already unpopular war, President Johnson made only a half-hearted and inadequate effort to rein in inflation by raising payroll taxes. Moreover, the economists' argument that the costs of unemployment exceeded the costs of inflation countenanced doing nothing. While Keynesian theory did call for higher taxes and interest rates to prevent inflation during boom periods, the CEA minimized the danger of inflation. Another factor undermining taxes as an instrument for restraining the economy was the rejection by Keynesians of the inhibitions against deficits. The theory highlighted the stimulative effect of deficits rather than the problems incurred by a growing public debt. The Fed became the sole agent for stabilizing prices.

The Fed zigzagged. The low unemployment rate of 1966 signaled worsening inflation, but the Fed was under pressure not to end the party. Using the prospect of a tax increase the next year as an excuse, the Fed boosted the money stock by a whopping 8.8 percent between 1966 and 1967. Reversing its policy, in April 1967 the Fed raised the discount rate—the rate it charged the banks for loans. Ignoring the falling real interest rates, Congress and the administration complained about the rise in nominal interest rates and continued to press for an easier monetary policy. Because economists were not yet fully aware of the importance of the real interest rate, the spiraling inflation in the face of a higher nominal rate surprised many. Reversing its policy again in 1968 the Fed relented by cutting its discount rate.[16]

Although unemployment rose in the recession of 1969–1970, inflation continued to heat up. Unemployment climbed to 4.8 percent in 1970, and the inflation rate was up to 5.5 percent. The economy was getting the worst of both unemployment and inflation, contradicting the Keynesian theory. The double disaster was a shock.

The higher priority was still to raise employment; therefore, the Fed added to the money supply even more than before. The money supply grew by 12.6 percent in 1971, by nearly as much in 1972, and inflation worsened. Out of desperation, in August 1972 Nixon ordered a freeze of wages and prices. When the controls were relaxed, inflation speeded up again; undeterred, the Fed continued to add to the money supply.

The growth rate of the money supply slowed to 6.7 percent in 1973 and to 5.4 percent in 1974, but it remained well above the growth rate of real GDP. The sharp rise in the price of oil in 1973 aggravated the inflation. Although real GDP fell in the 1974 recession, and unemployment rose to 5.5 percent, the inflation rate kept rising. Still attempting to reduce unemployment, the Fed sharply increased the money supply, and despite the recovery of 1976, the money supply continued its rapid climb. In 1977 the money stock grew by 10 percent, and prices rose by 6.9 percent. Because the unemployment rate—7.1 percent—remained high, the recovery did not persuade the Fed to restrain itself.

In October 1979, when the inflation rate reached 9.5 percent, the Fed finally reversed its policy, causing nominal interest rates to jump; and it tightened credit further in 1980. The money stock was still growing faster than real GDP, but the deceleration caused havoc. The nominal prime rate jumped from 9.1 percent in 1978 to 12.7 percent in 1979; it continued to rise until 1981, reaching a peak of 18.9 percent. Paul Volcker, the chairman of the Federal Reserve Board, became infamous for activating the worst recession since the 1930s.

Real interest rates remained high. The fall in inflation did not lower real interest rates to the early postwar level. Lenders' inflationary expectations raised nominal rates high enough to more than offset the current inflation. Nevertheless, real wages relative to real interest rates remained above the level of the 1920s and 1930s.

THE SUBSTITUTION OF CAPITAL GOODS FOR UNSKILLED LABOR

Private Domestic Economy

Low capital costs relative to wage costs induced businesses to acquire plant and machinery. Table 2.5 reports that the capital stock grew at a much faster rate between 1950 and 1990 than it had in the three decades from 1900 to 1930. For obvious reasons, I exclude the period between 1930 and 1950. The average annual growth rate of 3.8 percent in the more recent three decades much exceeded the growth rate of 2.6 percent in the earlier period. Although the earlier period is usually thought of as a golden age of growth, the postwar period experienced rapid growth as well. The 1950s may have caught up after the depression and the war. Yet in the 1960s and 1970s, when there was no longer an investment gap,

Table 2.5
Private Domestic Economy: Average Annual Rates of Growth of Labor Hours, Capital, and Capital per Labor Hour, by Decade, 1900–1990 and 1990–1994

	Labor Hours (Percent)	Capital (Percent)	Capital/ Labor Hour (Percent)
1900-1910	2.4	3.2	0.8
1910-1920	0.9	2.5	1.6
1920-1930	0.4	2.2	1.8
1900-1930	1.2	2.6	1.4
1930-1940	-0.7	-0.9	-0.2
1940-1950	1.4	2.5	1.1
1950-1960	0.2	3.3	3.1
1960-1970	0.8	4.3	3.4
1970-1980	1.6	4.1	2.6
1980-1990	1.7	3.6	1.9
1950-1990	1.1	3.8	2.8
1990-1994	0.8	1.9	1.1

Sources: Rates of growth for 1900-1950 were based on estimates in J. W. Kendrick, *Productivity Trends* (Princeton, N.J.: Princeton University Press, 1961), 334-35; rates for 1950-1990 were based on BLS, *News*, July 11, 1994; rates for 1990-1994 were based on BLS, *News*, January 17, 1996.

the growth was faster than in the 1950s. In the 1980s investment continued at a high rate despite the now high real interest rate. Clearly, the high cost of unskilled labor relative to the cost of capital goods remained important.

According to Benjamin Friedman, in the 1980s investment was inadequate.[17] But this judgment is inappropriately based on the percentage of GDP spent on investment. What matters for productivity is the growth of the capital stock per labor hour. Growth of the capital stock proportional or less than proportional to the growth of labor hours does not raise productivity. If firms expand their capacity by adding proportionally to capital and labor, nothing happens to productivity. Productivity rises when each worker operates more machinery. "More machinery" here refers to faster, more automatic machines; to machines with a larger capacity; or to more machines of the same kind.

The average growth rate of the capital stock per labor hour (column 3) between 1950 and 1990 was 2.8 percent per year, compared to 1.4

Table 2.6
Manufacturing: Average Annual Rates of Growth of Labor Hours, Capital,
and Capital per Labor Hour, by Decade, 1950–1990

	Labor Hours (Percent)	Capital (Percent)	Capital/ Labor Hours (Percent)
1950-1960	0.7	3.7	3.0
1960-1970	1.2	4.6	3.4
1970-1980	0.3	4.2	3.9
1980-1990	−0.3	3.1	3.4
1950-1990	0.5	3.9	3.4

Source: Rates of growth were calculated from estimates in BLS, News, January 17, 1996, 14.

percent between 1900 and 1930. The astonishingly high postwar growth resulted in each labor hour working with 3.2 times as much capital stock in 1994 as in 1948. True, the 1.9 percent growth rate of the capital stock per labor hour in the 1980s was below that of the earlier postwar decades, but it was higher than in any of the prewar decades.

Manufacturing

Over the period 1950–1990 the number of labor hours employed in manufacturing grew at the rate of 0.5 percent per year (see Table 2.6), which was less than half the rate for the private economy as a whole (see Table 2.5). Although some economists lament this decline of manufacturing's share of employment as "the deindustrialization of America," its share of total private output remained about the same. Moreover, only in the 1980s did the number of labor hours fall, but this was due to greater productivity—not to a fall in output, as implied by "deindustrialization." Between 1979 and 1990 manufacturing output grew by 24 percent, or at an average annual rate of 1.9 percent.[18] The gains by Japan, Germany, and other countries in world markets are not a sign of U.S. weakness. The United States could not expect to retain the large share gained immediately after the war when Japan and Germany were still recovering.

The growth of the capital stock between 1950 and 1990 was about the same in manufacturing as in the whole private sector. Because the number of labor hours grew far less, however, the growth rate of the capital stock per labor hour—3.4 percent per year—was greater than the average annual growth rate of 2.8 percent in the private sector as a whole. At the end of the period, the amount of capital goods employed per labor hour was 3.8 times as large as at the beginning.

Table 2.7
Manufacturing: Average Annual Rates of Growth of Capital per Production
Worker and per Nonproduction Worker, by Decade, 1950–1990

	Capital/ Production Worker (Percent)	Capital/ Nonproduction Worker (Percent)
1950-1960	3.7	−0.6
1960-1970	3.6	2.4
1970-1980	3.7	2.5
1980-1990	2.7	1.7
1950-1990	3.4	1.5

Sources: Rates of growth were calculated from estimates in BLS, *News*, August 29, 1992, 10;
   BLS, *Handbook of Labor Statistics 1989*, Bulletin 2340, 292; *Statistical Abstract of the
   United States 1992 (SAUS 1992)*, 405.

The rate of capital growth per production worker was much greater
than that of capital per nonproduction worker (see Table 2.7), indicating
that capital was substituted more for unskilled than for skilled workers.
Production workers consist largely of operatives, laborers, handlers, and
cleaners working in the factories as well as more skilled workers, such
as repair mechanics and tool-and-die makers. Overall, production workers are less skilled than nonproduction workers, who include supervisors, office workers, and professionals. The description of changes in
production methods in individual industries discussed later in this chapter shows that capital displaced production workers more than nonproduction workers.

Agriculture

In 1940 as many as 53 percent of black males were living in rural areas;
by 1950 the proportion had dropped to 39 percent; and by 1970 there
was a further drop to 19 percent.[19] Thus, the changes in production methods in agriculture over this period are of special interest.

We see the same forces at work in agriculture as in the economy generally. During the war, wages in agriculture went up tremendously,
much more than in manufacturing. Between 1940 and 1949, the real
wages of hired farm workers increased by 75 percent, compared to 39
percent for manufacturing production workers (see Tables 2.8 and 2.2).
Workers left the farms for the armed services and for manufacturing,
where the wages were much higher. In addition, farms were exempt

Table 2.8
Indexes of Farm Workers' Real Wages, Real Interest Rates, and the Wage/
Interest Rate Ratio (1929 = 100) by Decade, 1910–1989

	Wages	Interest Rate	Wages/ Interest Rate
1910-1919	90	–53	*
1920-1929	95	118	80
1930-1939	77	104	74
1940-1949	135	–70	*
1950-1959	157	15	1046
1960-1969	179	51	352
1970-1979	221	30	737
1980-1989	222	124	179

*Not shown because average real interest rate was negative in this period.
Note: Deflator is GDP implicit price deflator.
Sources: Index for wages was based on *SAUS 1994*, p. 676, table 1100 and corresponding
          table in earlier editions. For years prior to 1970 see *HSB*, ser. 177. For interest rate see
          Table 2.1.

from the wage controls imposed on firms in other industries. Over the
same period real interest rates were negative (see Table 2.8). Farm workers' real wages continued to rise in subsequent periods. In the 1960s the
minimum wage laws were extended to cover farming and resulted in a
rapid increase in farm workers' wages compared to wages in manufacturing. Otherwise, in the postwar period their wages kept pace with
those of manufacturing workers. As we saw earlier, in the first three
postwar decades real interest rates remained below the prewar level,
rising above it only in the 1980s. As a result, in the postwar period real
wages were much higher relative to real interest rates than they were
before the war.

The consequence was the substitution of capital goods for labor. During the 1940s, as workers left the farms for the armed services and employment in other industries, the number of tractors and motor trucks
on farms more than doubled; the number of grain combines nearly quadrupled; and the number of corn pickers more than quadrupled.[20] The
substitution continued after the war, as Table 2.9 shows. Over the period
1947 to 1990, while the output of agricultural products doubled, the
number of labor hours fell at an average annual rate of 3.1 percent. This
was made possible in part by the increase at the average annual growth
rate of 0.7 percent in the quantity of capital goods employed. The result
was an increase of capital per labor hour at an average annual rate of
3.8 percent. In 1990 the quantity of capital goods per labor hour was five
times as great as in 1947. The drop in number of labor hours was par-

Table 2.9
Agriculture: Average Annual Rates of Growth of Labor Hours, Capital,
Materials, Capital per Labor Hour, and Materials per Labor Hour, 1947–1990,
and Various Subperiods

	Labor Hours (Percent)	Capital (Percent)	Materials (Percent)	Capital/ Hours (Percent)	Material/ Labor Hours (Percent)
1947-1958	−4.4	1.7	1.0	6.1	5.5
1958-1972	−3.8	0.4	2.5	4.2	6.3
1972-1982	−1.7	1.0	−0.3	2.7	1.5
1982-1990	−2.8	−0.5	1.7	1.5	3.7
1947-1990	−3.1	0.7	1.3	3.8	4.5

Source: Based on data from BLS, Office of Productivity and Technology.

ticularly large in the periods from 1947 to 1958 and 1958 to 1972. In the
first period the number of labor hours fell by 61 percent, and in the
second by 69 percent.

Materials as well as machinery were substituted for labor. The materials, which include fertilizer and chemical weed killers, are an important
farm input. The growth in the quantity of materials used contributed
more to the increase in labor productivity than did the growth of machinery. The Bureau of Labor Statistics (BLS) estimates that in 1990 the
cost of materials made up 47 percent of the value of agricultural output,
compared to 34 percent for capital goods and 13 percent for labor.[21] The
growth of the quantity of materials used was particularly rapid in the
period from 1958 to 1972. Over the period from 1947 to 1990, the average
annual rate of increase was 1.3 percent, which resulted in a 4.5 percent
rate of growth for materials used per labor hour per year. In 1990 the
materials used per labor hour was over six and one-half times as great
as in 1947.

As Chapter 1 reports, the important changes in the production of cotton in the South during the 1950s and 1960s were the rapid spread of
the use of the mechanical cotton picker and the development of mechanical methods of applying chemical and oil herbicides.

Other Industries

Throughout the economy capital was substituted for unskilled labor.
Beginning with groceries and spreading to other types of retailing, the
self-service revolution, which required increases in inventories and floor
space, was another part of the economy-wide wave of substituting capital for unskilled labor. To permit customers to select their own goods,

Table 2.10
Selected Industries: Average Annual Rates of Growth of Output, Capital
Services, Labor Hours, Labor Productivity, and Capital per Labor Hour, 1947–
1990

Industry	Output (Percent)	Capital Services (Percent)	Labor Hours (Percent)	Labor Productivity (Percent)	Capital Per Hour (Percent)
Retail Trade	3.1	3.6	1.2	1.9	2.4
Wholesale Trade	3.8	5.2	1.8	2.0	3.4
Mining	1.3	2.8	−0.8	2.0	3.6
Construction	2.9	2.8	1.9	1.1	0.9
Transportation (1)	2.5	1.3	0.4	2.1	0.8
Communications (2)	6.6	6.1	0.9	5.8	5.2
EGS Services (3)	4.1	3.3	0.7	3.4	2.6
FIRE (4)	3.8	3.5	2.9	0.9	0.6
Services (5)	3.9	6.2	3.0	0.9	3.2

Notes:
(1) Railroad transportation, local and interurban passenger transit, trucking and warehous-
    ing, water transportation, transportation by air, pipelines except natural gas, trans-
    portation services.
(2) Telephone and telegraph, radio and television broadcasting.
(3) Electric, gas, and sanitary services.
(4) Finance, insurance, and real estate.
(5) Agricultural services, forestry, fisheries, hotels and other lodging places, business, per-
    sonal, and repair services, auto repair, services, and garages, motion pictures, amuse-
    ment and recreation services, health services, legal and other professional services,
    and educational services.
Source: Rates of growth were calculated from estimates provided by BLS, Office of Produc-
    tivity and Technology.

supermarkets must display much more merchandise than the service
grocery, therefore requiring more inventory and more space, both of
which are parts of the capital stock. The word "self-service" suggests
that customers' labor was substituted for that of employees. Emphasizing
the substitution of capital for unskilled labor does not deny the growth
of self-service; but it points out another aspect of the change in retailing,
one that was part of an economy-wide shift.

Between 1947 and 1990 labor hours employed in retail trade grew at
an average annual rate of 1.2 percent (see Table 2.10), which was a little
more than the rate of 1.1 percent for the private economy as a whole (see
Table 2.5). Despite the fact that employment was growing at a rapid rate,
capital was being substituted for unskilled labor. The capital stock per
labor hour increased at the average annual rate of 2.4 percent. Inventories
per labor hour grew at the average annual rate of 2.5 percent.[22]

Table 2.10 also reports the rates of growth of output, capital services, labor hours, labor productivity, and capital per labor hour between 1947 and 1990 for other industries. The capital stock per labor hour grew in all the industries listed. In wholesale trade, mining, communications, and services the rate of growth far exceeded the average for the private economy as a whole, which was 2.7 percent.

TECHNOLOGICAL ADVANCE

A more popular view than the one expressed here is that technological change was the cause of the fall in the demand for unskilled labor, and more specifically that microelectronics was responsible. Studies of manufacturing by Alan Krueger and by Eli Berman, John Bound, and Zvi Griliches support this view for the 1980s. The decline in the relative earnings of unskilled workers leads Krueger to conclude that the demand for their labor fell. He divides workers between college graduates (representing the more skilled workers) and high school graduates (representing the less skilled). He finds that the earnings difference between college and high school graduates increased from 38 percent in 1978 to as much as 55 percent in 1989.

Krueger attributes much of the growing wage gap to the increased demand for workers able to use computers. Between 1984 and 1989 the number of establishments that had personal computers grew from 10 percent to 35 percent.[23] Krueger estimates that between one-third and one-half of the increase in the earnings gap over this period was due to computers. Despite the growth in the number of computer users, the college earnings premium increased.[24]

Berman, Bound, and Griliches attribute two-thirds of the fall in production-worker employment in manufacturing from 14.5 million to 12.3 million, between 1979 and 1989, to technological change.[25] Investment in computers grew rapidly in the 1980s, and the industries that invested heavily reduced the production-worker share of employment more than other industries. The authors estimate that investments in computers accounted for between one-quarter and one-half of the decline in the employment share of production workers.[26]

What I call a change in the cost of capital goods embraces—but is not limited to—technological change, which includes only changes in production methods that are due to new knowledge. Berman, Bound, and Griliches do not limit their use of the expression in this way. Their procedure for estimating the change in employment due to technology includes the change due to mechanization generally and to greater use of skilled workers.

Moreover, contrary to these writers, the shift from unskilled to skilled workers even in the 1980s was due to their relative costs within the old technology. Krueger and Berman, Bound, and Griliches say that the growth in the use of computers took place largely in the latter half of the 1980s. But, as their own data show, virtually all of the shift from unskilled to skilled workers took place in 1980, 1981, and 1982.[27] The unskilled workers were displaced by skilled workers before the rapid growth of computer use.

CHANGES IN PRODUCTION METHODS

The following discussion is based largely on studies by the Bureau of Labor Statistics (BLS); they describe the automation of production in numerous industries.

Textiles

In 1993 the textile industry employed 39 percent fewer labor hours than in 1949.[28] Because output was as much as 3.5 times as large, productivity gains were largely responsible for the decline, not imports. Output per labor hour was 5.6 times as large. The number of production workers fell much more than the number of nonproduction workers. The number of nonproduction workers fell by only 17 percent.[29]

Unskilled jobs were eradicated by faster, more automated machinery. Many yarn mills adopted a continuous opening-blending-carding operation, eliminating the manual transfer of fiber from machine to machine and the process of picking; this increased output per labor hour three or four times.[30] The shift from ring to rotor spinning, which removed two processes of drawing and one of roving, raised productivity four to five times. Also, automatic doffing machinery replaced manual doffing, one of the most labor–intensive operations; and the new shuttleless looms were faster and required fewer operators and maintenance workers than shuttle looms. In addition, the new electronically monitored looms and the new continuous dyeing and finishing operations, which also used electronic controls, eliminated the need for unskilled workers. The changes increased the employment of skilled programmers and repairers.

Perhaps the most important cause of the displacement of unskilled workers was the mechanization of handling and transporting materials and of warehouse operations. Mills began to use computers for directing the movement of materials, whose handling and transport was increasingly mechanized. Some mills began to use robots to place filling yarn on a conveyor belt for transfer to the weaving shed. Another change that reduced the need for unskilled maintenance workers was the use of vacuum devices to clean the machines.

Moreover, the skill requirements for the less skilled jobs declined. The newer machines were more complex than those they replaced, but they were more automated and required less manual dexterity and speed of movement by operators.

The more modern mills employed more highly skilled technicians and engineers, and managers needed more technical skills. Thus, a plant manager had to analyze the computer information now available for every loom.

Motor Vehicles

Despite growing competition from imports, between 1957 and 1988 the output of the motor vehicle industry more than tripled. The number of production-worker hours grew by only 18 percent, and that of non-production-worker hours by 14 percent.[31] Productivity increased at the rate of 3.1 percent per year.

Machine lines that manufacture and assemble engines, transmissions, and other components became more automated. Numerical control, direct computer control, or programmable controllers operated the machines. Bolts were inserted and torqued automatically, and automatic equipment tested valves and speed controls. The number of robots increased, each replacing at least one worker per shift. The applications included spotwelding, painting, materials handling, and assembly operations. The quality of the work did not suffer. A robot painted with greater consistency than skilled painters. In 1983 about one-half of all assembly welding operations were performed by robots and other automatic welding equipment. Robots transferred parts between pallets or conveyors, loaded and unloaded machines, applied sealant around the edges of windshields; in engine plants they removed the burrs from holes drilled into crankshafts, and they tightened spark plugs. The robots displaced unskilled workers, but their maintenance and repair required skilled labor.[32]

New, more conventional machines, including metal-cutting and metal-forming machines, had automatic controls and were faster than their predecessors. Coats of titanium oxide, tungsten carbide, or ceramic composites enabled cutting edges to remove metal up to twice as fast as uncoated edges. New stamping presses enabled operators to save half the time required to change the dies. They were more expensive than the older machines and required more floor space.[33]

Among occupations, operatives showed the slowest growth. Automatic and programmable controllers were being used on many metal-cutting and metal-forming machines, and more of the handling and assembly operations were performed by robots or automatic devices. Simple checks to insure that bolts were installed were automated. Even complete tests of assembled engines were more automated. Welding and painting tasks were done by robots and advanced automatic equipment.

The changes reduced the number of jobs for drill press and punch press, lathe, and milling and planing machine operators, as well as those for welders, spray painters, and testing and inspecting operatives.

On the other hand, the increased use of complicated equipment required more sophisticated maintenance, increasing the demand for skilled millwrights, maintenance mechanics, and electricians to install, maintain, and repair robots, programmable controllers and other automated equipment. Greater use of computers, data networks, and statistical analysis affected management, professional, and technical workers, who now required training in computer and statistical techniques.

Tires

Between 1950 and 1988 the output of the tire and inner tube industry grew more than two and one-half times. The number of production-worker hours fell by as much as 29 percent, and the number of non-production-worker hours fell by 25 percent. Output per employee hour increased at an average annual rate of 3.5 percent.

The application of microelectronic technology quickened the pace of automation in several operations, including stock preparation and mixing of materials; component preparation or extrusion of treads; the application of liquid to steel, fiberglass, or polyester webs to form the piles; assembling components on building drums; the control of steam and temperature cycles in molding; and testing and inspection. When tire-building microprocessors were consolidated into a computer-controlled station, a computer program controlled the building of the tires after the components were taken to a station. Only one or two workers were needed to monitor a station, sharply reducing the labor requirements.[34] The use of microprocessors for testing diminished the number of workers employed in visual inspection.

Greater efficiency was gained in maintenance. Traditional craft workers were replaced by fewer multicraft workers. In one company, three basic classifications—mechanic-machinist, electrician-instrument repairer, and general craft worker—replaced the previous 10 or 12 crafts. The multicraft workers made the needed repairs in about 90 percent of the breakdowns. Salaried workers having specialized expertise in sophisticated hydraulic or electrical problems handled the remaining 10 percent of the problems.

The use of computers to coordinate microprocessor-controlled instruments and computer-aided design reduced the number of operators needed. The number of programmers increased, but the increase was not large. In one case the new computer technology reduced the need for skilled workers. The development of computer-assisted drafting eliminated the jobs of drafters, but those still employed needed more training in mathematics.

Gray Iron Foundries

Between 1954 and 1988 the output of gray iron foundries increased by 34 percent, the number of production-worker hours fell by 33 percent, and the number of nonproduction-worker hours grew by 10 percent.[35]

Manual handling of materials continued to be replaced by conveyors, trucks, cranes, and hoists. Between 1963 and 1977 the number of trucks and loaders nearly doubled, and average conveyor footage increased from just under 700 per foundry to 1,100. In automated molding systems, conveyors transport molds from the machine; the molds are poured and moved to shakeout, and bottom boards and flasks are returned in a continuous process to the molding machine.

Mechanization increased the employment of engineers, technicians, and maintenance workers relative to that of manual workers.[36] Production workers constituted a smaller fraction of the total work force, and, as automatic machinery and no-bake processes were introduced, the number of those performing manual tasks fell. Greater use of improved trucks, hoists, and conveyors required fewer hand laborers but more truck operators to move materials through production tasks. More maintenance mechanics and repairers serviced more complex equipment, and industrial robots assumed some functions, especially where heat, dust, noise, and fumes polluted the environment.

Electrical and Electronic Equipment

In 1993 the output of the electrical and electronic equipment industries was 11.5 times as large as in 1950, the number of labor hours was 2.2 as great, and the average annual rate of increase of output per labor hour was 3.8 percent.[37]

While many operations in manufacturing semiconductors were automated, the loading and unloading of trays of wafers remained labor-intensive. The fabrication and testing of equipment also continued to be labor-intensive. High equipment costs limited automation, but rising labor costs and the improvement of packaging technology increased the use of automated equipment. The shift from the production of electron tubes, which employed many assemblers, machine operators, and inspectors, to semiconductors increased the employment of engineers and technicians and reduced the employment of unskilled workers.[38]

The production processes of appliance manufacturing changed. Larger capacity presses fed from coils of sheet metal produced components at high speeds with little manual handling. The automation of assembly

lines shifted the tasks of workers to machine monitoring, machine loading and unloading, and machine maintenance.[39]

Hydraulic Cement

Between 1947 and 1988, the hydraulic cement industry reduced employment of its production workers by 63 percent and of its nonproduction workers by 12 percent. Yet the industry's output grew by 70
percent.[40]

New bag-filling machines, automatic palletizing, forklifts, and automated record keeping increased productivity in the filling, handling, and
loading of cement bags. Mechanization increased the employment of
control room operators and skilled maintenance workers, while reducing
that of operatives, transport equipment operatives, and laborers. The
new equipment included sensors which signalled impending breakdowns, but the more complex maintenance jobs required a knowledge
of electronics.[41]

Hosiery

Between 1947 and 1988 hosiery output increased by 264 percent, while
production-worker employment fell by 63 percent and nonproduction
worker employment by 36 percent.[42] Hosiery manufacturing employs a
relatively high proportion of unskilled workers. In 1982 production
workers were 90 percent of total employment, compared to 68 percent
in all manufacturing.[43]

The four-feed knitting machines, which replaced the two-feed machines, reduced the time required to knit a pantyhose blank from ten
minutes to one minute. The new machines had automatic lubrication
controls; automatic stop motion controls for needle and thread breakage;
and they used fewer knitters and fixers. The new double-cylinder
knitting machines for men's dress socks produced the true rib pattern
30 to 40 percent faster than the older machines.

In some mills the panty-sewing operation, which follows the knitting
of the blanks, was done by automatic line-closing machines, replacing
the manually operated sewing machine. The automatic gusset seamer
sewed in the crotch; the operator merely loaded the garment on the
seamer and monitored the machine. New toe-closing machines, which
combined the toe-turning and sewing operations, required less manual
work, especially for positioning. They doubled the output per operator
hour associated with the earlier sewing machines. New dyeing machines
employed half the labor of older machines by combining dyeing with
extracting. Maintenance was more complicated, requiring a knowledge
of electronic controls. New packaging machines reduced labor require-

ments to half that of the older manual operations by automatically folding, packaging, and labeling the hosiery. Also, mechanized conveyors replaced the manual movement of carts.[44]

Increasingly automated sewing machines reduced the number of operators, who constitute the largest occupational group, by about 20 percent between 1970 and 1981. Automated equipment replaced baggers, folders, boxers, and packaging-machine operators, who constitute the second largest group, by 50 percent. Automation reduced the downtime of seamless hosiery knitting machines and simplified the tasks of knitters. In 1981 there were 60 percent fewer knitters than in 1970. The skills required of fixers, who were involved in machine repair, maintenance, and style changes, increased. Over the same period, the number of boarders fell by 80 percent; automatic boarding machines simplified the tasks of many of the remaining boarders.

The demand for fixers, who were highly skilled, grew. Fixer training usually required three years plus an additional year for the highest grade.

Metal Cans

Can manufacturers replaced the three-piece can line with the two-piece line, which saved 25 to 30 percent of the labor required by eliminating some of the steps in the process, and by increasing operating speeds. The two-piece line also saved labor with automated conveyors between operations, which were monitored by sensing devices. In a three-piece line, consisting of nonadjacent parts, materials were handled between operations, perhaps by a forklift operator.[45]

Laundry and Cleaning

Industrial launderers and linen supply plants, accounting for 38 percent of the total employment of the laundry and cleaning industry in 1984, made major changes. Front-loading washing and cleaning machines, which tilted backwards, allowed automatic loading of soiled garments from overhead slings or chutes. The garments were loaded by hand or machine into slings and carried by overhead conveyors to the washing machines, which were loaded by overhead chutes. In the older process workers loaded the garments into carts by hand and pushed the carts to the machines, which they loaded manually. Front-loading washing machines were automatically unloaded into slings, which were transported by overhead conveyors. Automated washing and cleaning cycles added soap, bleach, and other supplies, and some equipment used solid-state controls. Increasingly automated sorting systems reduced labor requirements. New detergents, which cleaned at lower temperatures, reduced the number of rinse cycles, increasing the output per operator. Blended polyester-cotton fabrics and the use of steam tunnels for finishing work removed the need for pressers.[46]

Bakery Products

Continuous mix processing reduced labor requirements for dough mixing and makeup. The process mixed a flow of liquid ferment at high speed; and it extruded and panned the developed dough, which did not require further degassing, dividing, rounding, or molding. The older sponge and dough method required several additional processing stages. In particular, the new method eliminated the workers who transferred dough between the mixer and the fermentation room, and it reduced the number overseeing the mixing and makeup operations. One or two operators produced as much as six or seven in the older process.[47]

Concrete

Transfer systems which moved newly cast concrete through different operations reduced the number of forklift operators. Automatic cubers replaced manual or semi-automatic methods of cubing. The semi-automatic process required a worker to arrange the blocks before the machine stacked them; the manual process required four employees. Transfer systems and automatic cubers also reduced the number of material handlers and truck drivers.[48]

Contract Construction

Improved tractors, scrapers, shovels, graders, and other equipment moved soil and rock more efficiently. New truck designs raised hauler capacity and speed, and the development of all-wheel drive with equal weight distribution permitted greater machine traction and maneuverability. Front-end loaders with bigger bucket sizes replaced steam-powered shovels and reduced labor requirements. Continuous excavators, which dug, transported, and placed earth continuously displaced handling equipment and their operators. Improvements in cranes, conveyor belts, forklift trucks, helicopters and concrete pumps also saved labor.

Improvements in methods of asphalt and concrete road paving included simplified asphalt mixing methods, more efficient and mobile mixing plants, more versatile and powerful graders, electronically controlled pavers, and increases in the capacity of asphalt finishers. Improved slip-form paving methods eliminated the labor needed to place and take down fixed supports used with conventional pavers. A single slip-form paver replaced three conventional paving machines, reducing the number of machine operators and concrete finishers. Automatic controls increased the capacity of slip-form pavers. Mechanical devices, permitting a slip-form paver to place steel bars in pavement slabs automatically and faster, reduced the labor requirements incurred by manual operations.

The proportion of engineers and professionals and technical workers grew, while that of laborers, helpers, and tenders fell. Such functions as loading and unloading materials at the worksite, shoveling and grading earth, and stacking and carrying materials were mechanized.[49]

Wood Containers

Between 1977 and 1989 the number of production workers increased at the average annual rate of 0.2 percent compared to a rate of 2.9 percent for nonproduction workers. Mechanization of the manufacture of pallets, which are platforms that forklift operators use to move large crates and boxes, was chiefly responsible for the slow growth of the number of production workers. Gang resaws, which cut several boards from each log in a single pass, automatic feeding systems, and automatic stacking equipment eliminated the need for unskilled labor. Assembly was speeded by the hand-held nailing equipment. Automated pallet assembly systems raised productivity in the assembly operation by as much as 800 to 900 percent over hand nailing.

Gang resaws improved productivity in the manufacture of wooden boxes. Automated equipment was used to assemble boxes having large production runs. Improvements in conveyors and in other materials handling equipment also raised productivity.

Retail Trade

Point-of-sale terminals, which replaced mechanical and less sophisticated electronic cash registers, processed payments at checkouts more quickly, and they provided information to a computer for tracking inventories. The computers increased the productivity of stockroom employees. Scanners, which read bar code data at the terminal, removed the need for labor to affix price labels on individual items and speeded up the movement of customers through the checkouts.[50]

There was less manual material handling in warehouses and thus fewer helpers, laborers, and material movers. Employment in managerial, technical, and related occupations increased.

Wholesale Trade

Automated systems for the handling and distribution of goods reduced the number of labor hours in warehouses. Bar coding and other
identification technologies together with computerized equipment increased the speed and accuracy of the processing of information and the
movement of goods. Bar-code scanning in one wholesale establishment
raised the number of cartons handled daily by more than 50 percent.
Microprocessor-controlled conveyors generated, monitored, recorded,
and reported operational data, as well as moved materials. Material handlers, who became monitors of the conveyors' operations, had to be able
to handle the information necessary for adjustments to the conveyors.
The most advanced of the high stackers were semi-automated and computerized machines, which were programmed to store and retrieve ob-
jects in specified locations. Traveling on wire guides, except when
moving along the main aisles, they reduced the number of operators by
two-thirds to three-fourths.[51]

Certain common tendencies stand out. Mechanization advanced in all
the industries, and electronic controls were widely applied. Fewer laborers were needed to handle materials. Electronic sensors replaced visual inspection. Robots performed the repetitive, routine tasks formerly
done by assembly-line workers. On the other hand, the new capital
goods, especially those incorporating electronic controls, increased the
number of technical and managerial jobs. In general, the changes in the
methods of production reduced the employment of unskilled workers.

CONCLUSION

The inflationary, full-employment policies pursued by the Fed and the
different administrations during the period between 1950 and 1979 reduced real interest rates relative to the cost of unskilled labor, inducing
businesses to substitute capital for this input, which in turn raised unskilled unemployment to high levels. Even in the 1980s after the Fed's
credit crunch, the cost of unskilled labor relative to interest rates remained high compared to the 1920s, and the rate of growth of the capital
stock per labor hour continued to be high.

Part of the problem was the high level of wages of unskilled workers
at the end of the war, which was in part the result of the wage-
equalization policy during the war. To offset the effect of the high wages
on employment, the Fed had to lower real interest rates more than it
would have had to otherwise. The unemployment problem was cumulative. The effect of the high wages on employment prompted the Fed
and the administration to undertake an inflationary policy, which re-

duced real interest rates. This in turn raised the unemployment rate to an even higher level by inducing firms to substitute capital for unskilled labor.

NOTES

1. Edwin Mansfield, *The Economics of Technological Change* (New York: W. W. Norton, 1968), 63.

2. Frank Lynn, "An Investigation of the Rate of Development and Diffusion of Technology in Our Modern Industrial Society," *Report of the National Commission on Technology, Automation, and Economic Progress*, Washington, D.C., 1966. Cited by Edwin Mansfield, *Technological Change: An Introduction to a Vital Area of Modern Economics* (New York: W. W. Norton, 1971), 76.

3. Paul A. David and Peter Solar, "A Bicentenary Contribution to the History of the Cost of Living in America," *Research in Economic History*, 2 (1977): 16.

4. *Economic Report of the President (ERP)*, January 1962, 46.

5. Bureau of Labor Statisics (BLS), *News*, August 29, 1991, 13.

6. Irving Fisher, *The Theory of Interest* (New York: Macmillan, 1930), 43, 415.

7. Rudiger Dornbusch and Stanley Fischer, *Macroeconomics* (New York: Mc-Graw-Hill, 1994), 493–94.

8. Robert Mundell, "Inflation and Real Interest," *Journal of Political Economy*, 71 (June 1963): 281–83.

9. Milton Friedman, *A Theory of the Consumption Function* (Princeton, N.J.: Princeton University Press, 1957).

10. Based on *ERP 1970*, 186, 198; *ERP 1992*, 298, 328.

11. Raymond W. Goldsmith, *The Flow of Capital Funds in the Postwar Economy* (New York: Columbia University Press, for National Bureau of Economic Research, 1965), 91.

12. Benjamin M. Friedman, *Day of Reckoning: The Consequences of American Economic Policy under Reagan and After* (New York: Random House, 1988).

13. Daniel S. Hamermesh and James Grant, "Econometric Studies of Labor-Labor Substitution and Their Implications for Policy," *Journal of Human Resources*, 14, no. 4: 537.

14. Sherwin Rosen, "Short-run Employment Variation on Class-1 Railroads in the United States, 1947–1963," *Econometrica*, 36 (1968): 511–29; Zvi Griliches, "Capital-skill Complementarity," *Review of Economics and Statistics*, 51 (1969): 465–68.

15. Milton Friedman and Anna Jacobson Schwartz, *A Monetary History of the United States 1867–1960* (Princeton, N.J.: Princeton University Press, 1963), 619–20.

16. Anthony S. Campagna, *U.S. National Economic Policy 1917–1985* (New York: Praeger, 1987), 317–29.

17. Benjamin Friedman, *Day of Reckoning*, 7, 28–31.

18. BLS, Office of Productivity and Technology.

19. *Historical Statistics of the United States: Colonial Times to 1970, Bicentennial Edition*, 1975 (*HSB*), ser. A78.

20. Between 1940 and 1950, the number of tractors increased by 117 percent;

motor trucks by 111 percent; grain combines by 276 percent; and corn pickers by 314 percent. *HSB*, ser. K184, K185, K187, K188.

21. BLS, Office of Productivity and Technology.

22. Ibid.

23. Alan B. Krueger, "How Computers Have Changed the Wage Structure: Evidence from Microdata, 1984–89," National Bureau of Economic Research (NBER), Working Paper No. 3858, October 1991.

24. Krueger, "How Computers Have Changed the Wage Structure," 24–25.

25. Eli Berman, John Bound, and Zvi Griliches, "Changes in the Demand for Skilled Labor within U.S. Manufacturing Industries: Evidence from the Annual Survey of Manufacturing," NBER Working Paper No. 4255, January 1993, 1, 2.

26. Ibid., 29.

27. Ibid., 10. Pointed out by David R. Howell and Susan S. Wieler, "Trends in Computerization, Skill Composition and Low Earnings: Implications for Education and Training Policy" (New York: Graduate School of Management, New School for Social Research, October 1994), 7.

28. BLS, Office of Productivity and Technology, December 1995.

29. Ibid.

30. BLS, *The Impact of Technology on Labor in Four Industries: Textiles, Paper and Paperboard, Steel, Motor Vehicles*, Bulletin 2228 (May 1985): 1.

31. BLS, Office of Productivity and Technology.

32. BLS, *Impact of Technology on Labor in Four Industries*, 38.

33. Ibid., 40–41.

34. BLS, *Technology and Labor in Four Industries: Tires, Aluminum, Aerospace, and Banking*, Bulletin 2242 (May 1986): 1.

35. Based on BLS, *Productivity Measures for Selected Industries and Government Services*, Bulletin 2349 (February 1990): 92, table 167.

36. BLS, *Technology and Labor in Four Industries: Meat Products, Foundries, Metalworking Machinery, Electrical and Electronic Equipment*, Bulletin 2104 (January 1982): 10, 12, 16.

37. BLS, Office of Productivity and Technology, December 1995.

38. BLS, *Technology and Labor in Four Industries*, Bulletin 2104, 36.

39. Ibid., 43.

40. Based on BLS, *Productivity Measures*, 83, table 150.

41. BLS, *Technology and Its Impact on Labor in Four Industries: Lumber and Wood Products, Footwear, Hydraulic Cement, Wholesale Trade*, Bulletin 2263 (November 1986): 32–41.

42. BLS, *Productivity Measures*, 42, table 68.

43. BLS, *Technological Change and Its Labor Impact in Four Industries: Hosiery, Folding Paperboard Boxes, Metal Cans, Laundry and Cleaning*, Bulletin 2182 (February 1984): 7.

44. Ibid., 2–4.

45. Ibid., 21–22.

46. Ibid., 31–35.

47. BLS, *Technology and Labor in Five Industries: Bakery Products, Concrete, Air Transportation, Telephone Communication, Insurance*, Bulletin 2033 (September 1979): 2.

48. Ibid., 11, 16.

49. BLS, *Technological Change and Its Labor Impact in Four Industries: Contract Construction, Railroad Transportation, Air Transportation, Petroleum Pipeline Transportation*, Bulletin 2316 (December 1988): 6.

50. BLS, *Technology and Labor in Three Service Industries: Utilities, Retail Trade, and Lodging*, Bulletin 2367 (September 1990): 16–17.

51. BLS, *Technology and Its Impact on Labor in Four Industries*, 40–41.

3

The Substitution of Skilled
for Unskilled Labor

The sources of the growing inequality of incomes since the mid-1970s remain a puzzle. Some economists blame unions' diminished power, begging the question: Why the loss of power? As Chapter 2 shows, one source was the fall in the cost of capital goods due to the full-employment policy of the first three postwar decades. As we will see, other public policies also inflicted losses on unskilled workers.

The growing inequality is still a puzzle because observers commence with the 1970s; inequality started to increase in that decade. This is why some observers blame the slowdown of productivity growth, whose beginning is dated about 1973. The false inference is drawn that a rapid rate of growth fosters equality. What we have to understand is that the demand for unskilled labor fell due to public policies during the war and the first three postwar decades. Indeed, the rise of productivity reflected the fall in the demand for unskilled labor. The lower demand caused unskilled unemployment to rise and in the 1980s brought about a fall in the relative wages of employed unskilled workers. The roots of the growing inequality of the 1980s and 1990s were in earlier wage and employment policies.

During World War II the wages of unskilled workers got a great boost. By removing many workers from the market, conscription benefited those remaining in the civilian labor force, and the demand for munitions also raised unskilled workers' wages. There was also the New Deal egalitarian wage policy. The effect of the wage policy alone is hard to gauge, but it appears to have been large. It is unlikely that the demand for unskilled workers was so much greater than that for skilled workers that it alone accounted for the great narrowing of the skilled-unskilled wage gap.

Thus, the cost of hiring unskilled workers rose. And the postwar full-employment, educational, and minimum-wage policies also boosted the cost of unskilled labor relative to that of skilled labor. Subsidies for higher education reduced the demand for unskilled workers by reducing the cost of skilled labor, which deprived many unskilled workers of jobs. An obvious yet unnoticed effect of the subsidies was to increase the supply of skilled workers, which tended to reduce their wages, inducing employers to substitute them for unskilled workers. Moreover, education improved the skills of skilled workers relative to those of unskilled workers. While the schooling of the latter also increased, their skills did not benefit. In addition, the rise in minimum wages and the greater coverage of the minimum-wage laws in the 1960s reduced the number of unskilled jobs, especially on farms.

Businesses substituted skilled for unskilled workers. Supervisors do not become laborers, but they may enable fewer laborers to move parts from the receiving room to the assembly line, and together with time-and-motion engineers they can speed up the assembly line. Also, better planning cuts the number of operatives, the number of laborers moving materials, and the number of repair and maintenance workers. Better records of the number of laborers available at different times and places also improves productivity, as does inventory planning. Although programmers do not become delivery men, they are substitutes for delivery men, if they improve the scheduling and routing of deliveries.

These examples are selective, and hiring more skilled workers does not always eliminate unskilled jobs. Examples of pairs of skilled and unskilled workers can be chosen where no substitution is possible. Thus, adding lawyers does not increase the productivity of laborers. However, the survey of the related empirical literature by Daniel Hamermesh and James Grant concludes that skilled workers, represented by nonproduction workers, on the whole are substitutes for unskilled workers, represented by production workers. They also cite works indicating that highly educated workers are substitutes for workers with little education.[1]

The one-third of the labor force who are still unskilled are worse off. The contraction of the unskilled labor force was not sufficient to offset the effect of the lower demand. Although many youngsters became technicians instead of assembly-line workers, the substitution caused a net displacement of unskilled workers. As Chapter 1 points out, if one skilled worker produces as much as two unskilled workers, then an additional skilled worker results in one net displacement.

The early postwar years were a time of optimism for liberals. Wages had moved towards equality, jobs were plentiful, unions gained strength, assembly-line workers bought homes in the suburbs, cars, television sets, washing machines, and dishwashers; and the general level of education was rising. Education was the great hope for social democracy. In the emerging world messengers and dishwashers would read the same newspapers as their bosses, watch the same television shows, and listen to the same music.

The predictions were unduly optimistic, for, with most of the college students coming from middle- and upper-class families, the class divisions deepened. The greater expenditures for education helped prosperous families more than poor families. In 1992 only 26 percent of the 18 to 24 year-olds from families in the lowest one-third of the income distribution were full-time college students compared to approximately 51 percent of those from families with higher incomes.[2] The large flow of university and college graduates, which kept the skilled–unskilled wage gap from widening, blinded observers to the worsening class division. The harm caused unskilled workers by the larger number of college graduates did not come immediately, but it did come.

THE SUPPLY OF SKILLED AND UNSKILLED WORKERS

Even people who have not graduated from college succeed, but exceptions should not lead us astray. The number of clever, industrious, and aggressive dropouts who become high executives is small and keeps diminishing. For most people education remains the road to better jobs and higher incomes.

The prospect of a high time, of learning, and the hope that a college education would enhance their enjoyment of life were attractive, but the expected gain in earnings was also an incentive to attend college. In 1980 college graduates earned more than twice as much as elementary school graduates, and they earned 63 percent more than high-school graduates (see Table 3.1). In 1949 the difference in earnings between college and high-school graduates yielded a return on the investment in a college education of 13 percent,[3] which was much higher than yields of long-term securities. Including the nonmonetary benefits, the return was even higher. The investment includes, in addition to tuition fees, the earnings that a student forgoes by attending college. The yield from the investment in a high-school education also was high.

Nevertheless, high expected earnings do not explain the accelerated growth in the number of graduates, for, as we see later, the college earnings premium fell between 1939 and 1950. Because the return on an investment in education fell over this period, the high yield in 1950 does not explain the great spurt in the number of college graduates. Moreover, college was expensive, and in the early postwar years banks did not offer educational loans. Government subsidies cut the cost of higher education

Table 3.1
Mean Annual Earnings of Male, Year-Round, Full-Time Workers, Age 50–54,
by Educational Attainment (8 years of school = 100) and Index, 1980

Years of school	Earnings	Index
8	$16,594	100
12	$21,171	128
College		
1-3	$25,147	152
graduate	$34,452	208
Professional or graduate degree	$36,788	222

Source: Based on Daniel S. Hamermesh and Albert Rees, The Economics of Work and Pay
(New York: Harper and Row, 1984), 59.

to students and their families. It was public subsidies for higher education that drove up college enrollments.

Immediately following World War II the GI Bill increased federal subsidies for higher education sharply, and state and local government subsidies also grew. Between 1942 and 1950 government subsidies for higher
education in constant dollars grew at the average annual rate of 11.9
percent, while the real Gross Domestic Product (GDP) grew at the rate
of 7.4 percent. Later, the spectacular Sputnik triumph provoked the fear
of a Soviet lead in science, threatening our security. It may be recalled
that Kennedy's election campaign theme was the alleged missile gap.
Between 1950 and 1970 constant-dollar government expenditures for
higher education increased at the average annual rate of 8.7 percent,
compared to the GDP growth rate of 3.5 percent.[4] In addition, as families'
incomes rose, they spent more on education.

As a result, between 1940 and 1970 the number of people in the age
group 18 to 24 attending institutions of higher education increased from
9.1 percent to 30.6 percent.[5] The further consequence was that between
1950 and 1980 the number of college graduates in the age group 25 to
29 years rose from 7.7 percent to a whopping 22.5 percent (see Table 3.2).
The number of high-school graduates had increased sharply during the
1940s from 32.2 percent to 45.1 percent, and the 1950s and 1960s saw
another jump to 59.0 percent.

The torrent of college graduates greatly boosted the supply of managers and professionals (see Table 3.3). In 1994, as many as 65.7 percent
of male college graduates were so employed. The colleges also poured
new workers into the technical, sales, and administrative—including
clerical—occupations, which employed 22.2 percent of male graduates.
Of the nongraduates who had some college education, as many as 49.9

Table 3.2
Percent of All Persons Age 25–29 Who Completed High School or College,
Various Years

| | Completed | |
Year	High School Only	College or More
1940	32.2	5.9
1950	45.1	7.7
1960	49.7	11.0
1970	59.0	16.4
1980	62.9	22.5
1990	62.5	23.2
1994	62.8	23.3

Source: Based on Department of Education, National Center for Education Statistics, *Digest of Education Statistics 1995*, 17, table 8.

percent took white-collar jobs. As the number at the other end of the educational attainment scale—the high-school dropouts—dwindled, the supply of operators, fabricators, laborers, and service workers, which employed 50.7 percent of dropouts, shrank.

The entry of married women into the labor market was the other part of the transformation of the labor force. Productivity growth in the economy raised women's wages, increasing the cost of staying out of the labor force. Because remaining at home became more expensive, there was a huge jump in the number of clerical workers. The well-publicized policewomen, firewomen, and women telephone repairers climbing poles notwithstanding, most women took jobs as office workers, waitresses, supermarket cashiers, and nurses' aides—jobs their mothers had held. While the female share of the labor force went up from 28.1 percent to 45.7 percent between 1950 and 1990, the number of clerical workers rose from 12.0 percent of all employment to 16.0 percent. Over the same period the proportion of clerical workers who were female rose from 62.1 percent to 77.3 percent.[6] The increase in the number of clerical workers helped to eliminate some unskilled workers. With more information, planners could more easily recognize where the number of workers was excessive.

Immigration also harmed unskilled workers. This book does not investigate the effects of immigration, but it is clear that it worsened the condition of unskilled workers. Between 1991 and 1993 average annual immigration amounted to 0.48 percent of the U.S. population,[7] which does not seem to be large. But the percentage of the total population represented by the number of immigrants in one year is not the appropriate criterion. Most immigrants were unskilled and moved into New

Table 3.3
Occupational Distribution of Employed Males by Educational Attainment,
1994

	Total (Percent)	Less than High School (Percent)	High School (Percent)	Less than 4 Years College (Percent)	College Graduate (Percent)
Total	100.0	100.0	100.0	100.0	100.0
Mgr./prof.	29.5	4.9	10.8	23.2	65.7
Tech./sale/admin.	19.6	7.1	16.1	26.7	22.2
Service	8.3	12.6	9.8	10.1	3.5
Prec. prod.	19.7	27.0	29.1	22.1	4.3
Op./fab.	19.0	38.1	29.7	15.2	3.0
Farming	3.8	10.3	4.9	4.5	1.3

Notes:
Mgr./prof. = managerial and professional.
Tech./sale/admin. = technical, sales, administrative.
Prec. prod. = precision production.
Op./fab. = operators, fabricators.
Source: Based on *SAUS 1995*, 416, table 652.

York, Los Angeles, and other large cities. Because the unskilled make up one-third of total employment, the figure of 0.48 percent understates the immigrants' effect on the unskilled labor market. Immigration is adding as much as three times this percentage to the unskilled labor force for the country as a whole. In the larger cities, the percentage is much greater. Moreover, the impact of immigration on the unskilled labor market at any one time reflects the additions to supply over several years. The cumulative effect of immigration over time on unskilled unemployment thus has been substantial.

THE RELATIVE WAGES OF UNSKILLED WORKERS

The wartime jump in the demand for welders, riveters, lathe operators, assembly workers, and laborers, combined with the removal of men from the civilian labor force caused a large increase in unskilled workers' wages. The jump in the demand accompanied a fall in the supply of male unskilled labor. The flood of women into the labor market was insufficient to prevent an increase in wages.

Less well known is the effect of President Roosevelt's egalitarian policies.[8] The wartime controls over wages were chiefly intended to slow inflation, but the administration also used them to raise low wages. After January 1941 wage increases were limited to 15 percent, but the administration exempted low-wage workers from the rule. Also, employers could raise wages to 40 cents per hour without the permission of the National War Labor Board (NWLB), and the regional NWLBs could permit increases to 50 cents per hour. In addition, the NWLB raised low wages by reducing wage differences between plants. Ranges for each occupation in each region were established, and wages could be raised to the lower end of each range. The Board also allowed increases that eliminated differences between occupations within plants. Because labor was in short supply, there was enormous pressure on employers to raise wages. Effectively, the controls did not apply to low-wage workers. These exemptions allowed relatively large increases in low wages. In 1941 the average hourly earnings of production workers in manufacturing were \$0.73,[9] and, of course, the low-paid workers were receiving wages below the average. The combination of the large wartime demand for unskilled labor, the removal of men from the civilian labor force, and the egalitarian wage policy gave unskilled workers a big boost in wages which persisted after the war.

Between 1939 and 1950 manufacturing workers' wages rose over 70 percent more than the earnings of engineers and college teachers.[10] Also, the wage gap between college and high-school graduates narrowed. College graduates with 11 to 15 years of experience, who in 1940 had earned on the average 78 percent more than high-school graduates with the same years of experience, earned only 46 percent more in 1950.[11]

Changes in wages by occupational groups between 1939 and 1945 also reveal a rise in the relative earnings of unskilled workers (see Table 3.4). The index number 119 for 1945 for operatives/professionals means that operatives' wages relative to professionals' earnings rose 19 percent between 1939 and 1945. Operatives' wages relative to those of managers increased by 36 percent, they did much better than professionals and clerical workers, and laborers' earnings also gained on those of skilled workers.

Because a high proportion of blacks worked on farms, the change in the cost of farm labor during the war is of special interest. The wartime wage controls were not applied to farm workers, so their wages rose even more than those of production workers in manufacturing. Between 1940 and 1948 farms' wage rates for hired labor rose 43 percent relative to the average hourly earnings of manufacturing production workers. Another measure of the cost of farm labor indicates a relative increase of 61 percent.[12]

After the war years, unskilled workers advanced no further relative to skilled workers. They kept much of their wartime gains until the 1980s, when their relative wages worsened.[13] In 1990 they were back in the same position, relative to skilled workers, as in 1939.[14] Up to the 1980s unskilled workers lost jobs, but their relative earnings did not fall. With demand continuing to shrink in the 1980s, their relative wages also

Table 3.4

Indexes of Median Earnings of Male Operatives and Nonfarm Laborers Relative to Earnings of Male Professionals, Managers, and Clerical Workers, Various Years, 1939–1994 (1939 = 100)

	1939	1945	1960	1970	1980	1990	1994
Oper./prof.	100	119	120	107	113	97	91
Oper./mgr.	100	136	122	112	118	100	94
Oper./cler.	100	116	117	109	106	107	110
Lab./prof.	100	116	120	118	117	99	87
Lab./mgr.	100	132	122	123	123	103	90
Lab./cler.	100	113	116	120	110	110	106

Notes: Oper. = operator, prof. = professional, mgr. = manager, cler. = clerical, lab. = laborer.
Conversion factors were used to link post-1982 occupational median earnings by comparing median earnings in 1981, which were published under both classifications in Series P60, March 1983, no. 137, 117 and February 1984, no. 142, 117. The conversion factors do not change the basic results. The column for 1990 would read downward as 99, 102, 110, 100, 103, 111, 91, 94, 101 without the conversion. Note also that in 1987, the revised procedure raised median incomes of managers, professionals, technicians, machine operatives, transport operatives, and laborers, but not clericals. See P60, October 1989, no. 166. The data refer to year-round, full-time workers.
Sources: Based on Bureau of the Census, *Current Population Reports*, Series P60, Consumer Income, March 2, 1948, no. 2, 26; January 17, 1962, no. 37, 54; October 4, 1971, no. 80, 129; July 1982, no. 132, 132; August 1991, no. 184, 94; April 1996, no. 189, 15.

dropped. The entire impact of the shrinking demand for unskilled workers was on employment up to the 1980s, when it also reduced their relative wages.

McKinley Blackburn, David Bloom, and Richard Freeman attribute at least part of the relative decline in unskilled workers' wages during the 1980s to the weaker position of unions. Unskilled workers quit or did not join unions, and, according to the authors, their wages suffered as a result.[15] However, this conclusion assumes unreasonably that unions can remain strong even in a declining market for unskilled labor. The bargaining power of unions, who cannot buck the tide of labor demand, rises and falls with it.

Changes in minimum wages and in the coverage of the minimum-wage law partly explain the persistence of the wartime gains in unskilled workers' wages up to the 1980s. In 1966 federal legislation extended the coverage of the minimum wage laws to large farms, retail trade, construction, and the service industries. As a result, between 1965 and 1970 farm wage rates increased 16 percent relative to average hourly earnings in manufacturing.[16]

Cogan provides an analysis of the effect of the minimum wage increase and the extension of the law's coverage on black teenage employment. In 1950 46.6 percent of male black teenagers were employed, compared to 27.0 percent in 1970.[17] Almost all of the decline was due to the fall in employment in the South, where the proportion employed fell from 54.8 percent to 27.4 percent. In 1950 71.5 percent of all black male teenagers, including those not employed, lived in the South. Outside agriculture, the major employers of black male teenagers were retail trade, construction, services, and durable goods manufacturing. Employment of black teenagers in retail trade grew in the 1960s, despite the extended coverage of the minimum-wage law to retailing. Nevertheless, as Cogan shows, the minimum-wage law did slow the growth.[18]

Employment in durable goods manufacturing was concentrated in southern woodmills. According to Cogan, almost one in every five southern black teenagers not employed in agriculture was working in the woodmills.[19] At least part of the fall in employment in this industry was due to the increase in the minimum wage. In April 1956 the minimum was raised from 75 cents per hour to $1.00 per hour. In late 1955 74 percent of all production workers in the southern woodmills were earning less than $1.00 per hour; by April 1957 the number had dropped to less than 3 percent, and total employment in the industry had fallen 15 percent. Black male teenage employment fell by 74 percent between 1950 and 1974.[20]

The increases in the cost of labor–intensive production methods induced farm operators to use more machinery and chemicals, decreasing unskilled labor and, therefore, black employment. The minimum-wage law further increased unemployment among black teenagers.

THE IMPROVEMENT IN THE SKILL OF SKILLED WORKERS

Skilled workers' skills gained greatly from more schooling. The number of male professional and technical workers who had graduated from college increased from 54.6 percent in 1950 to 71.7 percent in 1982; among managers the number increased from 12.0 percent to 39.0 percent; among sales workers from 10.8 percent to 37.7 percent, and among clerical workers from 7.8 percent to 18.1 percent (see Table 3.5).[21] There can be no question that more schooling improved the skill of technicians, some sales workers, and clerical workers. Technicians include physician's assistants, librarians, laboratory technicians, practical nurses, biological and chemical technicians, among others. In the years before the war, unlike professionals, many had not completed college. Sales workers who informed customers about the qualities of complex goods also benefited, as did clerks who handled a variety of tasks.

Of course, the educational attainment of unskilled workers, also rose.

Table 3.5
Educational Attainment of Employed Male Workers by Occupation, 1950 and
1982

	4 Years High School		4 Years College or More	
	1950 (Percent)	1982 (Percent)	1950 (Percent)	1982 (Percent)
Total	19.4	35.8	7.8	26.6
Professional and technical	15.3	11.3	54.6	71.7
Managers	27.0	30.0	12.0	39.0
Sales	31.6	29.4	10.8	37.7
Clerical	34.8	43.6	7.8	18.1
Craft	22.0	50.6	1.8	5.8
Operatives (1)	16.6	47.8	0.9	2.7
Laborers	9.4	39.5	0.6	4.1
Service (2)	16.6	42.1	1.6	5.0
Farmers	11.4	36.9	1.4	6.7

Notes: (1) excluding transport operatives; (2) excluding household workers.
Source: SAUS 1984, 418, table 694.

The number of operatives who had graduated from high school grew from 16.6 percent to 47.8 percent, and the increases among laborers and service workers were similar.

It is doubtful, however, that the additional schooling improved the skills of unskilled workers. Floor cleaners are more likely to be high-school graduates than their predecessors, but the additional schooling has not increased their productivity. More schooling has enhanced the quality of life of assembly-line workers, but it has not speeded the assembly line or reduced the number of defects in production. This is so, although high-school graduates among unskilled workers earn more than dropouts. Part of the gain in earnings associated with more schooling is due to such characteristics as intelligence, reliability, and discipline, which high-earning operatives have along with more schooling. Employers know that the average high-school graduate is more dependable than the average dropout.[22] The schools provide employers with the service of screening potential employees. Moreover, skills vary within the large Census occupational classes. The operative who is a high-school graduate may perform more varied and more responsible tasks than the nongraduate. The high-school graduate is likely to be more skilled.

Nevertheless, the greater skill of high-school graduates among operatives does not imply that, as the percentage of high-school graduates increased, operatives became more skilled. The cross-sectional association between schooling and skill does not imply a historical association. The high-school graduates who are operatives need not be more skilled than the previous generation of nongraduate operatives. Indeed, the qualities of intelligence, reliability, and discipline of unskilled workers probably deteriorated over time. That this happened can be inferred from the change in the proportion of the population completing high school. In 1940 24 percent of the male population 25 years and over had graduated from high school, compared to 81 percent in 1994.[23] The gap in such qualities as discipline and dependability between high-school graduates and dropouts in 1994 was greater than in 1940. When a large majority of the population has completed high school, the minority that has not will have much less diligence, intelligence, and so on than those who do graduate. The same cannot be said about the difference between the two groups when nongraduates are a large majority. Although many of the nongraduates in 1940 were highly intelligent and reliable, poverty forced them into the labor force at an early age. This is not true today. While some still drop out for economic reasons, the proportion is much smaller. The dropouts today are likely to have problems that damage their job performance. But this also means that today's average high-school graduate may not have greater skill than the average dropout of 1940. Moreover, despite the larger number of unskilled workers who have completed high school, the dropout percentage among such workers remains high. In 1989 as many as 30 percent of operatives were dropouts.[24]

Also, the performance of unskilled workers does not gain significantly from schooling beyond the elementary grades. Machine operators, busmen, farmworkers, laborers, factory helpers, floor cleaners, and hospital orderlies need endurance, manual dexterity, strength, and energy, which do not benefit from more schooling.

In addition, the skill gap has widened with the advance of technology. Today's professionals know more than their predecessors even without more years of schooling. Engineers now know more about electronics, computers, and superconductivity; doctors have treatments for ulcers, gallstones, and heart disease, which were unavailable earlier; statisticians now have the technique of sequential sampling; chemists have acquired the technique of chromatography; and similar advances have occurred in other other professions. The occupations of aerospace engineers, computer systems analysts, operations analysts, and computer programmers, among others, did not even exist in the 1950s.

Not everyone may agree that unskilled workers' performance gained little from additional schooling. However, the conclusion that the relative cost of employing unskilled workers increased requires only that the relative skill of skilled workers improved. Whatever the increase in the skill of unskilled workers was, it is certain that skilled workers gained much more.

Although the skill difference grew, at the end of the 1980s the skilled–unskilled wage gap was no greater than in 1939. The increase in the supply of skilled labor swamped the effect of the change in relative quality.

AN ESTIMATE OF THE INCREASE IN THE RELATIVE COST OF UNSKILLED LABOR

My estimate of the rise in the relative cost of unskilled labor shows only that it has been substantial, no claim being made for its precision. The purpose is to explain the high unemployment in the 1980s; thus, the estimate is for the period between 1939 and 1980. Between 1939 and 1960 the relative wages of unskilled labor increased approximately 20 percent, no further rise occurring between 1960 and 1980.

In addition, the relative quality of unskilled labor fell. Edward Denison estimated that higher educational attainment improved the quality of the labor force as a whole by 39 percent between 1929 and 1980.[25] Assuming that the quality of unskilled labor remained the same, this is a minimum estimate of the gain in the quality of skilled labor. If the quality improved at a constant rate, the gain over the period from 1939 to 1980 was 31 percent.

Denison's estimate, which was based on the earnings in one year of the different educational attainment groups, does not include the contribution of advances in knowledge to the quality of labor. He estimated the contribution of technology to the growth of output independently of the contribution of the gain in skill. If half the growth of output due to advances in knowledge was embodied in skilled workers, then between 1939 and 1980 the quality of skilled labor improved by 25 percent.[26]

Summing the improvement in quality due to additional schooling and that due to advances in knowledge brings the total improvement in quality up to 54 percent. Adding this to the increase in the relative wage cost of unskilled labor brings the total increase in the relative cost of unskilled labor to 74 percent. Employers thus had a strong incentive to substitute skilled for unskilled labor, and the incentive grew over time with the quality of skilled labor.

SHIFT FROM UNSKILLED TO SKILLED EMPLOYMENT

In the postwar period professional and technical workers, managers and administrators, and clerical workers were substituted for operatives and nonfarm laborers. Thus, the white-collar share of total employment grew enormously from 38 percent in 1950 to 58 percent in 1995. The

Table 3.6
Average Annual Rates of Growth of Employment by Occupation by Decade, 1950–1990

	1950-1960 (Percent)	1960-1970 (Percent)	1970-1980 (Percent)	1980-1990 (Percent)	1950-1990 (Percent)	1990-1995 (Percent)
Total	1.1	1.6	2.1	1.9	1.7	1.2
Professional/ technical	5.1	4.0	3.4	3.2	3.9	2.3
Managers/ administrators	0.9	1.6	2.8	3.9	2.3	2.9
Sales	1.4	1.0	2.4	3.0	1.9	1.3
Clerical	2.5	3.4	2.8	1.4	2.5	-0.3
Craft	1.1	1.7	2.1	1.3	1.5	-0.2
Operatives	-0.1	1.5	-0.1	-0.1	0.3	0.2
Laborers	0.4	0.2	1.8	0.9	0.8	0.6
Service	2.4	1.5	2.9	2.1	2.2	1.4
Farmers	-3.2	-5.5	-1.5	-0.9	-2.7	1.3

Sources and methods: See Chapter 1, note 9. Data for 1995 from *Employment and Earnings*, January 1996, 169, table 9.

predominantly blue-collar workforce became predominantly white-collar. Table 3.6 reports the average annual growth rates for each occupation in each decade since 1950 and from 1990 to 1995.

The data for the period between 1950 and 1990 and for the individual decades show that unskilled employment was growing slowly. Over the entire period, the average annual growth rate of total employment was 1.7 percent. The growth rates of employment for operatives—0.3 percent—and laborers—0.8 percent—were much lower, and farm employment declined. In the 1960s the number of operatives did grow, and it is this decade that accounts for the growth over the entire period. At no time in the postwar period were the growth rates for these occupational groups close to that of total employment.

The rise in the demand for services, such as those provided by hospitals and restaurants, resulted in a rapid growth—2.2 percent per year—in the number of service workers. The growth took place despite the rise in the cost of unskilled labor. On the whole, however, the data reveal a decline in the demand for unskilled labor.

The demand for professional and technical workers grew very rapidly over the entire period. The average annual growth rate of 3.9 percent between 1950 and 1990 exceeded that for any other occupational group. Over the four decades employment in these occupations grew at more than twice the rate of total employment. Moreover, the growth has been remarkably persistent. During the 1980s the growth rate of 3.2 percent was well above that of total employment—1.9 percent—and it was exceeded only by the growth rate for managers and administrators. In the preceding decades the number of professionals and technicians grew even more rapidly both absolutely and in relation to total employment. The 1980s saw a small slowdown, but the demand for such workers remained very strong. In the most recent period, 1990 to 1995, the growth of employment in professional and technical occupations remained high at nearly twice the rate of total employment.

The growth rate between 1950 and 1990 for managers and administrators—2.3 percent—was relatively high. The growth of this group accelerated in the 1980s, when it reached 3.9 percent per year, more than twice the growth rate of total employment. The growth rate for clerical workers—2.5 percent—was also relatively high. The exceptionally high growth rate of the 1960s reflected the burgeoning number of women in the labor force. It remained high in the 1970s when women were still entering the labor force in large numbers. However, in the 1980s the growth rate fell to below that of total employment, and in the most recent period, 1990 to 1995, employment in clerical occupations actually fell. The developments in the 1980s and 1990s may reflect the effects of the greater use of computers in offices.

A popular view is that displaced operatives and laborers should be trained to be carpenters, electricians, plumbers, steam fitters, and other skilled blue-collar occupations. The federal administration appears to believe that training in these occupations would brighten the future of high-school students. However, the rate of growth of employment in the craft occupations as a whole—1.5 percent—over the period from 1950 to 1990 was below that of total employment—1.7 percent. In the 1980s the rate of growth—1.3 percent—was considerably below the overall employment growth rate—1.9 percent. In the most recent period—1990 to 1995, employment in craft occupations actually fell. Judging from this record, large training programs are likely to result in disappointment.

Between 1990 and 1995 the growth rate of total employment fell to the lowest rate—1.2 percent per year—since the 1950s. The growth rates of the most skilled occupational groups—professional and technical, managers and administrators—remained high. The growth rates of operatives and laborers remained low, well below the growth rate of total employment. The growth rate of sales workers fell to approximately the same rate as total employment. I have already commented on the decline in employment in clerical and craft occupations. Service occupations also present a surprise. The growth rate of employment in the service occupations fell sharply. In this period service employment grew only slightly more than total employment. On the other hand employment in farming occupations grew for the first time in the postwar period. Indeed the growth rate was about the same as that of total employment.

Forecasts by the Bureau of Labor Statistics (BLS) of employment by occupations reflect the same trends. Table 3.7 reports BLS estimates of the growth of employment between 1992 and 2005 for fast-growing and declining occupations, each of which employed more than 100,000 persons in 1992. The projected growth of total employment is 22 percent. A few unskilled occupations are expanding rapidly, including food preparation workers, home health aides, personal and home care aides, guards, child care workers, and nursing aides, orderlies, and attendants. Congress is likely to reduce the growth of expenditures for Medicare and Medicaid, which will cut the growth of employment in health care occupations; and the expansion of HMOs, which pursue economies more vigorously than fee-for-service providers, will have the same effect. Employment in other unskilled occupations is contracting rapidly, including service station attendants, sewing machine operators, metal fabricating machine operators, electrical and electronic assemblers, machine tool operators, farmworkers, various other types of machine operators, private household workers, telephone operators, packaging and filling machine operators.

Employment in skilled occupations is growing rapidly: computer engineers and scientists, systems analysts, special education teachers, medical assistants, therapists, preschool teachers, insurance adjusters, construction managers, management analysts, registered nurses, psychologists, social workers, and loan officers. Although the current drive to cut costs of health care is likely to reduce the demand for some of these skilled workers, it is skilled workers who are in demand. The only skilled occupation that appears to be declining is communication equipment mechanic.

OTHER WRITERS ON THE DEMAND FOR UNSKILLED LABOR

In *Losing Ground*, Charles Murray argues that the increase in welfare benefits between 1965 and 1975 induced many blacks to quit the labor force.[27] Why he looks only at blacks is a mystery, but I let that pass. Chapter 5 examines Murray's general argument in more detail. If Murray is correct that welfare payments were the predominant influence on black employment between 1965 and 1975, then the supply of black labor dropped. Murray's evidence of welfare's bad influence is simply that black unemployment grew as it became easier to receive welfare benefits and as they became more generous. Because he says nothing about demand, his analysis is incomplete. What about the displacement of unskilled labor by machinery, skilled labor, and imports? Moreover, black unemployment continued to climb after 1975, when the growth of welfare benefits stopped.

Table 3.7

Projected Percentage Rates of Change of Employment in Fast-Growing Occupations and in Declining Occupations and of Total Employment, 1992–2005

Total	22
FAST-GROWING OCCUPATIONS	
Home health aides	138
Personal and home care aides	130
Computer engineers and scientists	112
Systems analysts	110
Teachers, special education	74
Medical assistants	71
Correction officers	70
Travel agents	66
Child care workers	66
Therapists	61
Legal secretaries	57
Legal assistants & technicians (excluding clerical)	56
Teachers, preschool and kindergarten	54
Producers, directors, actors, entertainers	54
Guards	51
Insurance adjusters, examiners, investigators	49
Psychologists	48
Construction managers	47
Bakers, bread and pastry	47
Cooks, restaurant	46
Amusement and recreation attendants	46
Nursing aides, orderlies, and attendants	45
Food service and lodging managers	44
Teacher aides and educational assistants	43
Management analysts	43
Food preparation workers	43
Registered nurses	42
Hotel desk clerks	41
Social workers	40
Loan officers and counselors	40
Health technicians and technologists	40
Bill and account collectors	40
DECLINING OCCUPATIONS	
Stenographers	−1
Machinists	−1
Extractive and related workers (including blasters)	−2
Electrical equipment mechanics/installation/repair	−2
Purchasing agents	−3
Industrial machinery mechanics	−3
Custom tailors and sewers	−4
Bank tellers	−4

(continued)

Table 3.7 (*continued*)

Service station attendants	−5
Tool and die makers	−7
Sewing machine operators, non-garment	−8
Inspectors, testers, graders, precision	−10
Metal fabricating machine setters/operators/etc.	−11
Electrical and electronic assemblers	−11
Crushing and mixing machine operators and tenders	−12
Machine tool cut and form setters/operators/tenders	−13
Electrical equipment assemblers, precision	−14
Butchers and meatcutters	−14
Typists and word processors	−16
Farm workers	−16
Machine tool cutting operators and tenders	−17
Textile draw-out and winding machine operators and tenders	−18
Woodworking machine setters, operators, etc.	−20
Machine forming operators and tenders	−21
Farmers	−21
Packaging and filling operators and tenders	−22
Telephone operators	−28
Sewing machine operators, garment	−29
Private household workers	−33
Communications equipment mechanics/installation/repair	−38
Computer operators and peripheral equipment operators	−41

Note: Projected growth rates of fast-growing occupations equal or exceed 40 percent per year. Rates of growth are BLS Moderate estimates. Other estimates are Low and High. Only occupations with employment exceeding 100,000 in 1992 are included.

Source: Bureau of Labor Statistics, *The American Work Force: 1992-2005*, Bulletin 2452, April 1994, 59-71, table 2.

Adding the attraction of earnings from crime to that of welfare benefits, Finis Welch's economic analysis supports Murray's case.[28] Unlike this book, which focuses on employment, Welch's and other writings discussed here analyze changes in wages. Welch reasons that, if welfare benefits increase, fewer people will want to work at the same wage rate. A rise in welfare benefits will induce more of those nurse's aides who work unwillingly to choose welfare, and some of those welfare beneficiaries who are seeking work will stop looking. To employ the same number of unskilled workers, hospitals, restaurants, and apparel manufacturers will have to raise wages. Thus, an increase in welfare benefits will reduce the supply of unskilled labor, resulting in a *fall* in employment and a *rise* in wages. The combination of a fall in employment and a rise in wages signifies a fall in supply. Suppose that demand falls. As laundries add to their machinery, their demand for labor falls. Employment will *fall* and wages will also *fall*. The difference between a fall in supply and a fall in demand is that in the former case wages rise, and in the latter they fall. Welch shows that between 1970 and 1980 the percentage of black men who were employed or seeking work fell, but the wage rates of those who were employed rose. In short, employment fell, and wages rose. Thus, according to Welch, the supply of black male labor fell, and the cause was the increased availability of welfare benefits and the earnings from crime.

But other scenarios can explain the rise in wage rates and the fall in the percentage of black males in the labor force. The employment of skilled blacks may have risen. As we see later in this chapter, skilled blacks increased as a percentage of all blacks. In addition, they may have achieved greater seniority, they may have gained entry to unions, employers may have become less inclined to discriminate against blacks, and a decline in geographic wage differences may have resulted in a rise in blacks' relative wages.

Moreover, Welch does not analyze the labor market as a whole. Blacks are hired in the same markets as whites, and the wages of blacks move with the wages of whites as the demand and supply of unskilled workers as a whole change. By limiting his attention to blacks, Welch fails to include in the analysis the effect of the demand for unskilled labor as a whole. Because other changes may have brought about a rise in the wages of blacks, we cannot conclude from Welch's analysis that the rise of wages received by blacks was due to a decline in the supply of black male labor.

Further, a more persuasive argument would show that welfare benefits became more generous relative to the wages earned in low-wage occupations and similarly for the earnings from crime. Welch does not show either. He simply concludes from the combination of a fall in black employment and a rise in wages paid to working blacks that the cause of the fall in employment was a fall in supply. He then infers that welfare benefits increased and that the earnings from crime increased. The facts of whether welfare benefits actually increased are ignored. All that matters in this analysis is how employment and wages moved. As Chapter 5 shows, after 1975 welfare benefits fell, and they did not increase relative to earnings in unskilled occupations. I have no information on what happened to earnings from crime.

Also, Welch's analysis applies only to the 1970s. Unemployment rates of blacks continued to increase in the 1980s, when, as this chapter shows, the wage rates of unskilled workers fell relative to those of skilled workers. Also, the real wages of manufacturing production workers, consisting largely of unskilled workers, fell by 6 percent between 1980 and 1990.[29]

In a later paper that Welch did with Kevin Murphy, he turned to the skilled–unskilled wage difference.[30] Here Welch and his co-author deal with the appropriate groups. The analysis is not limited to blacks but deals instead with the wages and employment of all unskilled workers relative to those of skilled workers. Murphy and Welch represent the skilled workers by male college graduates and less skilled workers by male high-school graduates. If demand is responsible for an increase in the wage gap between college and high-school graduates, then it will be associated with an increase in the relative employment of college graduates. The analytical framework is the same as the one Welch applied in the earlier paper. However, in this context it is relative wages and relative employment that are the issue, rather than absolute wages and absolute employment, as in Welch's study of black employment. A *fall* in the relative employment of high-school graduates combined with a *fall* in their relative wages indicates a fall in the relative demand for unskilled labor. Looking at it from the side of skilled labor, a high demand for college graduates will raise their employment as well as their wages relative to the employment and wages of high-school graduates.

The paper focuses on changes in relative wages because it is clear that the relative employment of skilled workers increased. Murphy and Welch observe that the college–high school wage difference rose from 40 percent to 48 percent between 1963 and 1971. It fell to 38 percent during the rest of the 1970s. The 1980s saw a large increase. By 1989 the difference was as high as 58 percent. These estimates are for all age groups. For younger workers the increase in the difference in the 1980s was much greater than for older workers. For workers with ten years of experience or less, the difference increased from 28 percent to 69 percent.[31] Murphy and Welch conclude that the relative demand for unskilled workers did not change between 1963 and 1973. On the other hand, the 1980s saw a sharp decline.

This conclusion supports the view that the rise of black unemployment during the 1980s was due to a fall in the demand for unskilled labor. Welch's explanation for the rise of black unemployment during the 1970s in his earlier article would not apply to the 1980s. However, again, important facts are neglected. The conclusions depend entirely on the relative movements of wages and employment of the two groups of workers.

Using an analytical framework similar to Welch's and Murphy and Welch's, Lawrence Katz and Murphy conclude that the demand for unskilled labor fell over the entire period from 1963 to 1987.[32] In contrast to the paper by Murphy and Welch, they do not limit this conclusion to the 1980s. Katz and Murphy find that both relative wages and relative employment of unskilled workers fell. The period they examine includes Welch's period; and although demand was especially important in the 1980s, its influence predominated over the longer period.

According to Katz and Murphy, because the decline in demand was pervasive, it was due to neither a switch by consumers from low-tech to high-tech products nor a switch to imports. The authors infer that changes in the prices of nonlabor inputs and technical changes within industries were responsible.[33] They do not specify the cost of capital goods, but this is the major nonlabor cost of manufactured goods.

Katz and Murphy argue that imports do not have a pervasive effect. If imports had been an important element in the shift from unskilled to skilled labor, then output would have moved from import-competing industries to other industries, which did not happen. Similarly, there was no shift in output from low-tech to high-tech industries. Evidently, the causes were changes in costs for industries generally.

Katz and Murphy restrict their attention to wages, ignoring employment. But employment absorbed some of the effect. Between 1950 and 1988 in manufacturing as a whole the number of production workers declined from 82.2 percent to 68.3 percent.[34] This decline was pervasive throughout manufacturing. Most production workers being unskilled, fewer production workers would entail fewer unskilled workers. This book's analysis of the fall in the demand for unskilled labor in Chapter 2 and in the present chapter supports Katz and Murphy's conclusion that it was economy-wide, reflecting intra-industry shifts away from unskilled labor in favor of capital goods and skilled labor.

However, my analysis does not reject, as Katz and Murphy do, the importance of shifts in output away from unskilled-intensive products and toward skilled-intensive and capital-intensive products. Shifts in demand between industries also reduced unskilled employment. I have classified industries as unskilled labor–intensive if over 50 percent of their employees are unskilled. For this purpose, the unskilled occupations are identified as operators, fabricators, laborers, service workers, farmers, and farmworkers.[35] While the GDP in constant dollars grew at the average annual rate of 3.0 percent between 1957 and 1986, the output of unskilled–labor intensive industries grew at the rate of 2.0 percent.[36] I have estimated that unskilled workers constitute 31 percent of the labor force, which in 1986 was about 36 million persons. The unemployment rate among the unskilled that year was 9.6 percent. Had the unskilled-intensive industries grown at the same rate as the economy as a whole and the proportion of unskilled to total workers remained the same, then there would have been no unemployment among the unskilled. Thus, the decline of unskilled-intensive industries accounted for a large part of the unskilled unemployment. Further, Chapter 4 shows that the growth of imports of unskilled-intensive products from developing countries has contributed to the decline of these industries.

Robert Topel's findings for the period between 1967 and 1969 and from 1987 to 1989 support the hypothesis that the rise in unemployment among the unskilled was due to a fall in demand for unskilled labor. As

Table 3.8
Percent of White and Black Employed Persons in Unskilled Occupations, Decennial Years, 1950–1990

	1950 (Percent)	1960 (Percent)	1970 (Percent)	1980 (Percent)	1990 (Percent)
Total	41.8	39.6	36.8	34.0	30.7
White	37.9	35.6	33.7	30.6	27.0
Black	79.6	76.1	64.2	52.8	45.5

Sources: 1990 Census of Population, Supplementary Reports, 1990 CP-S-1-1, "Detailed Occupation and Other Characteristics from the EEO File for the United States," October 1992, 1-11, table 1; 1980 Census of Population, PC-0-S1-8, "Detailed Occupation and Years of School Completed by Age, for the Civilian Labor Force by Sex, Race, and Spanish Origin: 1980," March 1983, 7-17, table 1; 1970 Census of the Population Subject Reports, PC (2)-7A, "Occupational Characteristics," June 1973, 12-27, table 2, 1960 Census of the Population Special Report, PC(2)-7A, "Occupational Characteristics," 1963, 21-38, table 3; 1950 Census of the Population Special Report, PE no. 18, "Occupational Characteristics," 1956, 29-36, table 3.

Chapter 1 reports, Topel shows that the number of jobless weeks among low-paid workers rose more than among high-paid workers. His finding of a negative correlation between the change in the number of jobless weeks and the change in wages across wage groups is consistent with the demand hypothesis. Joblessness among low-paid workers increased more than among high-paid workers while their wages fell more.[37]

THE INCREASE IN SKILL AMONG BLACKS AND AMONG WHITES

Blacks as well as whites became skilled workers in the postwar period. I have estimated the shift in the unskilled proportion of black workers between 1950 and 1990. For this purpose I have defined unskilled workers to include operators, fabricators, and laborers, and those in service occupations, including private household workers, those working in protective service occupations, food service, and cleaning and building service. Skilled occupations include managers, professionals, technicians, and those in sales occupations and in administrative support.[38] A more careful estimate might reassign some of the more detailed occupations—such as police and firefighters, who are now included among the unskilled. Similarly, cashiers, who are now included among the skilled, might be reassigned. However, such detailed decisions would not affect the overall results significantly.

Table 3.8 shows that over the whole period the percentage of unskilled blacks fell from 79.6 to 45.5, compared to a fall from 37.9 to 27.0 whites.

The fall among blacks was especially large in the 1960s and 1970s. It is also evident that the decline in the number of unskilled workers among blacks was greater than among whites, which may have been due to the initial high percentage of unskilled blacks. But it should also be noted that the remaining large number of unskilled blacks may also be due to the initial large number. In any case, many blacks have moved up the skill ladder.

CONCLUSION

Public policy contributed importantly to the growth of unemployment among the unskilled during the postwar period. Chapter 2 discussed the role of the full-employment fiscal and monetary policies in reducing real interest rates relative to unskilled workers' wages. This chapter shows that government egalitarian and education policies induced employers to substitute skilled for unskilled labor by reducing the relative cost of skilled labor. The high wage rates paid to unskilled workers during the war persisted into the postwar period. The government's wage policy and the high demand for unskilled labor were responsible for the high wage rates. The extension of the minimum-wage law's coverage to include farmworkers and other workers not previously covered also added to unemployment. Further, federal, state, and local governments induced employers to substitute skilled for unskilled workers by subsidizing higher education, which increased the supply of skilled workers and reduced their wages relative to those of unskilled workers. The flood of college graduates depressed the wages of professionals, managers, and technicians. By reducing the cost of higher education to students and their families, the subsidies also encouraged students to extend their studies, which enhanced their skills. Scientific advances also added to the skills of skilled workers. Neither additional schooling nor advances in science added to the skills of unskilled workers. The unfortunate side effect of the government egalitarian and education policies was a diminishing demand for unskilled workers, resulting in the decline of unskilled employment, and thus of black employment. Although other factors also contributed, including the wartime demand for unskilled labor and the increase in the supply of female labor, government policies played an important part.

This chapter also shows that the number of skilled workers increased among blacks as well as among whites. The government's policies benefited skilled workers, including those who were black.

NOTES

1. Daniel S. Hamermesh and James Grant, "Econometric Studies of Labor-Labor Substitution and Their Implications for Policy," *Journal of Human Resources*, 14, no. 4: 529, 531.

2. Based on "School Enrollment," *Current Population Survey*, P20–474, October 1992, table 35, 137.

3. Gary S. Becker, *Human Capital: A Theoretical and Empirical Analysis with Special Reference to Education* (New York: Columbia University Press, 1964), 78.

4. Based on *Historical Statistics of the United States: Colonial Times to 1970, Bicentennial Edition*, 1975 (*HSB*), ser. H720–22.

5. Based on *HSB*, ser. H707.

6. Census of Population 1950, Occupational Characteristics, P. E. no. 1b; 1990 Census of Population, Detailed Occupation and Other Characteristics from the EEO File for the United States, 1990 CP–S–1–1. What the Census called "clerical workers" in 1950, it called "administrative support occupations" in 1990.

7. Based on Roger G. Kramer, "Developments in International Migration to the United States: 1994," Immigration Policy and Research Working Paper 21, November 28, 1994, U.S. Department of Labor, Bureau of International Labor Affairs, 6.

8. Claudia Goldin and Robert A. Margo, "The Great Compression: The Wage Structure in the United States at Mid-Century," *Quarterly Journal of Economics*, 107 (February 1992) no. 1: 24. They cite Hugh Rockoff, *Drastic Measures: A History of Wage and Price Controls in the United States* (New York: Cambridge University Press, 1986).

9. BLS, *Handbook of Labor Statistics—1975*, Bulletin 1865, 248, table 98.

10. Estimate based on David M. Blank and George J. Stigler, *The Demand and Supply of Scientific Personnel* (New York: National Bureau of Economic Research, 1957), 25.

11. Goldin and Margo, "The Great Compression," 7.

12. *HSB*, ser. K351, K705, K710, D802.

13. Blackburn, Bloom, and Freeman estimate that among white males between 1980 and 1987 the ratio of earnings of operatives and of handlers and laborers and service workers to those of managers and professionals fell by 12 percent. The fall in the earnings of high school dropouts and of high school graduates relative to those of college graduates supports the conclusion that the skill differentials in earnings grew in the 1980s. According to Blackburn, Bloom, and Freeman, the earnings of high school dropouts fell by 16 percent relative to those of college graduates, while the relative earnings of high school graduates fell by 11 percent. McKinley L. Blackburn, David E. Bloom, and Richard B. Freeman, "The Declining Economic Position of Less-Skilled American Men," in Gary Burtless (ed.), *A Future of Lousy Jobs? The Changing Structure of U.S. Wages* (Washington, D.C.: Brookings Institution, 1990), 36.

14. Goldin and Margo's observations of the ratio of the earnings of college graduates to those of high school graduates are similar. According to Goldin and Margo, the ratio of weekly wages of college graduates with 11 to 15 years experience to those of high school graduates with the same number of years experience in 1940 was 1.777; in 1950 1.461; in 1960 1.565; in 1963 1.584; and in 1987 1.635. Goldin and Margo, "The Great Compression," 7.

15. Blackburn, Bloom, and Freeman, "The Declining Economic Position of Less Skilled American Men," 60–61.

16. *HSB*, ser. K351, D802.

17. John Cogan, "The Decline in Black Teenage Employment: 1950–70," *American Economic Review*, 72 (September 1982): 623.

18. Cogan, "Black Teenage Employment," 630–31.

19. Ibid., 629.

20. Ibid., 629–30.

21. The data for 1994 are approximately the same as that for 1982. In 1994 29.5 percent of all employed male workers of the age 25 or over had obtained at least a bachelor's degree. The following are the percentages for each occupation: professional and technical 71.9; managers 53.0; sales 36.9; clerical 24.9; craft 6.5; operatives and laborers 4.7; service 12.1; farmers 9.6. In 1994 32.6 percent of all employed male workers 25 years of age or more were high school graduates who did not obtain a bachelor's degree. The following are the percentages for each occupation: professional and technical 7.1; managers 18.3; sales 26.7; clerical 32.7; craft 48.3; operatives and laborers 50.8; service 38.4; farmers 38.5. The estimates are based on *Digest of Education Statistics 1995*, Department of Education, 404, table 370.

22. Eric A. Hanushek, "The Economics of Schooling: Production and Efficiency in Public Schools," *Journal of Economic Literature*, 14 (September 1986): 1153

23. *Digest of Education Statistics 1995*, 17, table 8.

24. *HSB*, 2: 30, ser. H602–605, *Statistical Abstract of the United States 1991* (*SAUS 1991*), 139, table 225.

25. Denison's estimates indicate that education improved the quality of the labor force at the average annual rate of 0.64 percent between 1929 and 1980. Based on Edward F. Denison, *Trends in American Economic Growth, 1929–1982* (Washington, D.C.: Brookings Institution, 1985), 85.

26. Denison estimated the contribution of advances in knowledge to the growth of output of nonresidential business at 0.86 percent per year between 1929 and 1982. (*Trends in American Economic Growth*, 100.) He used 0.8 as the weight for labor. Accordingly, the average annual rate of gain in the quality of skilled labor was (.86/2)/.8, or .54 percent.

27. Charles Murray, *Losing Ground: American Social Policy 1950–1980* (New York: Basic Books, 1984).

28. Finis Welch, "The Employment of Black Men," *Journal of Labor Economics*, 8, no. 1, Part 2 (1990): 526–74.

29. Hourly earnings in current dollars from *SAUS 1992*, 742, table 1247. Deflated by Consumer Price Index (CPI).

30. Kevin M. Murphy and Finis Welch, "The Structure of Wages," *Quarterly Journal of Economics*, 107 (February 1992): 285–326.

31. Murphy and Welch, "The Structure of Wages," 285–86.

32. Lawrence F. Katz and Kevin M. Murphy, "Changes in Relative Wages, 1963–1987: Supply and Demand Factors," *Quarterly Journal of Economics*, 107 (February 1992): 52.

33. Katz and Murphy, "Changes in Relative Wages, 1963–1987," 55–56.

34. Based on Bureau of Labor Statistics, *Handbook of Labor Statistics*, 1989, 298, 300.

35. Based on Bureau of the Census, *1980 Census of Population*, 1, *Characteristics of the Population*, Chapter D, Detailed Population Characteristics, Part 1, U.S. Summary, PC80–1–D1–A, Section A: United States Tables 253–310, March 1984, table 283, 1–322 to 1–337.

36. The source for estimates of the average annual rate of growth of constant-

dollar GDP for individual manufacturing industries is the Bureau of Labor Statistics. The rates for other industries were calculated from estimates of GDP in constant dollars by industry in *Economic Report of the President 1990* (*ERP* 1990), p. 307, table C–11. To arrive at the average rate for the selected industries, the individual rates were weighted by employment of unskilled workers.

37. Robert Topel, "What Have We Learned from Empirical Studies of Unemployment and Turnover?" *American Economic Review*, 83 (May 1993): 111.

38. See Chapter 1, note 9.

4

The Substitution of Foreign for Domestic Unskilled Labor

No mere theoretical treatise high above the realm of policy, Adam Smith's *The Wealth of Nations* flayed the government for imposing restrictions on wealth-generating competition, among them barriers to imports. David Ricardo developed the theory of international trade by introducing the fundamental concept of comparative advantage, which furnishes the dominant justification for moving toward free trade. The concept is central to the explanation of the direction of international trade flows, and it underlies the case for free trade. The theory says that by producing those goods that give them a comparative advantage, countries will make the best use of their resources. It makes sense for a country rich in capital to produce aircraft, leaving the production of textiles to countries having an abundance of unskilled workers. The case for trade liberalization also gains strength from the idea that competition from foreign-based firms forces domestic firms to be lean. Without urgent foreign competition, CEOs may not dare to take the harsh measures necessary for maximum efficiency.

I will not dispute the theory of comparative advantage expressed in general terms. Thus, I have no objection to the statement that the United States has a comparative advantage in the production of movies, and it is difficult for other countries to acquire the needed resources. However, the usual statement features two inputs: labor and capital. In that form it is open to dispute, because capital is mobile. If the theory were stated more generally, it would not be objectionable. Some critical aspect of the U.S. movie industry, which is difficult to relocate out of the country, gives it a comparative advantage, not the international immobility of capital. Unfortunately, policy conclusions are drawn from the assumption that capital is immobile along with labor. This chapter discusses the theory as usually stated with both capital and labor as immobile factors. I will make one change in the representation of the theory. I will substitute "unskilled labor" for "labor."

Proponents of free trade assume wrongly that capital does not move internationally and that resources are fully employed in trading countries. Inasmuch as these assumptions are false, imports of manufactured goods from low-wage countries can harm U.S. workers. Thus, the long-standing policy of trade liberalization and the resulting misfortune of the unskilled unemployed stem from a bad theory. Trade liberalizers also rely on the false argument that U.S. jobs are protected by high productivity.

Asserting that trade liberalization has not harmed unskilled workers significantly, most writers favor the policy. Thus, according to Paul Krugman, Robert Lawrence, and Jagdish Bhagwati, unskilled workers have not suffered from the growth of imports. They blame the sharp decline in unskilled jobs in manufacturing industries and the widening income inequality in the 1980s on technological change and other factors independent of trade.[1] However, the verdict is not unanimous. Some economists, including Edward Leamer, Adrian Wood, and Jeffrey Sachs and Howard Shatz, realize that manufactured imports from developing countries have contributed.[2]

Despite the nearly universal approbation of the case for free trade, an old protectionist argument, known as the infant–industry argument, has experienced a revival. Its foremost expositor, Friedrich List, wrote that, while they learn a technology, establish market contacts, and gain scale economies, new industries need shelter against foreign, established industries.[3] Current protectionists point to the huge growth of Japan's computer chip and telecommunications equipment industries under government protection. However, having been taught in college to reject the infant-industry case, some protectionists invoke a strategic argument. They urge retaliatory quotas and tariffs against other countries to induce them to abandon their protectionism. Japan's mercantilist policy being the chief villain, the protectionists urge a tit-for-tat strategy.

Worried about the loss of skilled jobs, protectionists despair over other *developed* countries' trade policies. The framework is the nation's welfare; progress is measured by the Gross Domestic Product (GDP); and the greater the number of high-paying jobs, the better off the nation. Distressed by the flight of skilled jobs, Laura D'Andrea Tyson advocates retaliation against Japan's import barriers. She does not challenge the general principles of international trade theory; more to the point, Tyson and most economists would not suggest restricting imports from *developing* countries.[4] But it is the flight of unskilled jobs that should be the primary concern. Whether or not we adopt a retaliatory policy against other developed countries' import barriers, the higher priority should be to shelter our unskilled workers. And it is the imports from Hong Kong, China, Malaysia, and Mexico and other developing countries that have displaced American unskilled workers.

International trade theory has had enormous influence. Faithful to Ricardo, all administrations, beginning with Franklin Roosevelt's, have pursued trade liberalization. It was the Kennedy round of trade negotiations under the General Agreement of Tariffs and Trade (GATT) that brought about an especially large reduction in import barriers, and the rounds that followed lowered them further.

Trade liberalizers' assurances that imports are no threat do not persuade labor unions, who especially fear competition from low-wage, developing countries. For this reason, the American Federation of Labor and Congress of Industrial Organizations (AFL-CIO) opposed the North American Free Trade Agreement (NAFTA) and GATT. Because imports of agricultural and mineral products do not threaten U.S. workers, I distinguish between manufactured and other imports. Relying on the free trade doctrine, the administration and the majority in Congress dismissed the fear.

Imports have in fact harmed U.S. unskilled workers. Trade liberalization, which began to cut deeply into unskilled employment in the 1980s, exacerbated the effects of the wage-equalization, full-employment, education, and minimum-wage policies. In that decade, when the real interest rate was much higher than earlier in the postwar period and the growth of the skilled labor force had slowed, the growth of imports was largely responsible for the continued fall in unskilled employment. True, unskilled workers gained from the low prices of imports, but they lost more in earnings. The workers in the textile, apparel, toy, electronics, and other unskilled labor–intensive industries directly competing with imports from developing countries were not the only ones harmed. By shrinking the demand for their labor, these imports hurt unskilled workers generally. Because skilled workers gained, the bulk of the so-called national gain was effectively a tax on the poor third of the people, the benefits going to the richer two-thirds.

Unfortunately, trade liberalization has forced 37 million Americans to compete with 1.4 billion unskilled workers in developing countries.[5] As long as trade had a minor influence, the incomes of unskilled U.S. workers were determined by conditions within the country. In the 1970s trade liberalization began to cast unskilled Americans into the Third World. Imports from developing countries grew tremendously after the mid-1970s, especially those from China, Hong Kong, South Korea, Malaysia, Singapore, Taiwan, Thailand, Brazil, and Mexico.

The policy broke the nation's implicit wage and employment contract with unskilled workers. Imports are not entirely to blame for unskilled workers' worsening lot, but they contributed, and their effect grows. We all live by understandings based on what we are accustomed to. We expect to maintain our standard of living, and we react to disappointment with frustration and anger. The violence in the cities is caused by breach of the contract.

Inasmuch as the theory of international trade gives trade liberalization its legitimacy, it needs examination.

INTERNATIONAL TRADE THEORY

Ricardo said that free trade forces countries to produce those goods in which they enjoy a *comparative* advantage. A few words about absolute advantage may clarify the concept of comparative advantage. Smith argued that free trade permits a country to profit from other countries' superior productivity—from their absolute advantage. Suitable climate gives Portugal an absolute advantage in wine, and England has an absolute advantage in cloth. But what if all the absolute advantages are on one side? Will trade take place? If England can produce both cloth and wine, with fewer labor hours per unit of product than Portugal can, why should it trade? More to the point, does England benefit from trade?

Ricardo solved the puzzle neatly. With tariffs barring imports, the price of each product is proportional to the amount of labor required to produce one unit, the amounts differing in the two countries. Ricardo's assumption that labor is the only input gains simplicity at the cost of only a small error. Suppose that in England one yard of cloth costs two liters of wine, while in Portugal one yard of cloth costs three liters of wine. Suppose also that tariffs are scrapped. By selling cloth in Portugal, an English merchant can get three liters of wine for one yard of cloth instead of two liters of wine. By selling wine in England, a Portuguese merchant can get one and one-half yards of cloth in exchange for three liters of wine instead of only one yard. England's comparative advantage is in cloth, and Portugal's is in wine. The theory says nothing about England's efficiency in producing cloth relative to Portugal's. Even if England can produce more of both goods with a unit of labor than Portugal can, it will specialize in cloth, and Portugal will specialize in wine. Thus, in a free trade world comparative advantage directs which goods countries export and import.[6] The elimination of tariffs would enlarge the market for each product; and as Smith pointed out, the degree of specialization increases with the size of the market. Because specialization would lower prices and increase output, England would benefit from free trade. The price of each product would be lower in both countries.

Portugal's comparative advantage in wine comes from a warm climate and good soil, which are hard to move; thus, it could retain this advantage. To engage in trade, England must have a comparative advantage in another product. Given Portugal's advantage in wine, England's could be in any other product, which may be cloth. One country's comparative advantage in a product implies that other countries have a comparative advantage in other products.

Ricardo did not analyze the sources of comparative advantage. The modern theory of international trade does. Heckscher, Ohlin, and Samuelson extended Ricardo's theory by locating a country's comparative advantage in its resources.[7] A country exports goods requiring resources with which it is abundantly supplied. Subsequent applications of the theory have illustrated it by specifying two inputs: labor and capital. Substituting "unskilled labor" for "labor," the theory says that countries abundantly supplied with capital export capital-intensive goods, and similarly for those in which unskilled labor is plentiful. The United States's abundance of capital and its scarcity of unskilled labor give it a comparative advantage in aircraft and machinery. China's large supply of unskilled labor and its small supply of capital give it a comparative advantage in apparel. Later writers have specified human capital as an input. Skilled labor is regarded as a composite of unskilled labor and education, or human capital.

Both the old and the new versions of international trade theory assume that all inputs to production are immobile between countries. In particular the policy discussions based on the theory assume that labor and capital are internationally immobile. Thus, people do not move across frontiers in large enough numbers to affect the prices of goods; and capital, which includes money, other financial instruments, machinery, and other capital goods, is also confined within countries. Only goods and services move internationally. The other basic assumption is that labor and capital are fully employed, implying that workers displaced by imports are unemployed only briefly. The theory argues that, because both capital and labor are immobile, comparative advantage decides the direction of trade: efficiency rules.

The assumption concerning labor mobility may be close enough to the truth to pose little risk. Although Koreans have worked on Middle East construction projects; Germany has many Turkish guest-workers; and many Latin Americans migrate to the United States, such movements have not been large enough to depress wages in high-wage countries significantly. In the late 1980s only 80 million people, or 1.5 percent of the world's population, were away from their countries of citizenship, and much of the movement was in Sub-Saharan Africa.[8]

However, the assumption that capital is internationally immobile has led economists astray. The multinational corporations active in Malaysia do not apply for loans to local banks or sell securities there. They rely on their retained earnings from world-wide operations and sales of securities in the United States and other developed countries. This is similar for mutual and pension funds investing in developing countries.

Immense quantities of capital move daily between countries. In 1994 U.S. companies invested $9.9 billion directly in Asia and $12.2 billion in Latin America.[9] "Direct investment" refers to the purchase and construction of plants, as opposed to the purchase of securities issued by companies active in those countries. In addition, mutual funds, such as the Vanguard Group and the Scudder Global Fund, buy the securities of companies in developing countries, which are frequently referred to as "emerging markets." Of course, the United States is not the only foreign source of capital for developing countries. Between 1987 and 1991 Japan's average total direct foreign investment per year was $35 billion. Much of the investment was to establish plants in Malaysia, Indonesia, and Thailand.[10] Moreover, according to Sachs and Shatz, in the 1980s global foreign direct investment grew faster than international trade or world income. Hungry for capital, developing countries have liberalized the rules governing foreign direct investment. Also, international agreements protect foreign investors. NAFTA contains provisions for dispute resolution, guarantees of fair compensation for expropriated investment, and liberalization of access for foreign direct investment.[11]

The assumption of international capital immobility was unrealistic even when the theory was developed. The nineteenth century saw large capital movements. In the latter part of the century British capital helped finance the building of railroads and heavy industry in the United States, India, Canada, and Argentina. The flow of capital abroad was large enough to keep the yields on foreign investment remarkably low. Thus, in the United States in 1900 the yield on high-grade municipal bonds was 3.1 percent, which was not much more than the 2.8 percent yield on British Consols.[12]

My excuse for belaboring the obvious is that the assumption of international capital immobility is strongly entrenched in international trade economics. Why that should be is a puzzle for the historians of economic thought. Perhaps the proposition that comparative advantage determined trade flows was too intriguing to give up for the sake of the model's descriptive accuracy, and the proposition that low absolute costs yielded a competitive advantage was too obvious to be interesting. Moreover, if low wages were important, then there was nothing to distinguish international trade theory from general economic theory. Economists could use the framework that they apply to trade between Massachusetts and North Carolina to explain trade between the United States and Brazil. No one disputes that the textile industry moved from New England to the South in the 1920s because labor was cheaper in the South. Because in a free-trade world nothing distinguishes international from domestic trade, low wages can move industries between countries as effectively as within countries. But, on the basis of certain assumptions, international trade theorists deny the power of low wages to draw capital from one country to another, in the face of contrary evidence.

In any case, international trade theory with its false assumptions underlies many economic studies, including those cited by the administration in support of NAFTA. However, in the actual world, where capital is mobile and labor is immobile, relative wages matter. Capital moves to where wages are low. The low-wage developing countries take over the world markets for unskilled labor–intensive goods.

The importance of capital mobility should not be underrated for another reason. Because of capital mobility, unskilled workers lose their jobs quickly in industries competing with developing countries' exports. Were capital immobile, Mexico's exports would be limited by its existing capacity plus those additions paid for from the limited savings of its nationals. Manufactured imports from developing countries would grow slowly in a capital-immobile world, and American unskilled workers would not be displaced by a great flood of imports. Moreover, one should bear in mind that capital includes actual plants and equipment as well as financial capital. When a textile plant moves from South Carolina to Mexico, its workers lose their jobs immediately.

The theory's other important, false assumption is that of full employment in all countries. The conclusion follows that imports by developed countries only shift labor from apparel and other import-competing industries to machinery and other export industries. Free trade cannot inflict much harm if imports deprive workers of jobs only briefly. This reasoning is merely a circuitous way of dodging the employment issue. Assume full employment, then there is no employment problem.

The assumption is also vital in another context. Applied to developing countries it implies that as their manufactured exports grow, wages will rise. Manufacturers have to pay higher wages as they draw more workers out of agriculture. But, contrary to the assumption, much of the labor force in developing countries is unemployed or underemployed in agriculture. The official statistics do not distinguish between the underemployed and the employed, but underemployment along with unemployment results in a continuing large supply of workers at the same, low wage level. With many workers eager for jobs, manufacturers need not raise wages when they need additional workers.

Moreover, the population in developing countries continues to grow at a rapid pace. Between 1950 and 1990 the share of the world labor force in developing countries increased from 66 percent to 83 percent.[13] The supply of labor available to manufacturers in developing countries at what are low wages by the standards of industrialized countries promises to persist and depress the employment and wages of unskilled U.S.

workers. Even Mexico's surplus labor force is huge, and think of all Latin America and of East Asia.

If capital is mobile, what does determine the direction of trade? If an abundance of capital does not give a country a comparative advantage in capital-intensive products, then why does the United States export certain goods and not others? The United States possesses a comparative advantage in skill-intensive goods. It exports software, movies, machinery, aircraft, and pharmaceuticals. Software requires programmers, who are numerous in the United States. Movies require actors, producers, directors, editors, script writers, sound technicians, and photographers; the United States has plenty of people with the required skills. Moreover, this country gains a comparative advantage in the production of movies from a collection of particular skills. The movie industry is concentrated in Hollywood, where its writers, producers, directors, and so forth make up a community that enables them to keep abreast of changes in the industry more easily than if they were scattered. The concentration also enables firms to draw on the necessary resources as needed. Thus, even though capital is mobile within the United States, the movie industry does not relocate from Hollywood to South Carolina, where wages are lower. This applies to other industries as well.

Other countries have also developed industries employing clusters of valuable skills. India has many programmers, and it sells software to U.S. firms needing specially designed programs. The programmers are not spread out over India but are concentrated in Bangalore. Japan has built up a pharmaceutical industry by deliberately encouraging the development of the necessary collection of laboratory and clinical testing skills. France has cosmetics firms, which are clustered in Paris. Film animators have congregated in London. However, it takes time to build up the necessary minimum mass of skills to become competitive in the world market. While other countries are developing concentrations of necessary skills, U.S. export industries enjoy a comparative advantage in their products.

In large part, the advantages that industries have are due to historical accident. The United States developed an aircraft industry during World War II. The computer and associated industries also owe their early growth to special wartime needs. The first movie makers happened to be located in the area around Los Angeles. As the industry grew there, the number of producers, actors, directors, editors, and photographers living in the area also expanded, as did the number of outside firms supplying various inputs.

However, while the United States can produce certain goods at a relatively low cost, the unskilled workers who are displaced by imports do not benefit. They do not acquire the technical knowledge required by the export industries. The professionals and technicians in the movie, aircraft, and software industries benefit from trade liberalization. If these industries are to export their products, then other countries must be able to export to the United States. Even the unskilled workers employed by these industries do not benefit from trade liberalization. The parts of the production process that employ unskilled labor may be separated from those requiring skills. The aircraft industry can buy parts produced by unskilled labor from outside suppliers.

Moreover, the fact that the United States enjoys a comparative advantage in some industries does not protect unskilled workers generally against imports. As long as capital is mobile, firms will establish new plants in low-wage areas. They cannot create the concentration of skills necessary to develop computer programs in a new country, but they can establish plants to employ unskilled workers to assemble computers.

Then there is the case based on productivity, which I take up briefly here. A detailed examination is postponed until a later section. On the *Larry King Live!* program Ross Perot did not reply effectively to Vice President Al Gore's argument in their debate over NAFTA that the wages of Mexico's workers were one-seventh that of American workers because their productivity was one-seventh as great. What Gore did not mention was that it is the productivity of Mexico's industries competing directly with U.S. industries that matters, not the average productivity of Mexican workers, including those underemployed in agriculture. As we see later in this chapter, the productivity of workers employed in Mexican manufacturing industries is nearly as high on the average as the productivity of American workers in the competing industries. The wages of Mexican workers in manufacturing do not correspond to their productivity because unemployed workers and underemployed agricultural workers are ready to take their places.

THE STOLPER-SAMUELSON THEOREM

Although the main body of international trade theory supports free trade, there is a theorem that troubles its advocates. This theorem, formulated independently by Wolfgang Stolper and Paul Samuelson, says that trade drives wages in different countries together: trade depresses wages in high-wage countries, including the United States, and raises them in low-wage countries.[14] The theorem bothers Samuelson, a strong supporter of trade liberalization, enough for him to deny its importance. He maintains that trade's small influence on wages is overwhelmed by other forces. Nevertheless, trade liberalizers have felt obliged to refute the theorem.

Let us examine the theorem. Before trade occurs countries are isolated economically, and interest rates and wages are determined by a country's relative supplies of capital and labor. Because capital is scarce and labor is plentiful in China, capital there is expensive and labor is cheap; in the United States the converse holds. The conclusion about the effect of trade on wages is reached in two steps. The first is that trade pushes the prices of traded goods toward equality across countries. The price of a shirt will be approximately the same in the exporting and importing countries. Because transportation costs are too small to protect wages in high-wage countries, the theorem assumes that they are zero.

The second step is as follows. Because trade forces the prices of apparel and other labor-intensive goods down, high-wage countries will reduce the output of these goods. Some U.S. apparel manufacturers will go out of business, and the survivors will pay lower wages, resulting in a fall in U.S. workers' wages. The converse happens in China. Because labor is fully employed, wages there increase, as the demand for the labor-intensive products rises. Wages in the two countries converge.

Attacking the Stolper-Samuelson theorem, Jagdish Bhagwati and Vivek Dehejia say that, according to the theorem, the only way imports can depress U.S. wages is by driving down the prices of import-competing goods.[15] Because the debate concerns the harm to unskilled workers, the authors restrict their attention to this group. Although Bhagwati and Dehejia do not say so, the argument follows from the traditional full-employment assumption, which implies that imports will not depress wages by reducing employment. Thus, if imports depress wages, it is through a fall in the prices of import-competing goods. Choosing not to challenge the capital-immobility and full-employment assumptions, Bhagwati and Dehejia attack the theorem on other grounds.

According to the authors, because the prices of import-competing, un-skilled-intensive goods have not fallen relative to other prices, imports have not depressed unskilled workers' wages.[16] However, what is critical is the assumption of capital immobility, for without it falling prices are not necessary for this effect. If capital moves, then the production of unskilled labor–intensive goods moves to developing countries from the United States, which now imports these goods. The total supply of un-skilled labor–intensive goods in the United States does not change; therefore, the prices of these goods will not change.

Moreover, the prices of import-competing goods may be depressed by imports, even if they do not fall more than other prices. Imports are only one of the factors affecting prices; another important factor over a long period is productivity growth. Productivity growth in the aircraft industry has brought down the prices of aircraft, nearly all of which are supplied domestically, more than the prices of apparel, much of which is imported. Had imports been barred, apparel prices would be much higher than they are. Moreover, if trade does not reduce prices, what is the case for trade liberalization?

Further, in the industries hardest hit by imports relative prices did fall.

Lawrence and Slaughter find that the prices of unskilled labor–intensive goods as a whole rose relative to the prices of skilled labor–intensive goods as a whole. However, in the large industries most affected by import competition—apparel, footwear, and textiles—relative prices did fall. In the case of apparel, where imports grew to 44 percent of U.S. apparent consumption in 1994,[17] between 1975 and 1993 producer prices fell 17 percent relative to the producer prices of all finished goods.[18] What is more, it was not rapid productivity growth that reduced the relative prices of apparel. According to the BLS, productivity growth in the apparel industries was slower than in manufacturing as a whole.[19]

Moreover, using more appropriate measures of prices, Sachs and Shatz conclude that imports caused the prices of unskilled–intensive, import-competing goods to fall more than the prices of other goods. Their measure of skill intensity is the ratio of the number of highly educated workers to the number of less educated workers. Sachs and Shatz find that the net exports (total exports minus total imports) of unskilled-intensive industries fell sharply between 1979 and 1990. They point out that Lawrence and Slaughter analyze changes in gross output prices rather than the more appropriate value-added prices.[20] The value-added price is the price of the part of the output produced within the industry. It does not include the price of purchased components. In the case of aircraft, the value-added price excludes the price of the aluminum. The gross-output price, on the other hand, refers to the price of the aircraft as a whole. Between 1979 and 1990 the relative value-added price of unskilled labor–intensive, import-competing domestic products fell by 16 percent.

The increase in imports and the resulting price decline contributed to the fall in the wages of apparel production workers of 24 percent relative to the average for all manufacturing production workers.[21] It is important to observe that the comparison here is between unskilled apparel workers and unskilled workers in manufacturing as a whole. Moreover, the decline in wages was accompanied by a fall in employment. Production-worker employment in the apparel industry fell from 11.8 percent of the employment of production workers in manufacturing to 6.7 percent.[22] Further, the fall in employment was not due to a fall in consumer expenditures on clothing. Between 1975 and 1993 such expenditures measured in constant dollars grew from 4.7 percent of total personal consumption expenditures to 5.7 percent.[23] Thus, much of the fall in the wages and employment of apparel production workers was due to imports taking a vastly increased share of the market.

Bhagwati and Dehejia challenge the Stolper-Samuelson assumption that technology is the same across countries. Capital-intensive products in advanced countries, they point out, may be unskilled labor–intensive in developing countries. If this is so and trade depresses the U.S. prices of what are unskilled labor–intensive products in Mexico, then it need not depress U.S. wages. This argument relies only on possible differences, not on actual differences, and the industries of concern here are those that are unskilled labor–intensive in the U.S. In these industries the technology in developing countries is essentially the same as in the United States. Thus, as Table 4.2 reports, the differences in labor productivity between the U.S. and certain developing countries in the manufacture of shirts does not offset the wage differences.

Challenging what they consider to be an implication of the theorem, Bhagwati and Dehejia say that firms will respond to an import-induced fall in unskilled workers' wages by substituting unskilled for skilled workers. However, because the percentage of unskilled workers has fallen in most industries, they attribute the fall in wages to technical change. Chapters 2 and 3 suggest that the falls in the relative cost of both capital and skilled labor were critical for the decline in unskilled employment. But recognizing the contributions of these factors plus that of technical change does not deny that imports also reduced the demand for unskilled labor.

Bhagwati and Dehejia further say that unskilled workers may gain more from better utilization of scale economies and the resulting lower prices than they lose in wages. This argument too is in the realm of possibilities. There is no evidence that trade generates large economies of scale in many industries. Large plant size is not the source of developing countries' apparel and textile manufacturers' competitive advantage. True, firms in U.S. export industries, including aircraft, electrical equipment, pulp mills, construction machinery, food products machinery, and electronic computing equipment, tend to be larger than other firms; but only aircraft and electrical equipment appear to require a larger market than the U.S. to gain the full advantages of scale. And, the price cuts in these industries due to the elimination of trade barriers are unlikely to compensate U.S. unskilled workers for their wage and employment losses.

Then there is the X-efficiency argument.[24] Firms are X-efficient if they use no more labor or materials than necessary to produce a given output. The downsizing that has occurred recently in AT&T, General Motors, Boeing, IBM, Eastman Kodak, Lockheed-Martin, and other companies suggests that X-inefficiency has been rampant in American industry. In some markets the growth of imports appears to have driven domestic firms to greater efficiency. But the argument does not apply to the major unskilled labor–intensive industries—apparel, textile, and shoe manufacturing. The growth of imports was unlikely to improve the efficiency of these highly competitive domestic industries, in which profits were already low before the sharp increases in imports in the 1970s and 1980s.

Finally, the argument that imports cannot depress wages unless they

Table 4.1
Hourly Compensation in U.S. Dollars for Manufacturing Production Workers
and Indexes (U.S. = 100), 1975, 1992

	U.S. Dollars		Indexes	
	1975	1992	1975	1992
United States	$6.36	$16.17	100	100
Mexico	1.44	2.35	23	15
Hong Kong	0.76	3.89	12	24
Japan	3.00	16.16	47	100
Korea	0.33	4.93	5	30
Singapore	0.84	5.00	13	31
Taiwan	0.40	5.19	6	32
Sri Lanka	0.28	0.35*	4	2*

* For 1990.
Source: BLS, Office of Productivity and Technology, March 1993.

reduce the prices of import-competing goods needs the full-employment assumption. This unrealistic assumption does not justify increasing imports from developing countries. A realistic argument would conclude that manufactured imports from developing countries reduce wages and employment.

PRODUCTIVITY DIFFERENCES

The case usually presented for trade liberalization invokes international productivity differences as well as international trade theory. NAFTA's defenders try to assure anxious workers that their high productivity shields their high wages. Average hourly earnings of manufacturing production workers in Mexico in 1992 were $2.17 compared to $16.17 in the United States,[25] or a little less than one-seventh, but Mexican workers were one-seventh as productive as U.S. workers. Gary Hufbauer and Jeffrey Schott of the Institute for International Economics (IIE) recite the standard reassurance:

On average, high U.S. labor productivity pays for high U.S. wages. The U.S. worker earns high wages because of his high output, which in turn reflects his work skills, his complement of sophisticated capital equipment, and the highly articulated infrastructure of the U.S. economy.[26]

But it is the huge number of unemployed workers and of underemployed agricultural workers that depress manufacturing industries' wages in developing countries (see Table 4.1), not inferior productivity

Table 4.2
Labor Costs in the Manufacture of Men's Shirts, United States and Various
Developing Countries

	Person-Minutes per Shirt	Hourly Wage ($U.S.)	Wage Cost per Shirt ($U.S.)	Index of Wage Cost (U.S. = 100)
United States	14	7.53	1.76	100
Hong Kong	20	1.40	0.46	26
South Korea	21	1.53	0.53	30
Sri Lanka	24	0.35	0.14	8
India	23	0.40	0.15	9
Bangladesh	25	0.25	0.10	6

Source: Based on Walter Russell Mead, *The Low-Wage Challenge to Global Growth: The Labor Cost-Productivity Imbalance in Newly Industrialized Countries* (Washington, D.C.: Economic Policy Institute, 1990), 15.

in manufacturing. This was true in the early postwar years, even in Japan. Its export success was largely due to low wages, brought about by the availability of surplus agricultural labor. Between 1956 and 1971 agriculture's share of the labor force dropped from 41.9 percent to 17.7 percent,[27] so that as late as 1975 production workers in Japan earned only 47 percent as much as their U.S. counterparts.

The overall average productivity in developing countries is low, but it is the productivity in individual manufacturing industries that matters. And the productivity differences between developed and developing countries in the manufacture of unskilled labor–intensive goods do not compensate for the wage differences. The high U.S. wages in shirt manufacturing are not offset by high productivity (see Table 4.2). Apart from the United States, among the countries listed, South Korea has the highest cost; but even there the wage cost of a shirt is only 30 percent of that in the United States.

Moreover, Harley Shaiken found that in a Mexican automobile engine plant in 1985 labor productivity was as much as 75 percent of that in a U.S. plant.[28] Nor is Hufbauer and Schott's statement supported by Magnus Blostrom and Edward Wolff's estimates of productivity in several Mexican industries. In 1984 the productivity in Mexican textile mills was on the average 66 percent of that in U.S. counterparts: in food 51 percent; tobacco 75 percent; lumber and wood 111 percent; paper 68 percent; chemicals 60 percent; petroleum and coal 37 percent; rubber and plastic 185 percent; stone, clay, and glass 83 percent; primary metals 83 percent; fabricated metals 61 percent; non-electrical machinery 84 percent; electrical equipment 83 percent; and transport equipment 57 percent.[29] The average for all the industries studied by Blostrom and Wolff is 79 percent.

The low overall productivity of developing countries strengthens their manufacturers' competitiveness because it results in a huge, low-wage supply of unskilled labor. Instead of weakening their competitiveness, as some trade liberalizers argue, the low overall productivity is a source of strength to developing countries' manufacturing.

THE GROWTH OF U.S. IMPORTS

Multilateral negotiations under GATT in 1947 and 1967 reduced tariffs quite substantially on 44 percent and 67 percent, respectively, of dutiable imports by the United States. In both years the average reduction was 35 percent. After the Tokyo round of negotiations, tariffs were again cut by between 30 and 40 percent.[30] By 1981 the average tariff on dutiable imports had fallen to about 5 percent. Moreover, by 1993 the percentage of duty-free imports amounted to 41 percent of total imports.[31] The Fed's tight monetary policy beginning in 1979 also raised imports. Between 1980 and 1985 the yields on U.S. securities rose. As foreign investors eager to acquire them rushed to buy dollars, the real value of the dollar in terms of other currencies increased by 56 percent, sharply cutting foreign goods' dollar prices. Americans could buy trousers made in Hong Kong at much lower dollar prices. Because foreign sellers, who had become established in the U.S. market reduced their prices, imports did not drop back to the level of the 1970s after the exchange rates fell.

Manufactured imports from developing countries grew rapidly. As Table 4.3 reports, between 1965 and 1990 the output of manufacturing industries in developing countries in East Asia and Latin America grew much more rapidly than in OECD countries. Because trade liberalization and monetary policies opened the U.S. market, much of the growth was for export. Manufacturers based in the United States built foreign plants to produce for the U.S. market. Because textiles, apparel, radios, television sets, automobiles, and semiconductors require large inputs of unskilled labor,[32] manufacturers integrated their U.S. and foreign production. By the late 1970s more than 80 percent of U.S. semiconductor production was assembled abroad.[33] In 1990 shipments within transnational corporations made up as much as 33.6 percent of imports from Mexico.[34] Heading 9802.00.80 of the Harmonized Tariff Schedule spurred companies to shift operations abroad because it permits U.S.-made components of products further processed abroad to be imported duty-free. Transportation costs, which constitute a small part of the delivered price, do not bar trade in these products. In addition, the operations of manufacturing components, assembly, testing, and packaging can be separated easily into stages not requiring physical closeness. In addition, the

Table 4.3
Average Annual Growth Rates of Manufacturing Output in Various
Developing Countries and in OECD Countries, 1965–1980, 1980–1990

	1965-1980 (Percent)	1980-1990 (Percent)
India	4.5	7.1
China	8.9	14.4
Pakistan	5.7	7.7
Indonesia	12.0	12.5
Thailand	11.2	8.9
Malaysia	NA	8.8
Mexico	7.4	1.4
Brazil	9.8	1.7
Korea	18.7	12.7
Singapore	13.2	6.6
OECD	3.1	3.3

Source: World Bank, World Development Report 1992, 220-21.

assembly of these products requires large inputs of unskilled labor and small inputs of capital. Small wonder that manufacturing has grown much more rapidly in various developing countries than in OECD countries.

The growth rates of manufactured exports between 1965 and 1986, which ranged from 15.3 percent in China to 31.6 percent in Korea (see Table 4.4), show that much of the growth of manufacturing in the countries listed was for export. China's manufactured exports grew to 20 times its starting level; Korea's to 319 times. Accordingly, between 1980 and 1988 U.S. imports of manufactured goods from developing countries grew much more than those from the rest of the world (see Table 4.5). The rates of growth of imports from Mexico, Brazil, and the Asian newly industrialized countries (NICs) were especially high.

Imports have captured much of the U.S. market for a broad range of unskilled labor–intensive goods, including leather and sheep lined clothing; women's handbags and purses; textiles, not elsewhere classified (n.e.c.); women's nonathletic footwear; nonrubber footwear, n.e.c.; women's and misses' suits and coats; luggage, dolls, rubber and plastic footwear; leather gloves and mittens; games, toys, and children's vehicles; men's nonathletic footwear; fabric dress and work gloves; children's outerwear, n.e.c.; and waterproof outergarments.[35] Between 1982 and 1987 imports took between 26 percent and 88 percent of the U.S. market in these products. Among the industries with the highest penetration percentages were nonrubber footwear, n.e.c., with 87.8 percent; leather

Table 4.4
Growth Rates of Manufactured Exports by Various Developing Countries, 1965–1986

	Percent
Mexico	16.5
Brazil	24.0
Hong Kong	18.0
Korea	31.6
Singapore	20.4
Taiwan	28.0
China	15.3

Source: World Bank, World Development Report 1988, 248-49.

and sheep lined clothing with 66.3 percent; dolls with 65.9 percent; and women's handbags and purses with 55.7 percent.

Sachs and Shatz classify industries according to the intensity of unskilled labor, the measure being the ratio of production workers, their proxy for unskilled workers, to total workers. Periodicals and office and computing machines are two of the most skill-intensive industries; unskilled labor–intensive industries include footwear, girls' and children's outerwear, and other kinds of apparel. The United States has a large negative trade balance with developing countries in goods produced by unskilled workers.[36] Sachs and Shatz observe that imports from China are concentrated in the unskilled sectors.[37]

U.S. exports have also grown, but they consist of skill-intensive and capital-intensive goods. Edward Leamer has constructed a skill classification of industries based on the percentage of professionals and managers employed. The high-skill industries include aircraft, metalworking machinery, electrical machinery, and computers; while the industries ranking lowest include apparel, food products, furniture, and footwear. Leamer finds that between 1972 and 1985 the gains in the difference between exports and imports, or the net trade balance, were largest for the skilled-goods industries, and the net trade balance fell most for unskilled-goods industries.[38] Moreover, according to the Department of Labor, the industries enjoying a large increase in exports between 1982 and 1987 included the skill-intensive industries: oil field machinery; measuring and controlling devices, n.e.c.; pulp mills, aircraft equipment, n.e.c.; construction machinery, semiconductors and related devices; food products machinery, x-ray apparatus and tubes, and electronic computing equipment.[39]

The increase in imports of unskilled labor–intensive goods from developing countries resulted in job losses for unskilled workers. Sachs and

Table 4.5
Average Annual Rates of Growth of Manufactured Imports by the United States by Origin, 1980–1988

Origin	Percent
Total World	12.4
Developed Countries	11.1
Developing Countries	15.3
Mexico	17.2
Brazil	18.5
Asian NICs	16.0

Source: Based on Walter Russell Mead, *The Low-Wage Challenge to Global Growth: The Labor Cost-Productivity Imbalance in Newly Industrialized Countries* (Washington, D.C.: Economic Policy Institute, 1990), 11, table 4.

Shatz estimate that the rise in net imports (imports minus exports) between 1978 and 1990 resulted in a loss of 7.2 percent of production-worker jobs. Nearly the entire loss was the result of the increase in imports from developing countries.

Imports from developing countries are likely to continue growing. Foreign direct investment is growing; GATT and NAFTA will further reduce barriers to imports to the United States; these agreements will expand the protection to foreign investors by developing countries' governments; and the manufacturing capacity of these countries will grow.

THE GENERAL WELFARE

In their textbook, *Economics*, Paul Samuelson and William Nordhaus praise free trade:

If each country specializes in the products in which it has comparative advantage (or greatest relative efficiency), trade will be mutually beneficial. Real wages and incomes will rise in both countries. And these statements are true whether or not one of the regions is absolutely more efficient than the other in the production of every good.[40]

Trade liberalizers maintain that the United States can make better use of its labor than in apparel factories. They say that workers and the United States as a whole will gain from a shift from unskilled apparel, textile, and footwear jobs to skilled aircraft and machinery jobs. Unskilled work should be left to the countries with large numbers of unskilled workers. But a mythical market process underlies the analysis and the policy recommendations. Most important, the underlying assumption of full employment is simply not true. Displaced sewing-machine operators remain unemployed or find other unskilled jobs, displacing other workers. Policymakers make an ineffective attempt to help those directly displaced by imports by providing them with training programs, and they do nothing for the workers displaced by the trainees who do find jobs. As long as the demand for unskilled labor shrinks for other reasons, unemployment will rise as imports of unskilled labor–intensive products grow.

One reason economists are blind to what actually happens is their implicit assumption of homogeneous labor. The theory specifies only "labor," implying a homogeneous, pliable mass that flows easily from one use to another. There is also the implicit, false assumption that American unskilled workers are much more skilled than Mexican unskilled workers. In addition, economists and policymakers optimistically assume that displaced workers can easily be trained for other jobs. However, for unskilled workers to become skilled will require a large and unlikely increase in educational attainment. Trade Adjustment Assistance (TAA) and other training programs are ineffective. For practical purposes, trade liberalization has placed American unskilled workers in the world market for unskilled labor, where they have no special advantage.

By lowering prices, imports benefit consumers. However, most of the gain to consumers is a transfer from unskilled workers. Trade liberalizers assume that the United States is a single community, not a nation consisting of groups with conflicting interests. The conclusion that the community as a whole benefits requires a problematic summation of benefits and losses. According to the general welfare argument, the better use of labor and other resources resulting from trade produces benefits to the country as a whole, which exceed the losses to displaced workers. The rest of the community will still be better off, even if displaced workers are compensated for their losses. However, it is not clear that trade raises the GDP. It does so only if the displaced workers quickly get jobs paying as much or more than the jobs from which they are displaced. We are back in the never-never land of full employment.

Much of the case for trade liberalization rests on estimates of the cost of protection to the United States, such as the one William Cline of the Institute of International Economics (IIE) provides.[41] As he says about the textile and apparel industries:

The central policy questions may be stated simply: should the American public pay $20 billion or more annually in additional consumption costs in order to preserve approximately 200,000 more jobs in the specific sectors of textiles and apparel (but probably none economy-wide) than otherwise would exist?[42]

Let us examine Cline's argument. He estimates that in 1986 protection of the textile and apparel industries cost consumers $2,788 million and $17,556 million respectively. He also estimates that the elimination of the protection would reduce the number of textile jobs by 20.7 thousand and the number of apparel jobs by 214.2 thousand. These estimates of jobs lost do not include the losses to businesses supplying the textile and apparel industries. Thus, according to Cline, the cost per job saved in the textile and apparel industries by the quotas and tariffs in 1986 was $52,204 and $46,052 respectively. Pointing out that the average wages in these industries was about $12,000 annually, Cline concludes that the country would be better off paying the displaced workers several years' wages rather than maintaining the protection.

In my view, Cline considerably underestimates the number of jobs saved by the protection. I accept Cline's estimates of the effect of withdrawing protection on the prices of imports of textiles and on the prices of domestic textiles: 21.9 percent and 3.1 percent respectively. The import prices would fall by the amount of the tariff, and domestic prices cannot fall by a great deal because wages, which make up a large part of the total cost, are already very low compared to wages in other industries. The problem is with his estimate of the effect caused by removing protection on domestic output. Cline says that textile imports would increase by only 29.8 percent and the domestic output would fall by only 3.1 percent. These are underestimates. Domestic textile prices would have to decline nearly as much as imported textile prices for imports not to grow substantially, which, as Cline says, is unlikely. However, he then goes on to estimate a small increase in imports and a small decline in domestic production. A fall in import prices of as much as 21.9 percent will induce a large increase in imports and a corresponding large fall in domestic production. Consumers are bound to shift much of their purchases to imports. Domestic products are sufficiently similar to competing foreign products for the reduction in import prices to have an enormous effect. Domestic textile manufacturers will be unable to produce nearly as much as they do now when the quotas and tariffs are eliminated.

My chief quarrel with Cline, however, concerns the interpretation of the estimates for policy purposes rather than the estimates themselves. Part of the so-called cost to consumers of the tariff—24 percent—consists of the tariff revenue to the government; because the purpose of the tariff is protection, it should be disregarded. Of the remaining cost to consumers, Cline estimates that the transfer from consumers to workers whose jobs are saved makes up 66 percent. The rest consists of the gain in the GDP from an improvement in the allocation of resources plus the benefit to consumers from the ability to reallocate their expenditures to other goods.

Thus, most of the cost to consumers consists of the so-called transfer to workers. The issue of the direction of the transfer is obviously important, and Cline regards the transfer as going from consumers to workers. The industry developed and employed its workers in a national market; therefore, the appropriate view is that the elimination of protection results in a transfer from producers to consumers. Expectations have been formed on the basis of experience, and to change the market to include sellers in developing countries destroys their basis. Economists regard tariffs as transferring income from consumers to workers because for them free trade is the natural state. Governments impose tariffs. This is the wrong way of looking at tariffs. We should start with the proposition that people have certain expectations based on their experience. Government policies should not deprive them of incomes that they have come to expect. The correct view of trade liberalization is that it transfers incomes from producers to consumers, not that it removes a transfer from consumers to producers.

The other major problem concerns Cline's assumption that the number of jobs in the economy as a whole will remain the same, so displaced workers will have little trouble finding jobs. As I have mentioned, Cline estimates that the pure transfer (in his view from consumers to workers) makes up 66 percent of the cost of the protection to consumers. The remainder consists largely of the gain in total output resulting from shifting the displaced workers to other, better jobs. However, the estimated gain in total output depends on the full-employment assumption, which is valid only if the demand for unskilled labor is growing. But when the demand is falling, as it is, we cannot expect the displaced workers to be reemployed elsewhere. Without the full-employment assumption we cannot conclude that removing tariffs improves the general welfare. We can only conclude that it shifts income from workers to consumers.

Cline, like other economists, tries to avoid taking sides in conflicts over transfers because doing so entails preferring one group to another. Instead, economists argue the elimination of protection would leave consumers better off, even if they compensate displaced workers. However, the issue cannot be avoided. Because the efficiency loss from tariffs is nil or small, transfers are the issue. Why should poor factory operatives lose their jobs so that rich doctors can buy shirts at low prices?

The objection may be raised that those workers who do not lose their jobs gain from the lower prices. However, while some unskilled workers will not suffer joblessness, their wages will be depressed by the resulting fall in the demand for unskilled labor. The rise of unemployment due to imports will affect workers in the service industries, which do not compete directly with imports, as well as workers in the apparel and textile industries.

AN EXAMINATION OF CERTAIN POLICIES

The Elimination of Special Protection for Textiles and Apparel

As of September 11, 1991, exports of textiles and apparel by 41 countries were covered by the Multifiber Arrangement (MFA), which is an exception to GATT's prohibition of quotas. In 1990 these countries supplied 88 percent of all U.S. apparel imports and 69 percent of all textile imports.[43] The MFA specifies a quota for each of the signatories, nearly all of which are developing countries. The three largest suppliers of textiles in 1990 were China, South Korea, and Hong Kong. The six largest suppliers of apparel included these countries plus Taiwan, Mexico, and the Philippines.[44] The GATT agreement, which was passed by Congress in a special session in December 1994, phases out MFA over a period of ten years. When MFA expires the United States, apparel and textile industries will be without any protection.

The North American Free Trade Agreement

U.S. labor organizations opposed NAFTA, which will create a free trade area comprising Mexico, the United States and Canada, because of the threat to unskilled workers of unemployment and losses of wages. The administration's reply was that NAFTA will increase the total number of jobs, and it promises to provide funds for training displaced workers for new jobs.

Apparel

NAFTA will reduce the incentive of U.S. manufacturers to limit Mexican factories to the assembly of components made in the United States. The elimination of duties will make it more economical for Mexican factories to manufacture entire garments from fabrics produced either in the United States or Mexico. In 1994 only 10 percent of apparel imports from Mexico were completely manufactured there,[45] but with labor costs so low, Mexican factories will do more of the manufacturing. NAFTA may be particularly important for knit garments, which are difficult to cut for assembly abroad. Moreover, NAFTA adds to U.S. firms' inducement to move their operations entirely to that country by enabling them to increase their sales there. The assurance to foreign firms locating plants in Mexico of future easy access to the U.S. market further adds to the inducement. Bound by the agreement, the United States will not later turn around and raise tariffs against Mexican imports or impose quotas. For its part, the Mexican government seeks to persuade foreign-based producers to move their operations to Mexico by contracting to treat them as nationals. A major purpose is to encourage foreign investment; thus, the agreement guarantees foreign investors the freedom to move funds to the United States, protects them against expropriation, and removes performance requirements.

I cite some estimates of NAFTA's effect on Mexico's apparel exportation to the United States and the consequences for U.S. employment. These estimates, which preceded Congress's enactment of the agreement at the end of 1993, show that policymakers had ample warning that NAFTA would reduce employment in the United States. Thus, Leamer predicted that the exports of apparel will increase by as much as 2,762 percent by 2002 and that they will then constitute as much as 47 percent of the total output of the U.S. industry.[46] Because the U.S. apparel industry employed 1,024 thousand persons in 1991,[47] Leamer's estimate suggests that NAFTA will displace about 480 thousand workers.

The International Trade Commission (ITC) conducted a study based on interviews with 65 U.S. apparel companies having annual sales ranging from $10 million to over $500 million. About one third of the firms said that they planned to invest in Mexico.[48] This study concluded that the increase in imports will be much larger than an estimate of 57 percent,[49] but it suggested that a large part of the increase will displace imports from Hong Kong, Taiwan, Korea, and China. Nevertheless, the ITC predicted that the impact on total employment will be large in Puerto Rico, Alabama, and Mississippi, where the apparel industry accounts for 20 percent, 16 percent, and 15 percent, respectively, of total manufacturing employment.[50]

Automotive Goods

Nearly all of the Mexican automotive industry is owned by General Motors, Ford, Chrysler, Nissan, and Volkswagen. In 1989 the industry exported one third of its output of 641,000 autos to the United States and Canada, primarily from the U.S.-owned plants. The average output per plant is too small to realize the available economies of scale—less than half the standard output of modern plants throughout the world. Costs also are high because the plants produce four or five models rather than the one or two that more efficient plants do.

The most important restriction affecting trade with the United States was the limitation of foreign ownership to 40 percent participation. Under the Temporary Investment Trust Funds full foreign ownership was allowed in the maquiladoras on a temporary basis, provided that at least 80 percent of the output was exported.[51] Liberalization of the investment restrictions makes it more attractive for U.S. auto manufacturers to invest in Mexico.

General Motors, Chrysler, and Ford have built new assembly plants in Mexico; Chrysler has retooled its engine plant; and General Motors has added to and rebuilt its existing auto assembly plant, including a new stamping line to manufacture body panels. The Rockwell International Corporation has built a plant to make window regulators. Recently Honda announced it will build its first automobile plant in that country. According to Ciemex-Wefa, an econometric forecasting company, the Mexican auto industry, which currently employs 160 thousand workers, will add 50 thousand workers by 1998.[52]

General

Most of the studies concerning the impact of NAFTA on the United States predicted small effects on total employment. Predicted gains in industries employing skilled labor offset predicted losses in industries employing unskilled labor. In 1992 Hufbauer and Schott estimated for the Institute for International Economics (IIE) that in three years NAFTA would raise employment in the United States by 130,000.[53]

However, their corresponding estimate for Mexico, an increase in employment of 609,000, implied a decline in U.S. employment. This estimate implied a reduction of employment in U.S. consumer goods industries of the same number multiplied by the relative productivity of Mexican labor. The average of Blostrom and Wolff's estimates of the relative productivity of Mexican labor is 79 percent. Accordingly, the reduction in U.S. employment should be 609,000 times .79 or 481,000. The total reduction in U.S. employment would be this number minus the increase in employment in capital goods industries resulting from the growth of U.S. exports. The loss of U.S. employment may be a little less than 481 thousand because goods now coming from the Far East will come from Mexico. Accordingly, on the basis of the IIE estimate of the gain in Mexican employment, we can expect a fall in U.S. employment, rather than an increase.

Moreover, the authors' procedure was based on some critical and dubious assumptions. The first was that Mexican exports will increase at the same rate as the average growth rate of total exports for other developing countries that have liberalized trade, which the authors said was 11.2 percent per year. However, what we should be looking at is the average annual growth rate of exports of manufactured products by rapidly industrializing countries. The growth rates of total exports, which include agricultural products, oil, and other nonmanufactured products as well as manufactured products, will be much lower than the growth rates for manufactured products. In 1991 Mexico's exports were as follows: fuels, minerals, and metals 41 percent; other primary commodities 14 percent; machinery and transport equipment 24 percent; textiles and clothing 2 percent; and other manufactured products 20 percent.[54] The major part of the exports still consisted of primary products. But it is the growth of manufactured exports that is a threat to employment in the United States. Table 4.4 shows that between 1965 and 1986 the average annual growth rates for manufactured exports by rapidly industrializing countries was much higher than the IIE estimate of the growth rate of total exports in countries that liberalized trade. Indeed, the average annual rate of growth for Mexico itself was 16.5 percent. We also have seen that between 1980 and 1988 the growth rates for U.S. imports of manufactured products from developing countries and from Mexico, Brazil, and the Asian NICs were much higher. The IIE figure of 11.2 percent is very low.

The other critical assumption was that imports by Mexico will exceed exports by the sum of capital inflows. Initially imports of capital equipment will be large, but the imbalance is unlikely to keep up. One of Mexico's purposes in entering into NAFTA is to promote exports to pay off its foreign debts. A persistent and large unfavorable balance of trade would frustrate that purpose.

Other considerations suggest that Mexico's exports to the United States will grow more rapidly than those of other developing countries have grown in the past. Competition has become more severe, and Mexican wages are particularly low. In 1992 the average hourly compensation cost for production workers in manufacturing in Mexico was $2.35, compared to $3.89 in Hong Kong; $4.93 in Korea; $5.00 in Singapore; and $5.19 in Taiwan.[55] The devaluation of the peso has reduced Mexican wages since 1992. Moreover, there is much more slack in the Mexican economy than in the economy of either Spain or Portugal, with which it is frequently compared. Because Mexico is at an early stage of development, its exports should grow more rapidly.

The increase in manufactured exports from Mexico is likely to be considerably larger than from other developing countries for other reasons. The population in 1991 was 83.3 million, and growing at the rate of 1.9 percent per year. Thirty-eight percent of the population was under the age of fourteen. Moreover, a large part is still underemployed. The agricultural labor force was 36.5 percent of the total labor force in 1980; later figures are not available. By contrast, in Spain only 17.1 percent of the labor force was in agriculture, and in Portugal the percentage was 25.8.[56] Wages are likely to remain low for a long time.

The other factor not considered by Hufbauer and Schott is Mexico's proximity to the United States. A given reduction in import barriers has much more effect on imports from Mexico than on those from Spain. Trade tends to be greater between neighbors than between distant countries. The United States' first and third trading partners are Canada and Mexico.[57] Not only are transportation costs between neighbors low, but commercial contacts are more easily established and maintained. The effect of a reduction in import barriers between geographically close countries is likely to be greater than between distant trading partners.

As Leamer and Medberry point out, NAFTA is really a trade agreement between Mexico, southern California, and Texas.[58] As they also observe, the adjacency advantage is greatest for products that are costly to ship long distances. This is the reason a high proportion of production in the maquiladoras, which are located close to the U.S. border, consists of transportation equipment rather than apparel and footwear. Mexico's closeness encourages automobile manufacturers to establish assembly operations there rather than in Asia.

Imports resulting from NAFTA will impact the employment of manufacturing production workers only, who account for 11 percent of total employment. If NAFTA reduces employment by 500,000, then the employment of manufacturing production workers will fall by 4 percent. If these workers become unemployed, then the unemployment rate of unskilled workers will increase by 1.3 percentage points.[59] This is not an insignificant oamount, and the number of dislocated workers may be larger.

NAFTA was enacted at the end of 1993, and Robert Scott estimates that imports from Mexico grew by $23 billion, or by 59.3 percent, in the years 1994 and 1995. Because exports grew by $4.6 billion, net exports fell by $18.4 billion.[60] Using the Department of Commerce multiplier of 15,382 jobs created for each $1 billion of exports and of the same number of jobs eliminated for $1 billion of imports, Scott estimates that the fall in net exports resulted in a net loss of 283,607 jobs. Restricting our attention to the growth of imports, the resulting loss of jobs was 355,000.

Trade with Mexico in 1995 brought about large job losses in transportation equipment, electrical and electronic machinery, equipment and supplies, machinery, except electrical, food and kindred products, and apparel and related products. The losses in transportation equipment consisted largely of those in motor vehicles and parts. Those in electrical and electronic machinery, equipment, and supplies were made up largely of the losses in radio and television sets, communications equipment, and computers. On the other hand, trade created additional jobs in electronic components which are used as inputs in electronic products and in vehicles.[61] Clearly, the job losses were not confined to textile, apparel, and shoe manufacturing, which usually are featured in discussions of the effects of imports from developing countries.

Because the peso was devalued sharply in December 1994 and early in 1995, the share of the increase in imports in 1995 due to NAFTA is difficult to estimate. The peso lost more than 70 percent of its value against the dollar. Mexico suffered a large loss of jobs, and real wages fell. However, the prospect of NAFTA was partly responsible for the devaluation; therefore, part of the growth of imports apparently due to the devaluation was due to NAFTA. Expectations of NAFTA led to a great increase in investment in new capacity for export to the United

States. The devaluation came when currency traders realized that it was overvalued.

In any case, the loss of unskilled jobs resulting from the growth of imports from Mexico has hurt unskilled U.S. workers significantly. A loss of nearly 300,000 jobs over two years is substantial. Moreover, it is part of a continuing trend. Imports of unskilled-intensive goods are continuing to grow from developing countries, particularly from Mexico and China. NAFTA has contributed to the growth, and GATT promises to accelerate the pace.

NOTES

1. Paul R. Krugman and Robert Z. Lawrence, "Trade, Jobs, and Wages," *Scientific American*, 270 (April 1994): 44–49; Jagdish Bhagwati and Vivek Dehejia, "Freer Trade and Wages of the Unskilled: Is Marx Striking Again?", Paper prepared for the Conference on the Influence of Trade on U.S. Wages, American Enterprise Institute, September 10, 1993.

2. Edward E. Leamer, "Trade, Wages and Revolving Door Ideas," Working Paper 4716 (Cambridge, Mass.: National Bureau of Economic Research, 1994); Adrian Wood, *North-South Trade, Employment and Inequality: Changing Fortunes in a Skill-Driven World* (Oxford: Clarendon Press, 1994); Jeffrey D. Sachs and Howard J. Shatz, "Trade and Jobs in U.S. Manufacturing," *Brookings Papers on Economic Activity*, I (1994): 1–84.

3. Friedrich List, *National Systems of Political Economy* (New York: Longmans, Green, 1904).

4. Robert Z. Lawrence and Matthew J. Slaughter, "International Trade and American Wages in the 1980s: Great Sucking Sound or Small Hiccup?", *Brookings Papers: Microeconomics*, 2 (1993): 161–223; Laura D'Andrea Tyson, *Who's Bashing Whom? Trade Conflict in High Technology Industries* (Washington, D.C.: Institute for International Economics, 1992).

5. In 1990 the world labor force included 2.3 billion workers, of which 74.5 percent were in developing countries. I arrive at the figure of 1.4 billion by assuming that 80 percent of the workers in developing countries are unskilled. Cf. David E. Bloom and Adi Brender, "Labor and the Emerging World Economy," Working Paper 4266 (Cambridge, Mass.: National Bureau of Economic Research, January 1993), table 1. The authors cite International Labor Organization, *Economically Active Population 1950–2025*, Geneva, 1986.

6. David Ricardo, *The Principles of Political Economy and Taxation* (New York: E. P. Dutton, Everyman Ed., 1948), 77–88.

7. Eli F. Heckscher, "The Effects of Foreign Trade on the Distribution of Income," *Economisc Tidskrift*, 1919; Bertil Ohlin, *Interregional and International Trade* (Cambridge, Mass.: Harvard University Press, 1933); Paul Samuelson, "The Gains from International Trade," *Canadian Journal of Economics and Political Science* (May 1949).

8. J. Widgren, "International Migration: New Challenges in Europe," *Migration News*, 2 (1987), Geneva: International Catholic Migration Commission. Cited

by Bloom and Brender, "Labor and the Emerging World Economy," Working Paper 4266, 22.

9. *Survey of Current Business*, August 1995, 100.

10. *Wall Street Journal*, August 6, 1993, B7B.

11. Sachs and Shatz, "Trade and Jobs in U.S. Manufacturing," 43–44.

12. Albert H. Imlah, *Economic Elements in the Pax Britannica: Studies in British Foreign Trade in the Nineteenth Century* (New York: Russell and Russell, 1969), 61; B. R. Mitchell and Phyllis Deane, *Abstract of British Historical Statistics* (Cambridge: Cambridge University Press, 1971), 455; *Historical Statistics of the United States: Colonial Times to 1970, Bicentennial Edition*, 1975 (*HSB*), ser. X475.

13. David E. Bloom and Adi Brender, *Labor and the Emerging World Economy* (Washington, D.C.: Population Reference Bureau, 1993), 4.

14. Wolfgang F. Stolper and Paul A. Samuelson, "Protection and Real Wages," *Review of Economic Studies*, November 1941; Paul A. Samuelson, "International Trade and the Equalization of Factor Prices," *Economic Journal*, June 1948; Paul A. Samuelson, "International Factor Price Equalization Once Again," *Economic Journal*, June 1949.

15. Bhagwati and Dehejia, "Freer Trade and Wages of the Unskilled: Is Marx Striking Again?"

16. Lawrence and Slaughter find that, contrary to Stolper-Samuelson, the relative prices of manufactured unskilled-labor intensive products have increased slightly. They attribute the relative rise of skilled workers' wages to technological change, which increased the demand for skilled labor. Lawrence and Slaughter, "International Trade and American Wages in the 1980s: Giant Sucking Sound or Small Hiccup?", 192–207.

17. Estimate based on Department of Commerce, *News*, Bureau of the Census, Current Industrial Reports, Apparel, Summary for 1994, MQ23A, August 1995, table 6.

18. Bureau of Labor Statistics (BLS), Office of Productivity and Technology.

19. The BLS Office of Productivity and Technology estimates that the average annual rate of growth of labor productivity in the apparel industries between 1949 and 1988 was 2.4 percent compared to the average rate for manufacturing as a whole of 2.7 percent.

20. Jeffrey D. Sachs and Howard J. Shatz, "U.S. Trade with Developing Countries and Wage Inequality." Paper presented at American Economic Association meetings, January 6, 1996.

21. Based on *Statistical Abstract of the United States, 1977* (*SAUS 1977*), 403 and *SAUS 1994*, 423.

22. Based on *SAUS 1977*, 801, 875 and *SAUS 1994*, 423.

23. Based on *Economic Report of the President, 1995* (*ERP*, 1995), 293.

24. Jagdish Bhagwati and Vivek H. Dehejia, "Freer Trade and Wages of the Unskilled: Is Marx Striking Again?" in Jagdish Bhagwati and Marvin H. Kosters (eds.), *Trade and Wages: Leveling Wages Down?* (Washington, D.C.: AEI Press, 1994), 45.

25. BLS, "International Comparisons of Hourly Compensation Costs for Production Workers in Manufacturing," March 1993.

26. Gary Clyde Hufbauer and Jeffrey J. Schott, *NAFTA: An Assessment* (Washington, D.C.: Institute for International Economics, 1993), 13.

27. Hugh Patric and Henry Rosovsky, "Japan's Economic Performance: An Overview," in Hugh Patric and Henry Rosovsky (eds.), *Asia's New Giant: How the Japanese Economy Works* (Washington, D.C.: Brookings Institution, 1976), 17, table 1–2.

28. Harley Shaiken, "Wages, Productivity, and Trade: The Auto Industry in Mexico, Canada, and the United States." Presented at Allied Social Science Associations Annual Meeting, New York 1988, 8. Cited by Walter Russell Mead, *The Low-Wage Challenge to Global Growth* (Washington, D.C.: Economic Policy Institute, 1990), 18.

29. Magnus Blostrom and Edward N. Wolff, *Multinational Corporations and Productivity Convergence in Mexico*. National Bureau of Economic Research Working Paper No. 3141, 1989, 25.

30. Herbert G. Grubel, *International Economics* (Homewood, Ill.: Richard D. Irwin, 1981), 173–76.

31. *SAUS 1994*, 828, table 1331.

32. Joseph Grunwald and Kenneth Flamm, *The Global Factory: Foreign Assembly in International Trade* (Washington, D.C.: Brookings Institution, 1985), 7.

33. Grunwald and Flamm, *The Global Factory*, 7.

34. Sachs and Shatz, "Trade and Jobs in U.S. Manufacturing," 43.

35. U.S. Department of Labor, Bureau of International Labor Affairs, *Trade-Sensitive U.S. Industries: Employment Trends and Worker Characteristics*, Economic Discussion Paper 36, July 1991, 24, table B.1.

36. Sachs and Shatz, "Trade and Jobs in U.S. Manufacturing," 17–20.

37. Ibid., 52.

38. Edward E. Leamer, "Wage Effects of a U.S.-Mexican Trade Agreement," National Bureau of Economic Research, Working Paper No. 3991, February 1992, 16–17.

39. U.S. Department of Labor, *Trade-Sensitive U.S. Industries*, 16, table 2.

40. Paul A. Samuelson and William D. Nordhaus, *Economics* (New York: McGraw Hill, 1985), 836.

41. U.S. International Trade Commission (ITC), *The Economic Effects of Significant U.S. Import Restraints, Phase I: Manufacturing* (Washington, D.C.: Publication 2222, October 1989), 4–2, 4–3; William R. Cline, *The Future of World Trade in Textiles and Apparel* (Washington, D.C.: Institute for International Economics, 1987), 1, 188–97; Anne O. Krueger, "Free Trade is the Best Policy," in Robert Z. Lawrence and Charles L. Schultze (eds.), *An American Trade Strategy: Options for the 1990s* (Washington, D.C.: Brookings Institution, 1990), 68–96; Congressional Budget Office (CBO), *Trade Restraints and the Competitive Status of the Textile, Apparel, and Nonrubber Footwear Industries* (Washington, D.C., December 1991), xi, 42–47.

42. Cline, *The Future of World Trade in Textiles and Apparel*, 1.

43. CBO, *Trade Restraints*, 6.

44. Ibid., 11–12.

45. Ibid.

46. Edward E. Leamer, "U.S. Manufacturing and an Emerging Mexico," National Bureau of Economic Research, Working Paper 4331, 1993, tables 10 and 11.

47. *SAUS 1992*, 406, table 645.

48. U.S. ITC, *Potential Impact on the U.S. Economy and Selected Industries of the North American Free-Trade Agreement* (USITC Publication 2596, 1993), 8–6.

49. U.S. ITC Publication 2596, 8–7.

50. U.S. ITC, *The Likely Impact on the United States of a Free Trade Agreement with Mexico* (USITC Publication 2353, February 1991), 4–40.

51. U.S. ITC Publication 2353, 4–18.

52. Neil Templin, "Mexican Industrial Belt Is Beginning to Form as Car Makers Expand," *Wall Street Journal*, June 29, 1994, A1, A10.

53. Gary Clyde Hufbauer and Jeffrey Schott, *North American Free Trade: Issues and Recommendations* (Washington, D.C.: Institute for International Economics, 1992), 50–61.

54. World Bank, *World Development Report 1993*, 269, table 16.

55. BLS, "International Comparisons of Hourly Compensation Costs for Production Workers in Manufacturing, 1992," Report 844, April 1993, 8.

56. World Bank, *World Tables 1992*, 416, 546, 498.

57. Edward E. Leamer and Chauncey J. Medberry, "U.S. Manufacturing and an Emerging Mexico," Working Paper 4331 (Cambridge, Mass.: National Bureau of Economic Research, April 1993), 8.

58. Leamer and Medberry, "U.S. Manufacturing and an Emerging Mexico," 8.

59. Chapter 1 estimated that unskilled workers constituted 31.5 percent of all workers in the United States. Thus, the number of unskilled workers is 125 million times .315, which is 39.4 million. If 500,000 workers are added to the unemployed, the unemployment rate of unskilled workers rises by 1.3 percentage points.

60. Robert E. Scott, "1995 U.S. Trade with the NAFTA Countries" (Washington, D.C.: Economic Policy Institute, Draft Report, April 1996), 1.

61. Ibid., 2.

5

IQ, Welfare, and the Poverty Culture

Three theories blame blacks' alleged weaknesses for their high unemployment rate. Richard J. Herrnstein and Charles Murray in *The Bell Curve* point to blacks' allegedly inherited weak intelligence, implying that public policy is impotent.[1] The attention the popular press has given the book warrants an examination of the theory. Another reason I discuss the Herrnstein-Murray genetic theory is that my policy recommendations in Chapter 8 assume that the IQ can be raised significantly.

More popular than the IQ theory is the one that blames welfare, which is linked to black poverty particularly, supposedly because blacks more than whites find idleness attractive. Welfare payments preserve the "poverty culture" among poor blacks, who do not share whites' work values. Another argument implies that, inasmuch as welfare payments are generous, blacks are more rational than whites.

THE INTELLIGENCE ARGUMENT

IQ, Intelligence, and Economic Success

Herrnstein and Murray rest their case that blacks' intelligence is inferior on measures based on IQ tests, and—more controversially—they blame heredity, not environment. A major issue is whether IQ tests measure "general intelligence," and, indeed, whether there is such a thing as general intelligence as opposed to individual, specific abilities. The Herrnstein-Murray view goes back to a statistical analysis by Charles Spearman, who concluded on the basis of a factor analysis of scores on individual tests of space perception, verbal skills, reasoning ability, and arithmetic skills that general intelligence was a valid concept and that the summary IQ score was a good index.[2]

Doubting that the IQ measures any reasonably broad definition of intelligence, critics deny that it measures the ability to make appropriate choices in life situations—practical intelligence. They concede that the tests measure particular verbal, reasoning, and arithmetic skills, but they include in intelligence other skills. The intelligent business person, who knows when and where to advertise, when and how much to buy, and when and how much to cut prices, may bungle an IQ test. Urban poor children also have a kind of practical intelligence, consisting of the skills they must have to survive, but they fail IQ tests. Along with energy, determination, persistence, optimism, experience, education, and other attributes, practical intelligence is a factor in economic success. However, what the critics who contrast practical intelligence with the skills measured by IQ tests ignore is that the ability to make appropriate choices in one situation may not be useful in another. Whether inner-city children's skills are valuable in work situations remains an open question.

Herrnstein and Murray argue that the IQ is a good predictor of a person's earnings, chances of unemployment, marital success, and criminality.[3] The claim is based on observed relationships between these variables and the IQ. The authors divide the IQ distribution into five classes. They call those who score above the 95th percentile—the top 5 percent—Very Bright; the next 20 percent Bright; the middle 50 percent Normal; the next 20 percent Dull; and the bottom 5 percent Very Dull. The top IQ score for the Very Dull—75—marks the borderline for retardation. The percentage of the people who are poor increases as the score falls across groups. In 1989 30 percent of the Very Dull had incomes below the poverty line, compared to 16 percent of the Dull, the percentages in the top three classes were much lower, and the overall average was 7 percent.[4] Controlling for socioeconomic status, Herrnstein and Murray show that the chances of poverty fall sharply as IQ increases.

Undoubtedly the IQ is related to economic success, if only because schools screen job candidates for employers. The IQ tests originally were devised to predict success in school; thus, they measure skills that enhance school performance. And school performance is related to job success through educational attainment. More academically successful students graduate from college than students whose grades are poor, and college graduates' IQs exceed those of nongraduates. Employers generally do not check a job applicant's school performance, but they do pay attention to educational attainment. For many skilled jobs college graduation is a requirement. Some dropouts perform their jobs well when given the chance, but many cannot demonstrate their ability.

While the IQ provides some basis for predicting earnings, it is not a good gauge. Herrnstein and Murray's evidence shows only that it is a better predictor than their measure of the family's socioeconomic status, and both are poor predictors. A good gauge is reliable, which the IQ is not. A measure of economic success, such as income, tends to go up with the IQ, but many people with high IQs do not earn high incomes. The IQ errs too frequently and by too much to qualify as a good predictor, as an appendix to *The Bell Curve* reveals. In the appendix the authors use data on IQ, socioeconomic status, and age to predict whether an individual's income is above or below the poverty line. The three variables, which together are a better gauge than any one of them, explain only 10 percent of the variation in poverty status among whites. The IQ variable is the best of the three, but the three together provide little information, and the IQ alone provides even less. Over the entire range of IQs, the IQ plays a very small part in determining a person's economic success.

Many people with high IQs do not have the necessary interests, drive, persistence, energy, and luck to earn high salaries. Few become partners in large law firms, stock brokers, or CEOs. Former good students drop out of the race for high incomes, becoming low-paid lab assistants, guidance counsellors, and clerical workers. Because they did well in school, many become school teachers. The upshot is that the differences in earnings among people with high IQs are very large. Knowing a person's IQ does not give much information about his or her income.

These observations do not deny the important point: few people with low IQs achieve economic success. Apart from those with exceptional talents, such as sports and entertainment stars, a low IQ precludes success. The spread of earnings among people with low IQs is narrow. Few have high earnings. By contrast, the spread of earnings among people with high IQs is wide. Their earnings vary greatly. While not many earn large incomes, some do. Very few people with low IQs earn large incomes. If Herrnstein and Murray had concluded only that their chances of achieving economic success were poor, they would have a strong case.

The general conclusion up to this point is that while a high IQ does not assure economic success, a low IQ precludes it. It is not necessary to wade into the quagmire of whether IQ measures intelligence to reach this important conclusion.

As many as 25 percent of the black population fall into the Very Dull class, compared to 5 percent of whites.[5] Many blacks are unskilled because their IQs are low. Whether we choose to call the abilities measured by IQ tests "intelligence" or insist on including other attributes is immaterial.

The Heritability of the IQ

The theory that blacks' average IQ is partly inherited[6] supports the racist belief in black inferiority, and more important, the practical con-

clusion that education can do little to raise blacks' IQs. Despite Herrnstein and Murray's acknowledgment that heredity accounts for only part
of the racial IQ difference, they blame genetics for the ineffectiveness of
programs for improving black children's cognitive ability. Herrnstein
and Murray advance their genetic case diffidently, and since the book's
publication Murray has become even more hesitant,[7] but their pessimism
relies on it. The genetic argument is critical, for the alternative explanation, which relies on environment, is much more hopeful. After reading
many studies, Herrnstein and Murray conclude that heredity accounts
for between 40 and 80 percent of the variation in IQ among whites, the
rest being due to the environment. However, as they acknowledge, one
cannot infer from a study of whites that heredity causes the racial IQ
difference. Individual differences in scores within each of two groups
may be due to heredity without the difference between the averages for
the two groups being caused by the same source. Nevertheless, because
the alternative explanation would require a huge and unlikely environmental difference, the authors ascribe at least part of the racial difference
to heredity. They also point to the evidence of the difference in IQ scores
between whites and blacks within the middle class. Herrnstein and Murray suggest that middle-class black children have the same environmental advantages as their white peers.

Contrary to Herrnstein and Murray, black-white environmental differences may explain the racial IQ difference. Studies of school performance show that the most important factor by far is family background,
whose measures are based on income, education of parents, the presence
of both parents in the household, and the availability in the home of
such learning tools as a typewriter, a calculator, and books.[8] Consider
also the huge effort better-off mothers devote to children. Moreover, the
disappointment with Headstart may simply be due to the environmental
handicap faced by disadvantaged children.

One reason blacks in the middle class have lower IQs than whites in
the same class may be that the middle class embraces wide ranges of
income and education. Herrnstein and Murray do not make it clear who
is included. Does the middle class include all white-collar workers, all
continuously employed blue-collar workers, and all residents of suburbs?
If the middle class includes people in these groups as well as those in
highly skilled occupations, the difference may be due to a dispropor-
tionate number of blacks in less skilled occupations. The percentage of
blacks in the highly skilled of the skilled occupations—financial analysts,
marketing managers, engineers, mathematicians, physicians, college
teachers, and lawyers—is small. The large differences in income between
these occupations and those of less skilled, middle-class occupations may
give the favored children an important environmental advantage.

Moreover, the authors do not deal with evidence that contradicts the genetic theory. No significant difference has been found between those children born to German women fathered by black American soldiers and those fathered by white American soldiers.[9] The genetic argument is far from conclusive.

Whether or not genetics is important, low IQs probably have contributed to the rise of black unemployment. While blacks' scores have not fallen, the growing demand for skilled labor has raised the value of the verbal, arithmetic, and reasoning abilities measured by the IQ tests. The concomitant fall in the demand for unskilled labor has diminished employment opportunities for low-IQ persons.

THE WELFARE ARGUMENT

The tripling of the AFDC caseload between 1965 and 1975 drew demands for reform. The clamor died down as growth slowed between 1975 and 1989, but renewed speed of growth between 1989 and 1991 again provoked an attack. Much of the last spurt was due to the recession, not to any increase in benefits. Between 1989 and 1990 the caseload grew from 3.9 million to 4.2 million, and it jumped to 4.7 million the following year. Over the same period the number of families with incomes below the poverty level increased, as did the number of Food Stamp and Medicaid recipients.

Murray's earlier book, *Losing Ground*, which blamed the welfare system for the increase in black unemployment, supplied much of the intellectual ammunition for welfare reformers. Take welfare away, Murray said, and blacks would be forced to work, solving their crime and drug problems.[10] Why blacks particularly, Murray did not say. It is important, in any case, to examine his analysis carefully, because it provides the intellectual support for the drive by both Republicans and Democrats to reduce welfare payments.

Welfare Programs

Let us look first at the programs in question. The welfare programs are Aid to Families with Dependent Children (AFDC), Medicaid, Supplemental Security Income (SSI), General Assistance, Food Stamps, many jobs and training programs, and public housing programs.

The most prominent program, AFDC, pays benefits to single mothers. The federal government pays more than half the total cost, but the states administer the program and set the criteria for eligibility and benefit levels. The standards for determining benefits vary widely across the states. Neither family size nor the cost of living accounted for the difference in 1993 between the highest average monthly benefit per family, which was $568 in California, and the lowest, which was $120 in Mississippi.[11] Discouraging work, the benefits fall as earned income rises, the rate of reduction being set federally. Under the Omnibus Budget Reconciliation Act of 1981, the benefits fall by one dollar for every dollar earned by a recipient, which is to say the tax rate is 100 percent.

The AFDC rules also discourage two-parent households. Although the courts have forced the states to rescind the man-in-the-house rule, nearly all beneficiaries are single mothers. In half the states, while an adult male may be part of the household, he must not contribute to its support.[12] In the other half, where two-parent families are eligible under Aid to Families with Dependent Children and Unemployed Parents (AFDC-UP), severe eligibility requirements keep the number of beneficiaries small. The chief income earner must be without a job and have an employment history similar to that required for unemployment insurance. Not surprisingly, the caseload in 1985 was only 260 thousand families.[13]

Medicaid provides free or subsidized medical services only to the disabled, the aged, and AFDC recipients, not to all the poor. Couples generally are not eligible. The program is federally subsidized and regulated, but it is administered by the states.

The SSI program, which the federal government finances and administers and for which it sets standards, doles money out to the aged, the blind, and the disabled. State-sponsored general assistance helps the needy falling through the cracks of the federally financed system.

Nominally providing in-kind assistance, the Food Stamp program is really a cash transfer program. Because most beneficiaries spend more on food than the program's allowances, the coupons are the equivalent of cash. All the poor are eligible, regardless of family type or marital status. In 1993 as many as 10.8 million families received Food Stamp benefits, compared to 4.9 million AFDC families.[14] Set by the federal government at a uniform national level, the benefits are low.

Housing programs pay part of the rent for private housing and subsidize public housing for persons who qualify only on the basis of income and assets. About 20 percent of AFDC recipients receive housing subsidies in one form or another.[15] The Housing and Urban Development Act of 1964, which authorized local housing agencies to lease privately owned small units, was an effort aimed at economy and at reducing crime that the large public projects attracted. The beneficiaries paid rents equal to those for public housing units. In 1965 a rent supplements program was introduced, which paid the difference between market rents and one-fourth of the tenant's adjusted income.[16] However, not-in-my-backyard resistance has blocked the shift of subsidized housing to areas outside the inner cities. Furthermore, high costs have prevented the programs from supplying housing to many of the needy.

Table 5.1
Expenditures for Cash and Noncash Benefits to Persons with Limited
Income, 1992 (Millions)

	Total	Federal
Total	$289,880	$207,566
Medicaid	118,067	67,827
AFDC	24,923	13,569
SSI*	22,774	18,744
Food stamps	24,918	23,540
Housing	20,535	20,535
Other	78,663	63,351

* Supplementary Security Income.
Source: Based on *SAUS 1994*, 373, table 577.

Costs of the Programs

The cost of welfare arouses some resentment. In 1992 public programs
spent a total of $289,880 million, or 4.8 percent of the GDP, with the
federal government paying 72 percent (see Table 5.1). Medicaid requires
the largest expenditures by far, but no one seriously proposes eliminating the program. In those states that allow Medicaid benefits to families
not on AFDC, eligible families must have a major medical expense, and
they must spend their assets until they are poor. Thus, most Medicaid
beneficiaries are AFDC participants. Although the cost of Medicaid may
be cut by greater use of HMOs and by eliminating certain services that
typically are not covered by group health insurance plans, the debate
over Medicaid centers on whether others who are not currently beneficiaries should be covered.

Nor are the benefits paid under Food Stamps and SSI a serious issue.
The Food Stamps program is made invulnerable by the large number of
voters benefiting and the support of agricultural interests. SSI is not responsible for the welfare dependency of the disabled and the aged.

Let us look at some data on the number of AFDC recipients. In 1992
AFDC families made up a large proportion of poor families as defined
by the Social Security Administration (SSA)—61 percent (see Table 5.2).
Not everyone will agree on the poverty threshold, which in 1992 the
Social Security Administration (SSA) set at $11,186 for a nonfarm family
of three persons.[17] However, any reasonable change in the threshold will
not affect the conclusion that a large proportion of poor families are
AFDC participants. Moreover, it appears that nearly all eligible families
are beneficiaries. In 1992 the number of female-headed households with

Table 5.2
Families and Persons below Poverty Level, Average Monthly Caseloads of Major Means-Tested Programs (Millions)

| | Below Poverty | | AFDC | Food Stamp | Medicaid |
	Families	Persons	Families	Recipients	Recipients
1965	5.8*	33.2	1.1	0.4	---
1970	5.3	25.4	2.6	4.3	15.5
1975	5.4	25.9	3.6	17.1	22.0
1980	6.2	29.3	3.8	21.1	21.6
1985	7.2	33.1	3.7	19.9	21.8
1989	6.8	31.5	3.9	18.8	23.5
1990	7.1	33.6	4.2	20.1	25.3
1991	7.7	35.7	4.7	22.6	28.3
1992	8.0	36.9	4.9	25.4	31.2

* For 1966.

Sources: Moffitt, "Incentive Effects," 4; *SAUS 1977*, 345, table 543; *SAUS 1982-1983*, 440, table 727; 442, table 731; *SAUS 1992*, 456, table 717; 458, table 722; 459, table 724; *SAUS 1993*, 113, table 162; 381, table 604; 383, table 608; *SAUS 1994*, 116, table 162; 383, table 597; 383, table 608.

children, with money income less than the poverty line, was 3.7 million, and 4.9 million families were on AFDC.[18]

The Welfare Theory

The incentive argument, which is the chief thrust of the attack on the AFDC program, relies on Murray's analysis of the rising number of welfare recipients in the 1960s and early 1970s. Joining the Republicans, Clinton advanced the argument to support the welfare reform plank in his 1992 election platform, and he has continued to press it. In his State of the Union Message in January 1994, Clinton said: "If we value work, we can't justify a system that makes welfare more attractive than work if people are worried about losing their health care."[19] Clinton also said,

But to all those who depend on welfare, we should offer ultimately a simple compact: We'll provide the support, the job training, the child care you need for up to two years; but after that, anyone who can work must—in the private sector wherever possible, in community service if necessary. That's the only way we'll ever make welfare what it ought to be: a second chance, not a way of life.[20]

Clinton joins the multitude in condemning welfare beneficiaries for unduly preferring leisure to work, and he attacks the welfare system for paying benefits that exceed what beneficiaries can earn from work. Clinton suggests that rational welfare recipients would remain on the rolls rather than work at minimum wage. David Ellwood provides academic testimony in *Poor Support*, "When you give people money, food, or housing, you reduce the pressure on them to work and care for themselves. No one seriously disputes this proposition."[21] Clinton shares the widespread view that well-intentioned efforts to alleviate the problems of poverty create those problems. What especially shocks the welfare reformers is that as many as one-quarter of the recipients spend ten or more years on the AFDC rolls.[22]

In *Poor Support*, Ellwood evaluates how well off welfare recipients are on the assumption that an AFDC beneficiary has two children and lives in a state in which her benefits amount to $4,800 per year and $1,484 in food stamps, a total of $6,284. If she works full time, her child care would cost her $3,000. At a wage rate of $6 per hour, which Ellwood considers unlikely, her income would be only $2,700 higher than if she did not work. Allowing for the loss of Medicaid benefits, her gain would be even less. At a wage of $5 per hour, which Ellwood considers more likely, she would gain nothing.[23] In a more recent work, Ellwood takes into account the benefits under the Earned Income Tax Credit (EITC), which are paid only to families with earners, and for which AFDC recipients are not eligible. Even when EITC benefits are included, the gains from a full-time job remain small. In 1991 in Pennsylvania a single mother with two children could expect to net $1,923 from a job paying $10,000.[24] Some welfare critics argue that the estimates understate the benefits because they do not include the value of housing subsidies.[25] However, as mentioned above, only 20 percent of AFDC beneficiaries receive housing subsidies.

Moreover, because most beneficiaries do not remain on the rolls, they apparently do not conclude that AFDC benefits are as good a deal as the critics suggest. According to Bane and Ellwood, no more than 30 percent of welfare participants receive payments over periods lasting more than twenty-four consecutive months.[26] Ellwood seems to have changed his mind since writing *Poor Support*, on which the Clinton administration's proposal to limit AFDC payments to two years was based. For most recipients, welfare apparently is not a "way of life."

If welfare reformers are right, then the proportion of poor families participating in AFDC grew. Between 1965 and 1975 the proportion grew enormously from 19.0 percent to 66.7 percent, but between 1975 and 1985 the fraction dropped to 51.4 percent. The fraction went up again in 1989, rising to 61.0 percent in 1991. However, this increase was due not to AFDC but to the growth of the number of female-headed households and the recession.[27]

What about the growth in the number of female-headed households?

This growth has fed much of the expansion of the program since 1975, and, as I have mentioned, in half the states a man's support deprives a woman of eligibility. In these states the eligibility requirements discourage two-parent households. However, if AFDC were the villain, then the percentage of female-headed households on the rolls would have increased. If women did not marry because welfare enabled them to maintain households alone, or worse, with an employed husband they were ineligible for welfare, then as the number of single mothers increased, a higher percentage would have received AFDC payments. The participation rate of female-headed households did grow between 1967 and 1973, but after 1973 it fell continuously until 1987[28] and remained about the same thereafter.[29] Thus, any effect of AFDC payments on the number of female-headed households was over in 1973.

Other factors than AFDC benefits expanded the number of female-headed households. William Julius Wilson and Kathryn Neckerman point to the rise of unemployment among black males. They report that the black family was intact up to World War II, after which the unemployment rate of young and prime-age black men rose, and many quit the labor force. Joblessness destroys family stability, as the depression of the 1930s and of more recent years has established. Wilson and Neckerman also blame the falling number of marriageable men on the rising rates of male mortality at a young age and on incarceration. In the 1960s the ratio of marriageable black men to black women in the age group 16 to 24 years began to fall sharply.[30]

While Murray emphasizes the AFDC program as a cause of mounting black-male unemployment, he also argues that during the 1960s welfare benefits as a whole increased—including housing subsidies, and those of Food Stamps and Medicaid. However, the changes in benefits are not the only factor. We should also examine the changes in wages.

First, we look only at the benefits. Real AFDC benefits per beneficiary increased in the 1960s, but not after 1969. Indeed, the inflation after 1975 reduced them sharply. In addition, the sum of AFDC, Food Stamp, and Medicaid real benefits also fell after 1975 (see Table 5.3).

We must look at changes in earnings in unskilled occupations. For welfare payments to induce people not to work, they must increase relative to earnings from unskilled jobs. Even if welfare benefits grow, they will not be a work disincentive unless they grow faster than what recipients can earn from jobs. The benefits from AFDC, Medicaid, and Food Stamps taken together did not increase relative to unskilled women's earnings between 1975 and 1987 (see Table 5.3). Between 1969 and 1975 real AFDC benefits fell, as did the possible earnings in apparel factories and retail stores. Real earnings from cleaning jobs increased. In general, welfare benefits did not improve relative to possible earnings.[31] Moreover, of some interest is the fact that the earnings of apparel workers,

Table 5.3

Constant-Dollar Indexes of AFDC Benefits, Sum of AFDC, Food Stamp, and Medicaid Benefits, and of Earnings of Unskilled Occupations and of Manufacturing Production Workers, Various Years (1975 = 100)

	1969	1975	1985	1987
AFDC	105	100	81	80
Sum (d)		100	89	89
Earnings				
Apparel (a)	107	100	94	92
Retail (b)	101	100	92	90
Cleaners (c)	85	100	90	88
Mfg. prod. wrkrs (e)	97	100	103	101

Notes: (a) average hourly earnings of production workers in apparel and other textile products industries; (b) average hourly earnings of nonsupervisory workers in retail trade in the United States; (c) average hourly earnings of women janitors, porters, and cleaners in plants in the Northeast; (d) sum entered for 1987 is for 1986; (e) Manufacturing production workers' average hourly earnings.
GDP implicit price deflator used throughout.
Source: Data on welfare benefits from Moffitt, "Incentive Effects," 9, table 3; indexes of earnings based on BLS, *Handbook of Labor Statistics*, Bulletin 2340, August 1989, 312, 314, 361.

retail workers, and woman janitors, porters, and cleaners did not keep up with those of manufacturing production workers. The earnings in the kinds of jobs welfare recipients were most likely to get did not keep up with the average earnings of unskilled manufacturing workers as a whole.

The falling demand for unskilled labor evidently contributed more to the worsening black unemployment than the availability of welfare payments. Further, the welfare-incentive argument does not explain the increased disparity between the two races in unemployment rates and in labor force participation. Why welfare benefits should influence black workers more than white workers is not explained. As earlier chapters show, the explanation of the larger increase in black unemployment was due to the high proportion of blacks who are unskilled and the falling demand for unskilled labor. That the demand for labor makes a difference also is seen in the fact that disadvantaged minority youths did get jobs in tight labor markets during the recovery from 1983 to 1987. The unemployment rate remained high, but, as Richard Freeman shows, their position improved substantially.[32] In addition, black unemployment has fallen in the current boom.

What about the number of hours AFDC mothers work? The frequent comparisons between AFDC and other single mothers imply that they are lazy. In 1987 of all female family heads with children under 18, 54 percent worked, and of those working 74 percent worked full time. By contrast, only 6 percent of AFDC mothers worked, and of these 33 percent worked full time.[33] However, the comparison is not valid. The large difference is not surprising for the simple reason that most working mothers have greater skills. Nonwelfare mothers, including the briefcase-carrying single mothers made famous by former Vice President Dan Quayle's attack on television's Murphy Brown, can earn more. It is unreasonable to expect welfare mothers to match the performance of other single mothers.

Estimates have been made of how many hours welfare mothers would work, if their benefits were to stop. These unreliable estimates, which cover a wide range of hours, suggest little change. The estimates vary from one additional hour to 9.8 additional hours per week, the midpoint being 5.4 additional hours. Robert Moffitt reports that on average AFDC recipients work approximately 9 hours per week. Using the midpoint estimate of the effect of the elimination of AFDC on hours worked the average number of hours would increase to 14.4, which is not a large increase.[34] Moreover, because the AFDC program is intended to enable mothers to take care of their children, it is not clear that an increase in hours at work is desirable.

Another concern is that AFDC mothers rear AFDC mothers. A welfare mother's child is unlikely to disparage welfare, and a mother can provide information on how to use the system. On the other hand, by enabling the mother to spend more for food, the additional income may reduce the probability of a child becoming a welfare recipient. While daughters of welfare mothers are more likely than other women to have premarital births and become welfare recipients, the evidence of the effect of AFDC payments is inconclusive. The association may be due to the low skill and the unmarried state of the mother, for which studies have difficulty controlling.[35] Moreover, the probability of a daughter of a welfare mother becoming one herself is not as high as is frequently alleged. Approximately 80 percent of daughters who grew up in families receiving at least 25 percent of their income in the form of welfare payments do not themselves become welfare dependent.[36]

Do many of the poor exploit the welfare system? Some beneficiaries do, but we do not know that many make welfare a way of life. Many long-term beneficiaries may be illiterate or mentally retarded. Moreover, the fall in the demand for unskilled labor must account for some of the long-term dependency. Terminating AFDC payments may increase employment a little because some beneficiaries will desperately seek and get minimum-wage jobs, but total employment among the unskilled will not rise significantly. The basic problem is demand; thus, the elimination of welfare payments is not a solution.

Much of the discussion of incentives ignores men. Although some men live off their girlfriends' benefits and fathers are relieved of some of the burden of support, men's incentives probably are affected only marginally. Welfare reform does not address the big problem: male unemployment.

The major issue is not the effect of AFDC payments on the work incentives of welfare mothers. What we are seeking is an explanation of the rise of unskilled unemployment, and AFDC benefits do not provide it. Ellwood's comparisons between what a welfare mother could earn working and her welfare benefits suggest that the benefits have huge disincentive effects and, therefore, the elimination of welfare will raise employment substantially. Of course, some beneficiaries choose welfare over work, and some working single mothers not receiving welfare payments are on the margin. Cutting benefits will reduce the number of beneficiaries. However, these considerations do not explain the rise of unemployment among unskilled women, to say nothing of unskilled men. Nor do they imply that reducing welfare benefits will result in many beneficiaries becoming employed. Welfare reform will not get jobs for many of the beneficiaries.

THE CULTURE THEORY

The culture theory says that unemployed blacks are unwilling to work at unskilled jobs in fast-food restaurants, hospitals, and supermarkets. According to Michael Harrington, Kenneth Clark, Herbert Gans, and Oscar Lewis, realistic blacks in the poverty ghettos react appropriately to their dismal opportunities.[37] They refuse to do hard, menial labor for low wages in dead-end jobs. Their rational preference for the life in the streets is the source of the poverty culture with its disdain for "whitey's" values. The theory implies that an employment policy is hopeless. Lewis wrote:

The subculture develops mechanisms that tend to perpetuate it, especially because of what happens to the world view, aspirations, and character of the children who grow up in it. For this reason, improved economic opportunities, though absolutely essential and of the highest priority, are not sufficient to alter basically or eliminate the subculture of poverty. Moreover, elimination is a process that will take more than a single generation, even under the best of circumstances, including a socialist revolution.[38]

Lewis regarded the culture as a way of life which is passed down from generation to generation, producing people not prepared to take advantage of opportunities. Expressing the idea in another way, Paul Peterson says that joblessness in a community of the jobless is less opprobrious than where it is rare. His dramatic description of the appeal of street life follows:

The cultural explanation, perhaps the classic statement of the relationship between the underclass and the poverty paradox, holds that the style of life to which the urban poor has become attached is self-perpetuating. Street life in the ghetto is exhilarating—at least in the short run. In a world where jobs are dull, arduous, or difficult to obtain and hold, it is more fun to hang out, make love, listen to and tell exaggerated stories of love and danger, plan parties and escapades, and exhibit one's latest purchases or conquests. Gangs provide young people thrills, protection, mutual support, friendship, prestige, and enough income to allow them to buy fashionable clothes, alcohol, and drugs. When men cannot earn enough to support their families adequately, they avoid enduring relationships with their female companions. Women respond by becoming self-reliant, domineering. and mutually supportive. But without an adult male figure in the household, they are unable to protect their children from the alluring street life that promises short-term excitement, if not much hope for a prosperous future.[39]

If the culture theory is true, then black youths would remain on the streets even when jobs become available. But the black unemployment rate has its ups and downs. Even young black males—those who have no use for whitey's values—take jobs in tight labor markets. More to the point of the present study, the theory has nothing to say about the growth of black unemployment. The culturists claim to explain the high level, but not the growth. Despite identifying the lack of opportunity as a motivating force, the culturists do not say that the youths have become more pessimistic over time. The statement suggests that blacks always have been immersed in the poverty culture. The culturists may reply that blacks have grown more and more pessimistic as their prospects for good jobs have worsened, which comes close to what the demand theory being proposed here says. But to say only that prospects for good jobs have gotten worse is not enough for policy purposes. To be useful the theory must explain the sources of the worsening of job opportunities.

An implicit but important premise of the culture theory is that poor blacks live off welfare. The benefits enable them to refuse available jobs. If this were true, then welfare recipients would not accept jobs. We saw earlier that while some AFDC recipients remain on the rolls for more than 24 consecutive months, by far the majority take jobs sooner. The turnover rate of AFDC recipients on the rolls contradicts the impression conveyed by the culturists that the vast majority of poor blacks are trapped by anti-work values.

The culture theory emphasizes the geographic concentration of poverty. The descriptions of ghetto life refer to particular urban neighbor-hoods. Indeed, in the context of discussions of poverty "urban" has become a synonym for "ghetto." These writings give the impression that the majority of poor blacks live in neighborhoods where a high propor-tion of the residents are poor. However, the vast majority of the poor and even of the black poor do not live in such neighborhoods. According to Bane and Ellwood, if a high-poverty neighborhood is defined as a census tract with a poverty rate of 40 percent or more, then only 26 percent of all poor blacks live in such neighborhoods. Moreover, the vast majority of welfare recipients do not live in high-poverty areas in large cities. In 1980 fewer than 8 percent of persons receiving welfare pay-ments lived in such areas.[40]

The culture theory leads nowhere. It does not indicate a course of policy. The message is that nothing can be done to change the pessimistic attitudes.

CONCLUSION

None of the three deficiency theories of black unemployment explains its growth since 1975. Neither the IQ nor the culture theory even makes an attempt to do so. They seek only to explain the black-white difference in unemployment rates. But without an explanation of the growth over the postwar period, it is impossible to account for the current high level. Only the welfare–incentive theory seeks to provide a historical analysis, but its attempt is limited to the period from 1965 to 1975, and even for this period it provides only a partial explanation. None of the three the-ories takes into account the change during the postwar period in the demand for unskilled labor. As we have seen in the preceding chapters the demand for unskilled labor declined owing to the fall in the relative cost of capital, skilled labor, and imports, and the resulting substitution of these inputs and goods for unskilled labor.

NOTES

1. Richard J. Herrnstein and Charles Murray, *The Bell Curve: Intelligence and Class Structure in American Life* (New York: Free Press, 1994).

2. Charles Spearman, *The Abilities of Man* (London: Macmillan, 1927); A. R. Jensen, "How Much Can We Boost IQ and Scholastic Achievement?" *Harvard Educational Review*, 39 (1969): 1–123.

3. Herrnstein and Murray, *The Bell Curve*, 121, 131, 132.

4. Ibid., 276–78. We should also note that 34 percent of blacks have an IQ above 100, compared to 50 percent of whites. About 17 percent of whites have IQ scores above 115, compared to about 5 percent of blacks.

5. The black population is about 12 percent of the total population. A quota

system for admissions to colleges, graduate schools, and jobs as professionals based on population percentages would result in blacks in these favored positions having much lower IQs than the whites in the same positions. Thus, a quota system based on the share of the total population results in black students achieving lower grades in college courses. Quota systems may also result in black professionals and managers being less effective in occupations where school-taught skills and reasoning, mathematical, and writing skills are important.

6. Herrnstein and Murray, *The Bell Curve*, 295–311.

7. Charles Murray, "The Real 'Bell Curve,' " *Wall Street Journal*, December 2, 1994, A14.

8. Eric A. Hanushek, "The Economics of Schooling: Production and Efficiency in Public Schools," *Journal of Economic Literature*, 24 (September 1986): 1141–77; John E. Chubb and Terry M. Moe, *Politics, Markets, and America's Schools* (Washington, D.C.: Brookings Institution, 1990), 101–40.

9. Stephen Jay Gould, "Curveball," *New Yorker*, November 28, 1994, 142.

10. Charles Murray, *Losing Ground: American Social Policy, 1950–1980* (New York: Basic Books, 1984).

11. *Statistical Abstract of the United States 1995* (*SAUS 1995*), 388, table 612.

12. Robert A. Moffitt, "The Distribution of Earnings and the Welfare State," in Gary Burtless (ed.), *A Future of Lousy Jobs? The Changing Structure of U.S. Wages* (Washington, D.C.: Brookings Institution, 1990), 201–30.

13. Moffitt, "Distribution of Earnings," 207.

14. *SAUS 1994*, 385, table 601, 383, table 597.

15. Robert A. Moffitt, "Incentive Effects of the U.S. Welfare System: A Review," *Journal of Economic Literature*, 30 (March 1992): 5.

16. Sar A. Levitan, *Programs in Aid of the Poor for the 1980s* (Baltimore, Md.: Johns Hopkins University Press, 1980), 71.

17. *SAUS 1994*, 480, table 739.

18. Ibid., 479, table 735; 383, table 597. One reason the number of participating families exceeded the number of female-headed families with money incomes of less than $10,000 is that women went in and out of the program. Some months they earned enough to take themselves out of the program.

19. *New York Times*, January 26, 1994, A16.

20. Ibid.

21. David T. Ellwood, *Poor Support: Poverty in the American Family* (New York: Basic Books, 1988), 19.

22. Moffitt, "Incentive Effects," 24–25.

23. Ellwood, *Poor Support*, 138.

24. U.S. House of Representatives, Committee on Ways and Means, *1991 Green Book: Background Material and Data on Programs within the Jurisdiction of the Committee on Ways and Means* (Washington, D.C.: U.S. Government Printing Office). Cited by Mary Jo Bane and David T. Ellwood, *Welfare Realities: From Rhetoric to Reality* (Cambridge, Mass.: Harvard University Press, 1994), 72.

25. Michael Tanner, Stephen Moore, and David Hartman, "The Work vs. Welfare Trade-off; An Analysis of the Total Level of Welfare Benefits by State," *Policy Analysis* (September 19, 1995): 240.

26. Bane and Ellwood, *Welfare Realities*, 33.

27. Moffitt, "Incentive Effects," 11.

28. Ibid., 9.

29. *SAUS 1993*, 381, table 604.

30. William Julius Wilson and Kathryn Neckerman, "Poverty and Family Structure: The Widening Gap between Evidence and Public Policy Issues," Chapter 3 in William Julius Wilson, *The Truly Disadvantaged: The Inner City, the Underclass, and Public Policy* (Chicago: University of Chicago Press, 1987), 82–83.

31. The table below compares indexes of AFDC benefits and of the sum of AFDC, Food Stamp, and Medicaid benefits with an index of earnings of sewing machine operators.

Indexes of Real AFDC Benefits, Sum of AFDC, Food Stamps, and Medicaid Benefits, and of Real Earnings of Sewing Machine Operators, Various Years, 1968–1987 (1981=100)

	AFDC	Sum of Benefits	Operator's Earnings
1968			108.0
1969	125.6		
1971	125.1		101.8
1973	118.3		
1974			105.2
1975	119.5	113.2	
1977	118.3	113.5	
1978			102.0
1979	109.3	106.4	
1981	100.0	100.0	100.0
1982	96.1	101.0	
1983	94.4	103.0	
1984	94.4	99.5	95.7
1985	96.6	101.0	
1986	97.8	100.9	
1987	95.4		91.6

Note: GDP implicit price deflator used to deflate operators' earnings.
Sources: See Table 5.3 for AFDC and sum of AFDC, Food Stamp, and Medicaid benefits.
Operators' earnings index based on BLS Industry Wage Survey: Men's and Boys' Shirts (except Work Shirts) and Nightwear, Bulletin Nos. 1324, 1457, 1659, 1794, 1901, 2035, 2131, 2232, 2304.

32. Richard B. Freeman, "Employment and Earnings of Disadvantaged Young Men in a Labor Shortage Economy," in Christopher Jencks and Paul E. Peterson (eds.), *The Urban Underclass* (Washington, D.C.: Brookings Institution, 1991), 103.

33. Moffitt, "Incentive Effects," 12.

34. Ibid., 16.

35. Ibid., 37.

36. Frank Furstenberg, "The Next Generation: The Children of Teenage Mothers Grow Up," in Margaret Rosenheim and Mark Testa (eds.), *Early Parenthood*

and Coming of Age in the 1990s (New Brunswick, N.J.: Rutgers University Press, 1992). Cited by Joel F. Handler, *The Poverty of Welfare Reform* (New Haven, Conn.: Yale University Press, 1995), 50.

37. Kenneth B. Clark, *Dark Ghetto: Dilemmas of Social Power* (New York: Harper and Row, 1965); Daniel P. Moynihan, *The Negro Family: The Case for National Action* (Washington, D.C.: Office of Policy Planning and Research, U.S. Department of Labor, 1965); Oscar Lewis, "The Culture of Poverty," in Daniel Patrick Moynihan (ed.), *Understanding Poverty: Perspectives from the Social Sciences* (New York: Basic Books, 1968), 187–200; Herbert J. Gans, *Urban Villagers: Group and Class in the Life of Italian-Americans* (New York: Free Press, 1962); Oscar Lewis, *La Vida* (New York: Panther, 1965).

38. Lewis, "The Culture of Poverty," 199.

39. Paul E. Peterson, "The Urban Underclass and the Poverty Paradox," in Jencks and Peterson (eds.), *The Urban Underclass*, 12.

40. Bane and Ellwood, *Welfare Realities*, 89–90.

6

Race and Politics

Why have poor blacks fared so badly at the hands of the federal government? Postwar administrations have not adopted effective policies to deal with the problem of unskilled unemployment; NAFTA was enacted, despite the wide recognition that it harmed unskilled workers; and public assistance is being cut. What is the explanation?

One reason is that policymakers in neither party have had a correct analysis of the problem. They have not understood how the wage-equalization, full-employment, education, and minimum-wage policies affected unskilled workers. Instead of examining the consequences of these policies, policymakers have focused on welfare's alleged effect on work incentives. Indeed, this focus has blocked from view the general, economy-wide aspects of the problem. Even the welfare specialists in the Clinton administration have not understood the sources of black unemployment.

A contributing factor is the widespread animosity toward black welfare recipients, which is exacerbated by the anger at high taxes. Focus groups selected from among blue-collar whites apparently are enraged by what they see as black welfare recipients' exploitative behavior.[1] The current drive for cutting welfare payments reflects this rage. What is more, unskilled workers, white as well as black, lack political power. A sad fact of politics is that so large a group, consisting as it does of one-third of the labor force, is unrepresented in political battles affecting its members. Proponents of trade liberalization have simply disregarded their interests. The interests of skilled workers, who benefited from the growth of exports, prevailed.

Despite the claim of black organizations that they represent poor blacks, no organization represents them. The middle-class members of the National Association for the Advancement of Colored People (NAACP) and the National Urban League have exploited the problems of the inner cities to promote their own interests. The organizations have won programs from different administrations, which have benefited only their members, who belong to the middle class. They demand affirmative action and school integration, which do not benefit poor blacks. The underlying premise of these organizations' emphasis on affirmative action and school integration has been that inner-city problems are the product of race discrimination. But the unemployment of the unskilled is not due to discrimination.

The poverty programs were not a response to political pressure by black or other organizations. When the AFDC was enacted by Congress in the midst of the Great Depression, it was designed to help widows and their children. It was part of a package of programs for certain people in need of assistance, such as the blind, the elderly, and widowed women. The intention was not to provide assistance to the able-bodied poor, including single mothers who were not widows. Of course, during the Great Depression various programs provided relief to the unemployed. Employed voters favored them because they feared that they themselves were threatened. Also, they judged that the beneficiaries, who were out of jobs through no fault of their own, deserved assistance. Finally, the unemployed were politically powerful. With 24 percent of the labor force unemployed in 1932, they were a large fraction of the voters who supported Roosevelt.

BLACK POLITICS

A short history of the major black organizations' struggles may help us understand their neglect of inner-city problems. In the early 1950s the NAACP fought in the courts for blacks' constitutional rights. In the South their voting rights had been abrogated, and blacks in all parts of the country were suffering from discrimination in education and employment. The NAACP won its first important victory in 1954 when the Supreme Court in *Brown v. Board of Education* outlawed segregation in public education, asserting that it was inherently unequal.

Black organizations' efforts in the civil rights struggle were confined to the courts; they were not active politically. Without their help, President Johnson in 1964 pushed through the Civil Rights Act which prohibited segregation in public facilities and accommodations; outlawed discrimination by employers and unions; and prohibited the payment of federal funds to institutions practicing discrimination. The following year under Johnson's pressure, Congress passed the Voting Rights Act, prohibiting literacy tests and requiring the appointment of federal examiners to enforce voting rights.

In the 1960s poverty was a major concern of neither black organizations nor unions. Civil rights issues continued to command black organizations' attention and resources, and the unions fought for employed members of particular occupations and industries—not for the unemployed.

Thus, the initiative for the War on Poverty came from the administration. Martin Luther King's marches were protests against the violation of blacks' civil rights. It was only late in the 1960s, after Johnson had initiated the War on Poverty, that King planned a march for antipoverty legislation. His assassination in 1968 prevented the march from taking place.

To a large extent the War on Poverty was a fluke. Part of the appeal of the protests sponsored by black organizations relied on whites' sympathy for poor blacks, but the demands were only for civil rights. Kennedy did become concerned about the problem of poverty, but his interest was aroused by an article in a popular magazine, not by black or other political action. A review of Michael Harrington's *The Other America* in the *New Yorker* caught Kennedy's attention, and he ordered members of the administration to make policy recommendations. Action was not taken before Johnson took office.

Instead of black activism bringing about the poverty programs, the converse happened. The War on Poverty nurtured the activism by establishing community action programs, which gave blacks locally controlled organizations, resources, and a base. Rejecting the tradition of looking to social workers for leadership, David Hackett and Richard Boone of the President's Committee on Juvenile Delinquency proposed the community action programs. Urging that the programs encourage self-reliance, they suggested that the poor themselves run the operating agencies, which would coordinate welfare, housing, and job placement services in a single location in a poor neighborhood.[2]

Afraid of committing large funds without a preliminary trial, Hackett and Boone urged an initial, small pilot program. But Johnson, who recognized that a modest proposal had no hope of enactment, insisted that the credibility of a crisis appeal demanded a big program and large expenditures. Moreover, as a political practitioner, he knew that the chances of winning a majority in Congress were small unless many districts benefited. Johnson won the needed majority, and in August 1964 he signed the Economic Opportunity Act, setting up the Office of Economic Opportunity (OEO).

Pessimistic about gaining power through ordinary political processes, blacks seized on the community action programs, which gave them control over some institutions in the inner cities. The programs became the springboards for activist groups hostile to whites. The Black Panther party, whose members sported uniforms and fought gun battles with the police, was founded in an Oakland community action office, where Bobby Seale, the party's chairman, had a job. The community action programs also sponsored cultural activities expressing black rage. LeRoi Jones, the poet and playwright, received a grant to write a play in which Jack Benny's black valet killed his white oppressors.[3] Not having roots in the community, the activist groups did not survive the end of the community action programs.

In 1968 the issues of school and housing integration came to the fore, and the courts were again the battleground. In 1968 in *Green v. County School Board* the Supreme Court required public school systems to integrate the schools, and the Justice Department then forced cities to bus children.

The NAACP and the National Urban League continued to ignore the foremost problems. As late as the 1970s, Eleanor Holmes Norton was so unaware of the condition of the poor that she was surprised to learn of the large number of female-headed black families, and it was not before the early 1980s that Marion Wright Edelman discovered that 55 percent of black children were born out of wedlock.[4]

Arguing that the problem for the poor was joblessness, not school segregation, Bayard Rustin tried to persuade the NAACP and the Urban League to shift their attention. Because his following was small, race discrimination remained the chief concern. Sharing the ambitions of their white counterparts, middle-class blacks still found their way to professional and managerial jobs blocked, their children could not gain admission to the better colleges and universities, and they were excluded from suburban neighborhoods.

The black organizations' success in achieving their limited objectives has taken the heart out of their struggle for civil rights. Businesses, schools, and governments employ blacks, and black mayors, governors, and members of Congress are elected. The continuing discrimination is more subtle and therefore more difficult to fight in the courts and legislatures, leaving little for the civil rights organizations to do. The summit meeting of black leaders in June 1994 acknowledged that the organizations were doing nothing for the poor. So far, however, the organizations have not agreed on a program.

RACE POLITICS

The community action programs; the race riots, which came in the late 1960s; and the increase in crime, which was associated with blacks, aroused animosity toward blacks. In the first nine months of 1967 there were 164 race riots, including the one in Detroit, in which 43 people were killed. Johnson sent troops into the city to restore order.[5]

The demands of the civil rights movement exacerbated the hostility. Many whites had agreed to the demands for equal access to schools, housing, and jobs, but the insistence on busing and affirmative action imposed unacceptable costs, especially on unskilled white workers. In 1969 a court ordered busing in Los Angeles and Pasadena; the Department of Health, Education, and Welfare refused federal funds to Ferndale, Michigan because it was not in compliance. The Supreme Court allowed busing to be used as a method of integrating the schools, and going further, in 1972 a Virginia judge ordered students to be bused across county lines between the predominantly black schools of Richmond and two largely white counties. In Michigan a judge ordered busing between Detroit and surrounding districts. Although the Supreme Court in 1974 disallowed the decisions mandating busing between different counties,[6] protesters continued to demonstrate across the country. Anti-black feelings had been aroused, and they persisted.

Housing issues also provoked heated battles. Opponents of the Johnson administration's rent supplements program, under which poor blacks were to receive housing allowances usable anywhere, described it as a back door to integrating residential areas. The incursion of blacks to a neighborhood threatened to reduce the market values of its houses.

More than any other development, the growth of the welfare rolls aroused the resentment of whites, who saw their tax payments being used to support idle blacks. The marginal income tax rates had been established before the inflation of the 1960s and 1970s raised ordinary working-class families into high tax brackets. Although real wages were no higher than they had been in the 1950s, they now had to pay higher taxes. By the late 1970s inflation had raised the average income of a married couple, consisting of two prime-age, full-time earners to about $30,000, which in the 1950s had placed a family in the top 1 percent. The man earned about $20,000, and the woman about $10,000. In 1981, just prior to the income tax reductions, the marginal federal rate for this family was 33 percent. Adding 6.5 percent for social security and 5 percent for state and local taxes, the overall marginal rate was about 44.5 percent. Because the cost to a working wife included child care expenses, transportation, and additional food and clothing costs, she was lucky to keep half of her earnings. The conflicts over race transformed American politics, with the Republicans benefiting in the 1970s and 1980s.

In the late 1960s the Democrats acquired their pro-black reputation. Previously, southern Democrats, who had dominated the party, had prevented blacks from gaining influence. As the party's center of power moved north and the unions gained strength within it, the Democrats swung towards a liberal agenda.

The identification of the Democrats with slavery kept blacks in the Republican camp until the 1960s, but they never won a prominent role in the party. Since the 1920s the Republicans have been associated with business interests, and in the 1960s the Goldwater conservatives defeated the more liberal wing. After the Democrats sponsored the Civil Rights and Voting Rights Acts and the War on Poverty, blacks began to switch their political allegiance.

In 1972 the Democratic National Convention exacerbated whites' fears by adopting a more liberal platform on race. It supported school and housing integration, and affirmative action. Nominating George McGovern, the Democrats had become the pro-black party, threatening whites' schools and their property values. The convention also threatened to raise taxes by promising to work for a more equal distribution of income.

Capitalizing on whites' resentment against the taxes supporting malingering blacks, Nixon attacked welfare, thus tying the tax protest to this animosity. His attacks on busing and affirmative action further aggravated whites' hostility.

In 1980 Reagan continued to press these themes. Aiming his campaign at white blue-collar workers, he hammered away against high taxes, welfare, busing, and affirmative action. In 1978 the tax protest erupted in California with the passage of Proposition 13. The suburban middle class was already in the Republican camp, so Reagan had no need to tailor his appeal to win their votes. But he had to gain the support of blue-collar workers for the anti-union party of the rich—the party of the Taft-Hartley labor law. By condemning welfare and thus linking the tax protest to the anti-black resentment, Reagan's appeal succeeded.

The 1984 Democratic convention, which again identified the party with blacks, welfare, and high taxes, made it even more vulnerable to the Republican strategy. By winning the support of the platform committee for affirmative action, Jesse Jackson gained prominence, heightening the perception that black militants were powerful. Also, while the Democrats pledged themselves to raise public assistance, Democratic presidential nominee Walter Mondale promised to reduce the deficit by raising taxes.

Having found the right formula, the Republicans exploited bigotry even more in 1988. The Democratic candidate, Governor Michael Dukakis, had vetoed a bill prohibiting furloughs of first-degree murderers. While on furlough, in 1987, a convicted murderer, Willie Horton, attempted a burglary; when he was discovered, he beat up the householder and raped his fiancee. Nevertheless, Dukakis continued to support the furlough program. The issues of race and crime remained at the forefront, with the Democrats maintaining their liberal positions.

By 1992 the Democrats had learned that backing blacks' demands did not win presidential elections. Clinton, who had been a leading figure in the right-of-center Democratic Leadership Council (DLC), advanced a considerably more conservative platform than Dukakis had. Recognizing the widespread resentment against welfare and implicitly against blacks, Clinton proposed the requirement that beneficiaries must work after two years on welfare, and he avoided being tagged as an advocate of blacks' rights. Clinton softened his attack on Bush for condemning the Civil Rights Act by proclaiming his opposition to racial quotas.[7] Furthermore, he appealed to racist attitudes by emphasizing the crime issue, which traditionally had belonged to the Republicans. He promised to "put 100,000 new police officers on the streets."[8] Adding this number to the 800,000 already in the local and state police forces would not significantly enhance security against violent crime, but the Democrats no longer were vulnerable to the Willie Horton attack. In addition, Clinton refrained from supporting such traditionally Democratic platform planks as fair housing and affirmative action. He could not keep Jesse Jackson from making an impassioned address to the convention, but by ignoring him during the campaign he avoided giving the impression that blacks would have a prominent place in his administration.

Throughout the campaign Clinton directed his appeal to those he called the middle class. He probably recognized that even poor whites either thought of themselves as members or aspired to that status. The middle class did not depend on welfare but worked or looked for jobs, they lived in the suburbs, and, above all, they were white. When announcing his candidacy Clinton informed white workers that, despite his having attended Georgetown, Oxford, and Yale, he was one of them. Speaking of his family, he said,

By any standard, they were poor. But we didn't blame other people. We took responsibility for ourselves and for each other because we knew we could do better. I was raised to believe in the American Dream, in family values, in individual responsibility, and in the obligation of government to help people who were doing the best they could.[9]

The code words in this direct appeal for the support of white workers echoed those of the Republicans: "family values" and "individual responsibility." Not allowing the Republicans to have exclusive rights to protecting family values, after the campaign Clinton acknowledged the validity of Quayle's criticism of the idealized Murphy Brown. Because many single mothers were black, the message carried anti-black connotations. Clinton continues to ignore blacks and to adhere to the welfare and law-and-order themes.

Neither the Democrats nor the Republicans have addressed the issue of unskilled unemployment, which has been subverted by issues connected with welfare and race. Persistent unemployment has been regarded as a problem arising from welfare payments rather than from the declining demand for unskilled labor. Both parties agree that welfare's deleterious effect on work incentives is at the root of unemployment. And it is mainly blacks who are on welfare. Never explicit, this reasoning lies behind the hostility to welfare and stands in the way of an appropriate unemployment policy. Bigotry confounds the unemployment issue.

THE FUTURE

Jesse Jackson's Rainbow Coalition comes closest to representing the interests of unskilled blacks, but the Coalition weakens its bargaining power by identifying itself with the interests of blacks as blacks rather than as unskilled workers. The Coalition's energy is devoted to the struggle for affirmative action and fair housing. Moreover, it does not attempt to form a broad group of organizations representing all unskilled workers.

The only other organizations representing unskilled workers are the unions. An alliance of the Coalition with the unions would have had a better chance of defeating NAFTA than the separate groups. Having no alternative, such an alliance cannot threaten to withdraw from the Democratic party. But it can oppose candidates in primaries, and its political weight would be greater than that of the Coalition and of the unions separately.

The Coalition does not appear to be ready for joint action with unions. It does not see itself representing the interests of white as well as black unskilled workers. Instead, it alienates and antagonizes white unskilled workers by emphasizing affirmative action and other racial issues. Unskilled blacks are hurting themselves by going along with middle-class blacks. The Rainbow Coalition would benefit its supporters by focusing on the issues where they have the same interests as white unskilled workers rather than by emphasizing divisive racial issues.

The unions have not attempted to develop their political strength as representatives of unskilled workers. They have taken positions on policies affecting unskilled workers generally, such as NAFTA. But they have campaigned as representatives of the workers in particular industries.

If the Rainbow Coalition and the unions representing unskilled workers recognize their mutual interests, they will be far more effective. The unions can do far more to counter the Republicans' racist appeals. They can educate their white members to recognize their mutual interests with black unskilled workers and to ignore the appeals exploiting their resentment against welfare cheats and employment preferences based on race. The Coalition for its part can reduce its emphasis on racial issues and base its appeal on the interests its members share with those of white unskilled workers.

NOTES

1. Stanley B. Greenberg, *Middle Class Dreams: The Politics and Power of the New American Majority* (New York: Times Books, 1995), 11, 136.

2. Nicholas Lemann, *The Promised Land: The Great Black Migration and How It Changed America* (New York: Random House, 1992), 133.

3. Ibid., 180.

4. Ibid., 281–82, 288.

5. Ibid., 190.

6. Thomas Byrne Edsall with Mary D. Edsall, *Chain Reaction: The Impact of Race, Rights, and Taxes on American Politics* (New York: W. W. Norton, 1992), 88.

7. Bill Clinton and Al Gore, *Putting People First: How We Can All Change America* (New York: Times Books, 1992), 64.

8. Ibid., 72.

9. Bill Clinton, Announcement Speech, Old State House, Little Rock, Arkansas, October 3, 1991. Reprinted in Clinton and Gore, *Putting People First*, 197.

7

Current Public Policy

It was Clinton's election campaign proposal in 1992 that triggered measures to limit the length of time single mothers could receive welfare payments and to mandate training for them. The proposal was widely understood to refer to black women who, Clinton said, were making welfare a way of life. Thus, a liberal Democrat, appealing for the support of whites angry with so-called black deadbeats, initiated the drive to limit welfare—not conservative Republicans. Claiming success for the Arkansas workfare program, Clinton hailed it as a model for welfare reform. However, his claim was unwarranted. The fact that assistance in searching for jobs helped a few welfare recipients find employment did not mean that the program reduced total unemployment. The findings of studies reviewed in this chapter do not justify welfare reformers' belief that a small amount of training and assistance in job searches will substantially reduce unemployment among the unskilled. The studies ignore completely the fall in the demand for unskilled labor. With the demand dropping, no conceivable training program will be effective.

CURRENT POLICIES

Having proliferated haphazardly in response to the pressures of particular problems and interest groups, the federally funded uncoordinated mess of numerous, overlapping training programs incur large costs and accomplish little. The federal government spends about $25 billion annually on 154 training programs distributed among 14 departments and agencies; most are sponsored by the Departments of Education, Labor, and Health and Human Services.[1]

The programs provide counseling and assessment services, occupational training, basic skills training, job placement, on-the-job training, and job-search training. Furthermore, they assist in the search for jobs by Native Americans, the homeless, migrant workers, school dropouts, the handicapped, single parents, criminal offenders, Alaskan and Hawaiian natives, veterans, the economically disadvantaged and unemployed youths out of school, and workers displaced by imports, the downsizing of defense expenditures, and the implementation of the Clean Air Act.[2] The programs duplicate populations, goals, and services. The nine programs specifically targeting the economically disadvantaged seek to increase their employment, and four of them attempt to reduce welfare dependency. The Job Opportunities and Basic Skills (JOBS) program is designed to help AFDC recipients, and the Job Training Partnership Act (JTPA) title IIA program served 136,000 AFDC recipients in 1991. The Department of Agriculture's Food Stamp Education and Training program is intended to help food stamp recipients, and the Department of Labor's JTPA program served more than 100,000 food stamp recipients.

The government has a patchwork of parallel administrative structures. Within the 14 departments and agencies sponsoring the services, 35 interdepartmental offices channel funds to state and local programs. Thus, the Departments of Agriculture; Education; Health and Human Services; Housing and Urban Development; and Labor administer the nine programs serving the economically disadvantaged. Each has its own staff to plan and monitor the programs. Each program has its own policies, procedures, and requirements, and each administers the delivery of service through a separate network of local offices. The JTPA program funds about 630 local offices, and JOBS and Food Stamp Education and Training programs also fund numerous local offices.[3]

The history of the Food Stamp Education and Training program sheds some light on how the patchwork of programs grew. In 1985 Republicans insisted that food stamp recipients work, while Democrats proposed a training program. The compromise created the employment and training program for food stamp recipients. To ensure that the program met the Republican goal at least partly, the Agriculture Department ordered that at least half the food stamp beneficiaries participate, which meant that $40 million would be spread over training 10 million people.[4]

Aware that the funds were inadequate for training so many people, in 1986 some state food stamp directors urged the Department to reduce the participation requirement, but the proposal was rejected. Only after Abt Associates reported in 1989 that the program was ineffective, did Congress and the Agriculture Department reduce the requirement to 10 percent.[5]

Despite the change, the Food Stamp training program continues to be a sham. The 1985 law creating the program was intended to get benefi-ciaries into jobs and reduce government aid. *The Wall Street Journal* de-scribed a training session in Baltimore as follows:

The counselor carefully explains the program's sole requirement: Apply for two dozen jobs in the next 60 days, or risk losing your food stamps. Ten of the job "contacts" must be in person. Their meeting that morning counts as one job contact, Ms. Johnson [the counselor] adds. If they walk across the hall to the state's employment bureau, that will count as another contact. Shops across the street are another quick stop. "You just have to get through this," she urges.[6]

Secretary Reich says that studies of the program show it to be a failure, which he ascribes to the small expenditures on training per participant.[7]

The program continues because it has strong defenders in Congress representing agricultural interests. Evidently, farmers' organizations fear that withdrawal of the training requirement would threaten the Food Stamp program. According to the *Wall Street Journal*, Senator Patrick Leahy of Vermont, chairman of the Senate Agriculture Committee, said that he would "fight any proposal that makes it more difficult for the people we are trying to help."

Despite the Clinton administration's express desire to consolidate the programs, political pressures continue to increase the number. Thus, to win votes for NAFTA, the administration created a program for workers displaced by the resulting imports.[8]

The absence of clear entry points to the system and of a defined path from one program to another and differences in eligibility requirements between programs create confusion. Conflicting eligibility requirements have blocked attempts to coordinate the programs. Nine programs for the economically disadvantaged used six different definitions of "low income"; five different definitions of family or household; and five def-initions of what is included in income. Potential beneficiaries must complete a long application form for each program. Employers have to deal with over 50 programs, which are slow to respond, and they com-plain that they have difficulty finding qualified workers.[9]

Mandatory Training Programs

Many states are administering federally funded mandatory training programs for welfare recipients. The argument is that the states can op-erate such training programs better than federal agencies. More impor-tant, the legislation assumes that if AFDC recipients were provided training and faced a cutoff date when they would no longer receive ben-efits, they would seek and find jobs. However, the outcome of the pro-grams that the states have operated does not support the optimism.

Attempts by the federal government to reduce the number of welfare recipients through state-operated employment search and training programs go back to 1967. To handle the rising number of AFDC participants, Congress enacted the Work Incentive Program (WIN), which provided assistance in finding jobs. In 1981 the Omnibus Budget Reconciliation Act permitted states to require recipients to work in public sector jobs for as many hours as would make up for their benefits at the minimum wage. The Act gave the states an option to convert WIN into a block grant and to use workfare, giving them flexibility in administering what was often regarded as a rigid, bureaucratic program. The Family Support Act of 1988 enacted the JOBS program, requiring the states to offer education to AFDC recipients who have not graduated from high school or who do not have basic literacy skills. In addition, the states must provide job training and placement services. They must also provide two of the following: assistance in job searching, on-the-job training, and workfare.[10]

These mandatory training and work programs have not succeeded in getting many welfare recipients into jobs. The Family Support Act requires that all states operate a JOBS program for AFDC recipients. But Congress has been unwilling to appropriate the funds necessary to train many recipients. Due in part to limited resources, only 10 percent to 15 percent of AFDC families have participated. Moreover, even if larger expenditures were made, the programs are unlikely to succeed. Contrary to the impression that most AFDC mothers are long-term dependents, as Chapter 5 reports, the majority are recipients for short spells. For many participants the periods in which they get benefits are too short for them to benefit from the training programs.

The Manpower Demonstration Research Corporation (MDRC) has studied the performance of programs in Arkansas, Baltimore, Cook County, San Diego, Virginia, and West Virginia. Except for West Virginia, which compelled recipients to work, the states only demanded participation in the program. The training consisted of guidance in searching for a job, not of instruction in specific work skills. With the assistance of counselors, welfare recipients were required to look for a job for two to four weeks. The first week of a two-week program might provide three-hour daily group sessions to help develop job-seeking skills. In the second week, under supervision, the participants would make telephone calls to prospective employers for two or three hours daily. If they were not successful, the participants might do unpaid work for up to three months in entry-level jobs in public or nonprofit agencies, performing maintenance, clerical, park upkeep, or human services functions. They worked the number of hours that their welfare payments would pay for at the minimum wage rate. If at the end of this period the participants were still not employed, the training and work require-

Table 7.1
Employment Effect of Welfare Employment Programs in Seven Areas

Area	Year	Experimental Group Mean (Percent)	Control Group Mean (Percent)	Difference (Percent)
Arkansas	1	20.4	16.7	3.7
	2	23.9	20.3	3.6
	3	24.5	18.3	6.2
Baltimore	1	34.7	31.2	3.5
	2	39.5	37.1	2.4
	3	40.7	40.3	0.4
Cook County	1	22.6	21.4	1.3
San Diego I	1	42.4	36.9	5.5
San Diego saturation	1	34.7	26.9	7.7
	2	34.7	29.3	5.4
Virginia	1	34.7	31.0	3.8
	2	39.3	33.3	6.0
	3	38.7	34.1	4.6
W. Virginia	1	12.0	13.1	−1.0

Source: Judith M. Gueron, "Work and Welfare: Lessons on Employment Programs," *Journal of Economic Perspectives*, 4 (Winter 1990): 92-93.

ment would cease, or periodically the program would require them to do some minimal job search.[11]

Judith Gueron, of the MDRC, concluded in 1990 that most of the state-administered workfare programs were successful because they led to increases in employment and earnings. President Clinton's claim that the Arkansas program succeeded calls attention to it. Unlike the other states, which imposed an obligation on only one-third of AFDC participants with school-age children, Arkansas required women with children aged three years or over to work. At the end of the first year of the Arkansas study 20.4 percent of the experimental group who had gone through the program were employed (see Table 7.1), compared to 16.7 percent of the control group, who had not gone through the program. The effect of the program thus is estimated as the difference—3.7 percent. The program was a success, according to Gueron, because this difference was large enough to rule out chance. Gueron also considers it a success because the differences between the experimental and control groups in average earnings, AFDC payments, and the number on welfare were also statistically significant. The Baltimore, San Diego I, San Diego Saturation, and Virginia programs were also rated successful. Only in West Virginia, where the labor market was depressed, was the program rated a failure. In general, the programs had a positive effect.

But the statistical significance of the difference in the success in finding and keeping jobs between the experimental and control groups only demonstrates that an effort to help recipients find jobs will have a small effect. Indeed, the effect is so small that for all intents and purposes the programs have no effect. The statement that the results are statistically significant means only that the differences between the experimental and control groups are too large to be due to chance.

Moreover, the studies do not show that when large numbers of recipients are trained many will become employed. No conclusion about the effect of large training programs can be reached from a study of small training programs. Such a conclusion requires an investigation of the unskilled labor market along with a study of the effect of assistance in job searching. As previous chapters have shown, the unskilled labor market is unlikely to absorb a large number of additional workers. The problem is not lack of training or lack of motivation, it is lack of unskilled jobs.

In 1994 the MDRC hailed the training program in Riverside County, California, a great success. Let us look at this program, which was supposed to provide a guide for future training programs. A high percentage of the AFDC beneficiaries of the Riverside program lacked basic education.[12] On the other hand, the program had certain advantages. Riverside emphasized the objective of getting its beneficiaries into jobs; it had a charismatic director; the program promised employers trained applicants immediately; the employers cooperated; the staff was closely supervised; and its members were rated according to their success in placing trainees in jobs. The MDRC undertook a study to determine whether the emphasis on job placement produced better employment results than an emphasis on training. The results of the Riverside program were contrasted with those of programs that emphasized training. Each program was examined individually. The results for an experimental group in each program were compared with those for a control group. According to the MDRC, on the grounds that over a three-year period the earnings of those in the Riverside experimental group increased 49 percent more than those of the control group and welfare payments fell 15 percent more than those of the control group, the program was a success.[13] Moreover, the results were better than those for the programs that emphasized training. The lesson was that a program dedicated to placing welfare beneficiaries in jobs and in which staff members' performance was rated accordingly would succeed.

Joel Handler is skeptical about Riverside's success. He points out that the difference in employment between the experimental and the control group in Riverside was only 9 percent. More important, about two-thirds of the members of the experimental group were not working at the time of the third-year interview, and almost half never worked during the entire three-year period.[14] Moreover, as in the case of the other studies mentioned earlier, the results indicate only that some effort applied to getting jobs for a small group of beneficiaries helps them marginally.

Even if the results were more favorable, policymakers could not infer that a greater concentration of effort by job placement training programs will get many welfare beneficiaries off the rolls. As was noted earlier, the studies do not attempt to evaluate the effect of the demand for unskilled labor on the number of trainees who find jobs. Even in the case of Riverside the success was only temporary and thus may have been due more to market conditions than to the program.

Moreover, the MDRC's conclusion that a placement program is more effective than a training program is dubious. The success of a single program, whose staff is highly dedicated, does not permit any conclusion about the best policy to follow. The results may be due to the staff's dedication and other peculiar factors than to the placement policy. Not many staffs are likely to be very energetic over a long period. To reach any conclusion about the effectiveness of the policy would require a sample of programs. The experimental group would have to be those programs pursuing a placement policy, and the control group would consist of other programs. If the purpose of the studies is to evaluate different types of programs, the samples are too small. The appropriate observation units are the programs. Riverside was compared to five other programs, which emphasized training rather than placement. The sample size for programs emphasizing placement was one, and the sample size for those emphasizing training was five. Treating individual beneficiaries as observation units, the MDRC rated the results significant, but the appropriate comparison is between two samples of programs.

The evaluations of the training programs do not warrant President Clinton's optimism. The studies provide no basis for the belief that training will greatly expand the employment of welfare women. The meager success of a few small training programs due to some effort to help participants find jobs does not warrant optimism about large programs. Depressed markets for unskilled labor will not grow to accommodate many additional workers.

Nonmandatory Training Programs

The first government sponsored nonmandatory training program came with the Area Redevelopment Act of 1958, providing loans to businesses in depressed areas for training unemployed workers. In 1962 Congress passed the Manpower Development and Training Act (MDTA) to assist workers dislocated by mechanization. Following the passage in 1964 of the Economic Opportunity Act, the focus shifted to reducing poverty, and the MDTA program began to train welfare recipients and disadvantaged young people. The program provided classroom training for 140,000 persons and on-the-job training for 125,000 persons.[15]

The MDTA program included the Job Corps for disadvantaged youths, which continues. In 1977 five of six trainees were school dropouts averaging below sixth grade reading and mathematics levels; only one-half came from intact families; the typical family size of students was nearly twice the national average; the per capita family income was less than one-third that of the mean for the total population; four of ten participants had been arrested by the police at some time; and more than one-third had never held a job that required at least 24 working hours per week, for longer than a month. According to Sar Levitan, the description is still accurate. Levitan also says that three out of every ten students complete a Job Corps program.[16]

Notwithstanding the small proportion of students completing it, this intensive and costly program is one of the most successful. In 108 centers across the country the Job Corps brings youths out of destructive surroundings, placing them in residences and offering them highly structured programs. Training is provided for business occupations, automotive trades, construction trades, welding, health occupations, culinary arts, and building maintenance. Other services include health care, social skills training, and placement services. The average length of stay for trainees is about 7.6 months. The number of trainees that the Corps can accommodate at one time is about 39,000, and in 1991 about 100,000 received some training. The program is costly. Total appropriation for 1991 amounted to $867.5 million, and the average cost per slot was about $16,000.

The program has had modest success in placing its graduates. In 1991 about 75 percent of all students were placed in a job or in school, and the average starting wage for those placed was $5.11 per hour.[17] Since the unemployment rate among black youths between the ages of 16 and 19 was 36.3 percent in 1991 and among those between the ages of 20 and 24, 21.6 percent,[18] the Job Corps can be viewed as having had some success. However, the proportion of the students who are still employed three or four years after graduation is not known. One study in 1982 estimated that average gain in earnings for graduates in the first four years was $4,639, or an average per year gain of $1,160,[19] which is not much.

During the Nixon administration, Congress passed the Comprehensive Employment and Training Act (CETA), replacing MDTA. Shifting the operation of employment and training programs to the states, the Act provided for grants to state and local governments to train unemployed and disadvantaged persons. It also provided for temporary public service jobs. The Carter administration raised expenditures, which by 1981 amounted to $8.4 billion (1994 dollars).[20]

During the Reagan administration, Congress passed the Job Training Partnership Act (JTPA), which eliminated CETA's public service employment program and substantially reduced expenditures for training. While it provided funds for training dislocated workers who were not disadvantaged, the disadvantaged have constituted by far the majority of participants. About 15 percent of the disadvantaged participants get help in job searching, 45 percent receive classroom training, 15 percent of all participants receive on-the-job training, and 6 percent of the disadvantaged participants receive work experience. Community colleges and private vocational and proprietary schools provide the classroom training. The students consist of adult women, who usually receive 16 weeks of vocational instruction, and youths, who receive remedial education. Employers providing on-the-job training receive a wage subsidy of up to 50 percent over six months. The work experience component consists of a short-term job in the public or nonprofit sector. Most participants are youths and adult women who have not had recent job experience.[21]

Apart from the Job Corps, the programs have failed dismally. Tens of thousands receive three to six months of job training under JTPA, the funding for which in 1994 amounted to $2.3 billion.[22] In 1986 Abt Associates found that JTPA produced a modest increase in the earnings of adults throughout the 2 1/2 year follow-up period, exceeding the cost of the services under the program. On the other hand, the earnings of out-of-school male youths did not increase. Among adult women, adult men, and female youths, JTPA increased the number attaining a high-school diploma or General Equivalency Diploma (GED), but it had no discernible effect on male youths.[23] Evidently, programs like the JTPA will not significantly reduce unskilled unemployment.

Other programs offer help to workers displaced by imports, reductions in defense expenditures, environmental protection, and other sources of dislocation.[24] For a firm's workers to qualify for the Trade Adjustment and Assistance (TAA) program, they must show that imports have contributed importantly to their unemployment. Beneficiaries receive payments for up to 52 weeks after they exhaust their unemployment insurance benefits. Vocational training centers and local community colleges provide the training, which usually lasts more than a year.[25] In 1991 there were only 20,000 participants, significantly fewer than the 500,000 in 1980. Stricter requirements reduced the program's size.[26]

The Department of Labor's own Office of Inspector General (OIG) found that only half the recipients of benefits in the TAA program enrolled in training programs. Of these only 40 percent found training-related jobs, and only 20 percent were paid suitable wages, defined by the OIG as 80 percent or more of their former wages.[27] In short, the OIG said that the TAA program failed to meet its objectives. Moreover, a study by Mathematica concluded that the training did not increase employment or wages.[28]

Secretary Reich concluded that conventional, short-term training programs for disadvantaged youths do not work. The trainees do no better than other disadvantaged youths either in getting jobs or in earnings.[29] According to Secretary Reich:

But here's the problem: the system we have in place to ensure that every worker learns and constantly upgrades his or her skills is not a system at all. It's a rag-tag collection of programs—a hodgepodge of initiatives, some of which work, many of which don't. In its place this country needs—and this Administration intends to create—a true system of lifelong learning. We'll scrap what doesn't work, and build on what does.[30]

THE CLINTON ADMINISTRATION'S PROPOSALS

Mandatory Training and Work Programs

Lacking a clear conception of the sources of unskilled unemployment, the Clinton administration flounders in the welfare morass. Despite Secretary Reich's condemnation of current training programs, the Clinton administration's proposals for welfare reform depend on continuing them. The administration proposes to terminate AFDC payments after two years and to require recipients to train for jobs. At the end of the two years, the welfare mothers would be required to take jobs which, if necessary, local governments would provide. Moreover, under the Clinton administration's proposals AFDC recipients would have a lifetime limit of benefits of five years.

Debates within the Clinton administration have centered on what would happen to AFDC recipients at the end of the mandatory training period. One side argues that the prospect of termination must be real for the training to be effective, to which the other side replies that the government cannot abandon those who cannot get a job. The Republican Congress has proposed making block grants to the states. The effect would be to reduce the assistance provided to welfare mothers. The probability is that the states will mandate training for a specified period and then require the beneficiaries to take state and local government jobs if they do not find jobs in the private sector.

Although cutting off welfare, of course, will drive some beneficiaries to seek and find jobs, the welfare reformers will be amazed to find that the reform will increase the number of those who over some period receive benefits. Because the policy change will not create jobs, former beneficiaries will displace other unskilled workers, and the newly displaced will be added to the rolls. The average length of stay on welfare will fall, but the total number of people who receive benefits over any period will rise.

The requirement that welfare recipients work after two years of training either in the private economy or in the public sector will entail larger public employment programs than the welfare reformers anticipate. With the demand for unskilled workers falling, firms are unlikely to employ many welfare recipients who will be thrown on the labor market. In 1992 4.9 million families were receiving AFDC benefits. Assuming that one-third of the recipients find jobs in the private sector and that another one-third are exempt from the employment requirement, the states will have to provide about 1.6 million workfare placements.

Nonmandatory Training Programs

Lauding the Job Corps and the program at the Center for Employment Training (CET), based in San Jose, California, Secretary Reich wants to expand programs that appear to work. CET fosters close ties between secondary schools and the business community. Also, Reich is impressed with a study showing that a year or more beyond high school reaps increases in earnings. The administration therefore proposes to expand the Job Corps and programs that combine classroom learning with on-the-job training.

Because the administration is also impressed by the success of the German apprenticeship system, some comments on this system may be useful. At an early age, students are sorted into three classes of schools: hauptschule, realschule, and gymnasium. The hauptschule students remain in school until grades 9 or 10, when they enter a three-year apprenticeship to become carpenters, auto mechanics, and office assistants, and they are paid between 22 and 33 percent of full-time professional wages. Realschule students are in school until grade 10, when they take further vocational training to become laboratory technicians, precision mechanics, and personnel managers. Gymnasium students remain in school until grade 13 and then proceed to university.[31]

In the United Kingdom, Japan, and Sweden, which also have skill-training programs for youths who do not go on to college, schools and employers work together and use national standards to certify competency in skills. By contrast, in the United States training certificates affirm only the completion of a program. The U.K., German, Japanese, and Swedish governments provide remedial education, training, and job placement for most jobless out-of-school youths. Japanese youths not going on to college get jobs through their schools, which are agents of the public employment service and have ties with employers. In Sweden youngsters choosing a vocational field are trained in school and with an employer. The U.S. employment and training programs are available to relatively few.[32]

The foreign governments provide extensive assistance to jobless youths. The United Kingdom guarantees every jobless 16- and 17-year-old out-of-school youth up to two years of work experience and training. Sweden guarantees education, training, or work to every jobless out-of-school teenager. Sweden's municipal authorities develop an individualized plan for the education, training, and employment of every 16- and 17-year-old not in school or working. The public employment service assumes responsibility of youths 18 years old and over, providing placement, training programs, and jobs.[33]

When the administration calls attention to the European and Japanese vocational schools and their link to employers as a model for U.S. policy, it assumes that youths in this country have trouble finding jobs because they lack appropriate training, and the market for semi-skilled jobs does not work well. In contrast to European youths who are not college-bound, American youths in a similar position lack good training in a particular vocation and they lack information about available jobs. However, as this book argues, it is the falling demand for unskilled labor that is the problem, not lack of training or of information.

The administration's proposals cannot achieve their goals. It proposes to use the Job Corps as a model. However, the Corps provides training in basic skills, which are useful only for blue-collar occupations, and they are declining. On the present small scale, the program has been marginally successful, but a much larger program will have less success. Although the graduates may continue to be placed even after there are many more of them, they are likely to displace other potential construction workers, welders, and auto mechanics. Tests of the effectiveness of the Job Corps in placing its graduates will show success, according to the standard techniques of evaluation, because the number of jobs found by graduates will exceed the number found by other disadvantaged youths, and the difference may be statistically significant. But the Job Corps will not add to total employment. Moreover, if the program is greatly expanded, it is likely that whatever difference is observed will vanish.

Education

The long-run objective must be to increase the number of disadvantaged youths who become skilled workers. Without exceptional motivation, unskilled adults will not do the work necessary to become professionals, technicians, and managers. However, there is hope for youths. The hope of any society rides on its children's education, and the inner-city schools have concerned policymakers since the 1960s. I review the policies of the Clinton administration against the background of the history of educational policy.

The large white-black difference in educational achievement provoked anxious debate in the 1960s. The children in the predominantly black inner-city schools performed poorly, they were undisciplined, had high truancy rates, and many dropped out. The extreme problems of blacks in the inner cities spurred moves by the Johnson administration. The Elementary and Secondary Education Act (ESEA) of 1965, part of Johnson's War on Poverty, provided funds to districts to aid education on the basis of the number of poor children.

During the 1980s it was anxiety over the performance of public schools generally, kindled by the declining SAT scores of high-school graduates in the 1970s, that provoked debate. A better measure of students' performance than the SAT scores was the National Assessment of Educational Progress (NAEP) of 17-year-olds, which found performance in science and in mathematics to be deteriorating during the 1970s. By 1992 performance in mathematics returned to the 1973 level, but performance in science did not.[34] The recently passed Goals 2000: Educate America Act was the outcome of anxieties over elementary and secondary school education generally and of efforts by the Reagan, Bush, and Clinton administrations. Nevertheless, the discussion in Congress featured the special problems of the inner cities. The discussion of the School-to-Work Opportunities Act also stressed these problems.

Under Goals 2000, the federal government will provide funds to school systems to meet national academic standards. This policy is consistent with the popular view, with which teachers' associations agree, that students are not performing well because the schools are not demanding enough. The universal remedy for the problems of education is higher standards. A resolution at the American Federation of Teachers' (AFT) 1992 convention said that the poor achievement level of a huge number of students leaving school reduced their employment prospects. According to the resolution, because many students never overcome the social problems that they bring with them to school, the percentage of high-achieving graduates is the smallest of any of the industrialized countries. The resolution also ascribed the better performance of students in other countries to national standards. It said that the greater effectiveness of teachers there is due to a national curriculum, which enables the schools to use the same textbooks and to base assessments of students' performance on a specific curriculum. Other countries have had more educational success than this country because their schools have grouped students by achievement level, with all students being given challenging work. In this country demands on the "slow" groups are much less.

College entrance standards are higher than here, and employment standards are clearer. All students are expected to work hard, and their teachers and parents push them. Moreover, with the legal system supporting school regulations, schools do not suffer the disruptions common in the United States, and they are relatively safe.[35]

The Clinton administration agrees that higher standards will improve students' performance, particularly that of minority children. Appearing before the Senate Labor and Human Resources Committee, Education Secretary Richard W. Riley said that the racial performance gap was unacceptably large. Asserting that students who took more difficult courses, did more homework, and watched less television performed better, he concluded that more challenging standards and curricula would enhance students' performance.[36]

At the same hearing, Senator Christopher J. Dodd described some of the difficulties facing the schools. He said that about 35 percent of children entering kindergarten are unprepared for it, one out of five students has to repeat the first grade, and 50 percent of high school students do not go on to higher education. In Connecticut 10 percent of all 16- to 19-year-olds are high school dropouts. One out of five children brings a lethal weapon to school every day. Referring to schools in disadvantaged areas, Secretary Riley responded that one of the goals of the bill was safe, disciplined, and drug-free schools and that $75 million was to be appropriated for the safe-schools effort. Senator Dodd responded in turn by referring to some research that was being done by the Yale Child Study Center in cooperation with the New Haven Police Department as part of a project on community policing and training in conflict resolution. Senator Edward M. Kennedy added: "A lot has been done with the metal detectors, but one of the very interesting studies indicates that in schools which have comprehensive health services, there has been a very significant reduction in violence and guns."[37]

Senator Kennedy asked Secretary Riley the following question: "Could you briefly walk us through how this legislation would impact a poor school district or a poor school that is attempting to improve the educational accomplishment and achievements for the students in a major urban area in the United States?" Secretary Riley's reply was:

First of all, it is a standards-driven measure which would automatically begin to raise expectations for all children. The whole concept of the bill, as permeated through it, is that all children can learn, and it is a process then of raising expectations for children to start with. We aren't going to have some watered-down curriculum for some and some tough curriculum for others.[38]

The assumption underlying the Act thus is that the major reason for the relatively poor performance of children in disadvantaged areas is the low standards of the schools there. Under the Act funds will be appropriated to assist the states in improving their school systems, which will include vocational schools. Standards will be set by the Goals Panel with the assistance of the related labor organizations and industry trade associations. The Act calls for special assistance to districts in which there are many disadvantaged children.

Unfortunately, the schools in disadvantaged areas are unlikely to accomplish much, even if they are prodded. When classes are constantly disrupted; students lack motivation; and the parents themselves are uneducated, providing no discipline for their children, imposing higher standards cannot raise the performance level significantly.

The School-to-Work Opportunities Act is directed at the young people who do not go to college. In presenting this bill Senator Kennedy emphasized that the United States is the only major industrialized nation lacking a comprehensive and effective school-to-work transition system. The Act is designed to encourage the development and expansion of programs to ensure that all students who do not complete a college program enter the workforce with the needed basic academic and occupational skills. The goal is to orient secondary education toward providing hands-on, experiential learning through connections with employers. Title II provides for small federal grants to states to develop and implement their school-to-work systems. To be eligible a program must include a plan of study at school which integrates academic and vocational learning. It must also provide a program of work-based learning, including job training, paid work experience, and workplace monitoring. The program must also match students with employers who can offer work-based learning opportunities and help students find appropriate jobs or pursue further education or training.[39]

The guiding principles for School-to-Work are that a lack of vocational training is the basic problem for youngsters not going on to college and that present employment agencies perform poorly. Following the model of the German apprenticeship system, the argument is that students would get good training and employers would hire the students they train if the schools worked with employers. However, school-to-work programs cannot correct the basic problem of decreasing demand for unskilled labor.

School-to-Work, like Goals 2000, is unlikely to succeed in disadvantaged areas. The conditions that will doom Goals 2000 will have the same effect on the School-to-Work effort.

Earned Income Tax Credit

Long a popular proposal by economists, a negative income tax would provide a guaranteed minimum income; a tax schedule reducing benefits as income rises; and an end to benefits at some income level.[40] The goal being to guarantee families a minimum income, the proposal does not include a work requirement. The reduction in benefits as earned income increases—effectively a tax—is obviously necessary, and a low tax rate encourages work.

However, the very existence of a negative income tax would reduce the work incentive. Those who are working and earning below the eligibility income level may quit working. To fix the tax rate schedule and the eligibility income so as not to reduce the work incentive may be impossible. In 1975 Congress solved the problem by enacting an income subsidy limited to low-income workers—the Earned Income Tax Credit (EITC). To be eligible a family must include a worker as well as dependent children. The requirements for 1994 were as follows. Beneficiaries had to work, earn less than $23,760, and have dependent children. The income levels were adjusted for changes in the cost of living, so the maximum changed with the cost of living index. The basic credit for a family with one child was 23 percent of the earned income. The credit rose with income up to $7,990. The maximum basic credit amount was 23 percent of $7,990 or $1,838. It remained at that dollar level up to an income of $12,580. The basic credit fell as income increased beyond this level. It was phased out completely at the maximum of $23,760. The basic credit percentage increased with the number of children. Supplements were provided for children under the age of one and for premiums paid to provide a child's health insurance coverage.[41]

The administration proposed to increase the basic credit in 1995 for families with one child to 34.4 percent up to a maximum of $2,062, which would be reached at an income of $6,000. The proposed change would not add much to the credit for families with one child. The proposal was more generous toward families with two or more children. The maximum credit for these families would reach $3,371 at $8,500, the phaseout would begin at an income of $11,000, and the maximum income of recipients would be $28,000.[42]

The bill, finally passed, is slightly less generous to families with one child, but it is more generous to larger families. Under the bill, in 1996 and the following years families with two or more children were to receive a credit up to $3,370 at an income of $11,000 and the maximum income of recipients was to be $27,000 (in 1994 dollars). However, Congress has since reduced the benefits sharply.

CONCLUDING REMARKS

Refusing to recognize that training is not the answer when the demand for unskilled labor is declining, the administration's offer of training programs is merely a sop to dislocated workers. Unless the dislocated workers become professional, technical, and skilled clerical workers, many will not get jobs. The EITC is a good idea. It raises the income of low-wage workers without raising the costs of unskilled labor to employers. It also strengthens the work incentive of unskilled workers. Effectively, therefore, it increases the supply of unskilled workers to employers, thereby reducing the cost of employing them.

However, the EITC alone, even with the benefits urged by the administration, will not accomplish the task of raising the employment of unskilled workers. A large jobs program is needed immediately. The program will be expensive if it is to provide jobs for many unskilled unemployed. But the net costs, taking into account the resulting reductions in the costs of drugs, crime, and welfare, will be lower than the expenditures for the program.

NOTES

1. Linda G. Morra, "Multiple Employment Training Programs: Conflicting Requirements Underscore Need for Change," testimony before the Subcommittee on Employment and Productivity, Committee on Labor and Human Resources, U.S. Senate, March 10, 1994, GAO/T-HEHS-94–120.

2. General Accounting Office (GAO), Health, Education, and Human Services Division, B-252883, January 28, 1994. "Multiple Employment Training Programs: Overlapping Programs Can Add Unnecessary Administrative Costs," report to Ranking Minority Member, Committee on Appropriations, U.S. Senate, GAO/HEHS-94–80, 22.

3. Morra, "Multiple Employment Training Programs," 3, 4.

4. Kevin G. Salwen and Paulette Thomas, "Job Programs Flunk at Training but Keep Washington at Work," *Wall Street Journal*, December 16, 1993, A11.

5. Ibid., A11.

6. Ibid., 1.

7. Robert B. Reich, "Getting America to Work: What's Working and What's Not Working in Workforce Policy," remarks before the Center for National Policy, Washington, D.C., January 27, 1994. U.S. Department of Labor, Office of Information, *News*, 3.

8. Salwen and Thomas, "Job Programs Flunk," 1.

9. Morra, "Multiple Employment Training Programs," 4, 5.

10. Judith M. Gueron, "Work and Welfare: Lessons on Employment Programs," *Journal of Economic Perspectives*, 4 (Winter 1990): 84–5.

11. Ibid., 88–89.

12. Joel Handler, *The Poverty of Welfare Reform* (New Haven, Conn.: Yale University Press, 1995), 68.

13. Ibid., 69.

14. Ibid., 71.

15. Robert J. LaLonde, "The Promise of Public Sector-Sponsored Training Programs," *Journal of Economic Perspectives*, 9 (Spring 1995): 150.

16. Sar A. Levitan, "Statement," *The War on Poverty*, hearings before the Joint

Economic Committee, 102nd Congress, September 25, 1991, 247.

17. GAO, Human Resources Division, "Job Corps Costs and Outcomes," memorandum from Clarence C. Crawford, Associate Director, Education and Employment Issues, to Representatives Ralph M. Hall, and Richard K. Armey, February 19, 1993, B-223699, GAO/HRD-93–16R.

18. *Statistical Abstract of the United States 1993 (SAUS 1993)*, 413, table 652.

19. Charles Mallar et al., "Evaluation of the Economic Impact of the Job Corps Program: Third Follow-up Report," report prepared for U.S. Department of Labor under Contract No. 23–34–76–06, Mathematica Policy Inc. September 1982. Cited by LaLonde, "The Promise of Public Sector-Sponsored Training Programs," 163–64.

20. LaLonde, "The Promise of Public Sector-Sponsored Training Programs," 151.

21. Ibid., 153.

22. GAO, "Multiple Employment Programs," report to the Chairman, Subcommittee on Employment and Productivity, Committee on Labor and Human Resources, U.S. Senate, January 1994, GAO/HEHS-94–78, 13, tables.

23. Abt Associates, Inc., *The National JTPA Study: Overview: Impacts, Benefits, and Costs of Title II-A* (Bethesda, Md.: Abt Associates, 1994), 5.

24. GAO, "Multiple Employment Programs," 12.

25. Walter Corson, Paul Decker, Philip Gleason, and Walter Nicholson, *International Trade and Worker Dislocation: Evaluation of the Trade Adjustment Assistance Program*, 1993. Contract No. 99–9–09805–75–071–01, MPR Reference No. 7875. Department of Labor, Employment and Training Administration, Office of Strategic Planning and Policy Development. Submitted by Mathematica Policy Research, Inc., 153.

26. Congressional Budget Office, *Displaced Workers: Trends in the 1980s and Implications for the Future* (Washington, D.C., February 1993), 33.

27. U.S. Department of Labor, Office of Inspector General, *Trade Adjustment Assistance Program, Public Law 93–618, As Amended: Audit of Program Outcomes in Nine Selected States, Fiscal Years 1991/1992*, Report Number 05–93–008–03–330 (Washington D.C.: September 30, 1993), 1, 2.

28. Corson et al., *International Trade and Worker Dislocation*, 155.

29. Reich, "Getting America to Work," 3.

30. Ibid., 2.

31. James Heckman, "Assessing Clinton's Program on Job Training, Workfare, and Education in the Workplace," National Bureau of Economic Research, Working Paper 4428, August 1993, 17–19.

32. Statement of Franklin Frazier, Director, Education and Employment Issues, Human Resources Division, GAO, *School-to-Work Transition Strategies*, hearing before the Subcommittee on Education and Health, Joint Economic Committee, U.S. Congress, 101st Session, June 14, 1990, 11.

33. Ibid., 11–14.

34. National Center for Education Statistics, *Report in Brief: NAEP 1992 Trends in Academic Progress* (Washington, D.C.), 8–9.

35. American Federation of Teachers, *U.S. Education: The Task before Us* (Washington, D.C., November 1993).

36. Statement of Secretary Richard W. Riley, Goals 2000: Educate America Act,

hearing before the Committee on Labor and Human Resources, U.S. Senate, 103rd Congress, 1st Session, on S. 846, May 4, 1993, 6, 10.

37. Ibid., 20.

38. Ibid., 10.

39. Statement by Senator Edward M. Kennedy on the Conference Report on the School-to-Work Opportunities Act of 1994, April 21, 1994.

40. Milton Friedman, *Capitalism and Freedom* (Chicago: University of Chicago Press, 1962), Chapter 12; James Tobin, "The Case for an Income Guarantee," *The Public Interest*, 4 (1966): 31–41.

41. Samuel Y. Sessions, Statement before the Ways and Means Subcommittee on Select Revenue Measures and the Ways and Means Committee on Human Resources, U.S. House of Representatives, March 30, 1993, Department of the Treasury, Washington D.C.

42. Ibid., 9.

8

Policy Recommendations

The primary long-term goal of turning a greater number of disadvantaged youths into skilled workers cannot be achieved without radical reform of the schools serving them. Because the demand for unskilled labor is declining, the short-term goal of providing jobs for unemployed unskilled workers will require a public employment program. In addition, the government should close domestic markets for textile, apparel, and other manufactured products to imports from developing countries.

EDUCATION

The Quality of Education

To begin with I briefly state my arguments, some of which admittedly are obvious. However, many studies of student performance reach wrong conclusions because they omit them; thus, they need stating.

First, children must apply themselves to their studies. Second, they are unlikely to do so unless their parents are involved in their education. Third, some disadvantaged parents are involved. Fourth, small school and class size, which enable teachers to work closely with students, help disadvantaged youngsters. Fifth, public school systems resist change.

Studies of students' performance ignore the contribution of their effort. Instead, policy discussions center on types of programs and the quality and quantity of the resources devoted to education. Treating schools as producers, economists apply the same model as they use for manufacturing. A can manufacturer, who employs more labor and more machines, will produce more cans. By analogy a school with more teachers per student and more lab equipment will produce more education. According to the model, education should benefit from smaller classes (more teachers per hundred children), more skilled teachers (higher salaries), more equipment, and better facilities. One reason the expectations are not confirmed is that the model omits student effort, which may be promoted by the qualities of programs not captured by the economic models.

What the students put into their studies matters, as differences in test performance between American and other countries' students demonstrate. Americans do worse because they exert less effort. John Bishop reports that in the Second International Math Study, American high-school seniors answered 39.8 percent of the questions correctly, compared to 59.8 percent for British students; they also performed less well on physics and chemistry tests.[1] According to visitors to classrooms in different countries, European students generally appear to work harder than U.S. students. They pay closer attention and are more likely to do their assignments. Moreover, American high-school students get a bad report on their attitude. Studies describe them as docile, compliant, and without initiative; and high school teachers complain about lack of student interest.[2] Also, comparisons between schools with high-achieving students and those with low-achieving students blame low achievement on lack of effort. In Chicago high schools with high-achieving students, about 75 percent of class time was spent on actual instruction, while the average for schools with low-achieving students was 51 percent.[3] Further, one study comes to the unsurprising conclusion that homework improves students' performance. In some high schools assigning homework is a hopeless endeavor. Teachers give up and have students read assigned books in class because many would not do so at home.[4]

The importance of effort explains Eric Hanushek's conclusion, based on a survey of the literature, that the primary influence by far on children's school performance is family background which is measured by income, education of parents, the presence of both parents in the household, and the availability in the home of books, a typewriter, and a calculator.[5] These studies arouse pessimistic doubts about how much children will benefit from larger expenditures for education. Moreover, the Coleman Report found that after controlling for family background, school resources explain only a small fraction of the variation in student achievement.[6] Other studies find that the effectiveness of school resources is difficult to measure,[7] and many studies produce statistically insignificant results.[8] Policymakers confront a truly pessimistic literature.

However, the studies do not explicate the connection between family background and student performance. So important is family background that it obliterates the effect of other variables, including expenditures per student, class size, average teacher salary, teacher education, and teacher experience. There are two reasons for this result. First, family background is important, and, second, it is correlated with the variables measuring the quality of schools. Family background is largely a matter of income, and affluent families live in suburbs where the schools have experienced, well-trained teachers and small classes. The correlation of family background with class size, education of teachers, and other measures of school quality in the population as a whole make it difficult to isolate the effect of the quality of schools.[9] The effect of the variables associated with school quality therefore is difficult to assess.

We should take a closer look at family background. Well-off, educated, verbal parents rear verbal children who are interested in history, literature, and other school subjects; books in the home facilitate reading, parents help with homework and limit the time their children spend watching television. Moreover, parents warn their children that to maintain their standard of living they will have to attend college and a professional school, which requires that they do well in high school. Thus, the link between family background and school performance is through parental involvement and student effort.

However, family background, of which a good measure is family income, is not the only determinant of parental involvement, which as we see later, may be enhanced by a school's organization and policies. The statistical investigations of students' performance, which use measures of family background to represent parental involvement, say nothing about the influence that schools have on parents. Schools cannot raise parents' education or income, but they can encourage their involvement. Even poor parents can monitor homework, and they can warn children of the economic consequences caused by failure to get into a college. Schools may directly demand that parents be involved, and an indirect method is encouraging parents to participate in their governance. Parents active in parent-teacher associations are likely to supervise their children's homework.

Moreover, the studies do not provide a basis for dismissing the effect of large reductions in class size. The differences in class size between suburban school districts may not be large enough to affect student performance significantly, especially after controlling for family background. This does not mean that large reductions in class size will not affect student performance. Small classes may accomplish much more than large classes, but the difference may not be revealed by studies of the general population of schools. These studies may fail to show the effect because class sizes are concentrated around the average. If the average size is 30 a difference of five students per class may not affect the quality of teaching significantly.

Moreover, the effect of class size may be more pronounced for disadvantaged students than for other students. The conclusions concerning the general population of students may not hold for disadvantaged children. By compensating for lack of parental involvement, small class size may help disadvantaged children more than affluent children. Intensive classroom teaching may replace the advantages of a good family background. The performance of disadvantaged students may improve enormously if they are in classes that are much smaller than the ones they are in now.

Although most studies dismiss the effect of small class size on student performance, an important one reaches the opposite conclusion for elementary grades. At the behest of Governor Lamar Alexander and the Tennessee legislature, between 1985 and 1989 Frederick Mosteller conducted a study gauging the effect of small classes on student performance. The state provided funds to reduce class size from kindergarten through the fourth grade in 79 schools. The classes were chosen at random from schools throughout the state. From 13 to 17 students constituted a small class; regular was from 22 to 25, and the third group was this range taught by a teacher with an aide. It should be noted that even the regular classes were smaller than the early-grade classes in many cities. Elementary public-school classes in New York have over 30 students.

The study found that small classes raised reading and math scores. Students in the small classes performed better than those in both groups of larger classes. The effects continued into junior high school, where the students were in large classes. The main conclusion is that small class size in the earliest grades improves learning in those grades and the benefits continue in later grades.[10] One reason children in small classes learn more, according to the study, is that teachers maintain order more easily. It should be noted that Mosteller succeeded in controlling for family background by comparing the performance of children in small classes with that of children in large classes within the same school. The children in the same school came from families in the same small area who had similar incomes.

Of special interest is the finding that minority students benefited more from small classes than other students. Minority children gained about double the benefit that majority children did. The study found that the additional gain occurred in the first two years of the experiment; subsequent gains were the same in both groups.

As we see later, the experience of New York City's school choice program supports the conclusion that class size is important. This experience plus that of the Catholic schools, which is also discussed later, indicates that the organization of the schools and the quality of programs may encourage student effort.

Recognizing the importance of student effort has the obvious policy implication that disadvantaged children should be encouraged to work hard at their studies. Parental involvement should be fostered, and potentially good students should be rescued from the disorder in their schools. One of the gains from small class size is that teachers are better able to maintain order, as Mosteller's study found.

Good students should be safeguarded from peer pressures not to study. Many disadvantaged children, who might be good students, are persuaded not to apply themselves by the many children who refuse to do so. According to Jonathan Kozol, early educational deprivation destroys the learning skills of many secondary-school students. He goes on to say: "Knowing one is ruined is a powerful incentive to destroy the learning opportunities for other children, and the consequence in many schools is nearly uncontrollable disruption." He reports that in 1989 the New York City Office of School Safety started buying handcuffs.[11] Not limited to New York, the incidence of student disorders has increased nationally. According to Robert Rubel, while there was no problem up to 1964, the number of student disorders increased enormously between that year and 1971 and then remained at a high level.[12]

As we see later, a school choice program may succeed in separating good students from disorderly ones. The goal of separation is controversial; thus, proponents of choice do not acknowledge it. Teachers' organizations, who oppose school choice, argue that the private schools may appear to perform well because they exclude problem children—they do not have as much of a problem to begin with. Accordingly, the selectivity practiced by private schools invalidates comparisons with public schools. Also, separation is unfair to the public schools, who have all the problems dumped on them, and it is unfair to the problem children, who no longer have the benefit of associating with normal children. However, the primary goal should be to improve the education of children, even if the benefits are limited to good students.

Public, Catholic, and Alternative Schools

What are the possibilities of improving the education of disadvantaged youngsters? The pessimism about ghetto parents, who are described as irresponsible, is unwarranted. That many disadvantaged parents are involved in their children's education is evidenced by the large number of applications for admission to New York's alternative schools, which demand more from their students than the traditional public schools. Because the alternative schools have places for only about 9 percent of the New York secondary school population,[13] the number of applications far exceeds the number of places available.

Some disadvantaged parents are sufficiently ambitious for their children to pay the fees required to have them attend Catholic schools. But, because the tuition fees at Catholic primary schools in Bedford-Stuyvesant are over $2,000, only 3 percent of the children of the appropriate ages in the area are enrolled.[14] Bedford-Stuyvesant has no Catholic high schools, and those close to the area charge about $4,000.

The debate over the proposal that the federal government provide vouchers usable in private as well as public schools provokes the discussion of issues relating to student performance. Vouchers are urged as the cure for the failure of public schools generally—not only of those in disadvantaged areas. Although proponents point to the disaster in the disadvantaged areas, they urge vouchers for all areas, including affluent suburbs. According to John Chubb and Terry Moe, the problem arises from the public schools' monopoly of educational services.[15] Vouchers would open the gates of the education market to more private schools, resulting in competition that would force the public schools to improve their services. Opponents reply that if this is true then private-school students should perform better than public-school students. Unless private schools, which sell their services in a competitive market, provide a better education than public schools, we cannot expect school choice to have a good effect.

Much of the debate over school choice, therefore, features the performance of private and public schools. Because Catholic schools teach the majority of private-school students, they have been compared with public schools. A major study by James Coleman, Thomas Hoffer, and Sally Kilgore concludes that Catholic schools produce higher cognitive achievement than public schools.[16] The authors credit the Catholic schools' greater insistence on order, homework, and less tolerance of absenteeism. The moral is that discipline is what matters. Corroborating this explanation, Paul Hill, Gail Foster, and Tamar Gendler report that in one Catholic school cutting classes is punished by detention; a serious reprimand follows talking back to a teacher; cheating, stealing, and fighting lead to expulsion. Moreover, the schools enforce a dress code. Boys are required to wear ties and jackets.[17] The zoned public schools do not have the option of expulsion, and in these schools the lack of discipline is a serious problem. I note later that the classes in Catholic high schools are no smaller than those in zoned public schools. The schools' good results do not appear to be due to a larger number of teachers per hundred students.

A recent study by Anthony Bryk, Valerie Lee, and Peter Holland also reaches conclusions favorable to Catholic schools. These authors emphasize the programs offered by Catholic schools and the possibility of close ties between teachers and students. By contrast, the public high schools offer more choice in courses, differing greatly in both subject matter and difficulty.[18] Also, because Catholic-school teachers are less specialized in particular subjects, they spend more time with individual students. In addition, they do the counseling that in large public schools is performed by social workers and psychologists. The students feel that the teachers care about them.[19] Further, the schools actively promote parental involvement, which helps. More important is the authors' report that disadvantaged students benefit from the schools' academic demands more than well-off students. Andrew Greeley agrees that the quality of instruction in Catholic schools is superior to that in public schools and that disadvantaged children gain more than other children.[20]

But not all studies agree. According to Karl Alexander, the advantage students gain in private schools, including Catholic schools, is too small to be important.[21] The American Federation of Teachers (AFT) infers from data from the National Assessment of Educational Progress (NAEP) that the performance of private-school students is only slightly better than that of public-school students, and when controlled for parental education and income, the advantage vanishes completely.[22]

However, Alexander and the AFT ignore the evidence that disadvantaged students benefit more from Catholic schools than other children. Their studies compare the performance of private-school students generally with that of public-school students generally. I assume that the data on the performance of private-school students largely reflect that of Catholic-school students. The Catholic schools' insistence on discipline, homework and attendance; the small size of Catholic schools and the resulting closer relationship between teachers and students; the highly structured organization of Catholic schools, and their greater focus on academic subjects appear to be more important for poor children than for other children.

The studies by Bryk, Lee, and Holland, and by Greeley, as well as the evidence of the Mosteller study suggest that improvements in the quality of schools confer greater benefits on disadvantaged children than on other children. The studies of Catholic schools show that their organization and programs are important even when class size is the same as in public schools. Mosteller's study shows that small class size benefits disadvantaged children even when the organization and programs are unchanged. One may infer from these studies that improvements in the quality of the schools' services, which may take the form of changes in organization and programs or of a reduction in class size, will improve the performance of disadvantaged children.

The classes in Catholic high schools are no smaller than those in the public schools. The classes in Brooklyn's Catholic high schools have between 30 and 35 students, which is about the same as the average for zoned public schools in New York.[23] The performance of the schools thus is not due to small class size. However, the Catholic schools are much smaller than the public high schools, which may explain part of the superior performance of their students. The Catholic high schools in Brooklyn have between 250 and 1,250 students.[24] The average number of students per zoned public high school in Brooklyn is about 2,700. The largest has 4,000 students.[25] A school of 500 students is more likely to be a community than one of 3,000. The principal of a Catholic high school may at least know the names of most of the students and may be able to help teachers with those having problems.

Part of the superiority of the Catholic schools apparently is due to a greater emphasis on academic programs. Although the zoned public schools in New York profess to emphasize academic training, in practice they try to meet many different demands. Special programs in one New York school include parenting, ethnic music and art, and temporary housing for homeless students.[26]

Other differences between the Catholic and the zoned public schools also may be important. In the latter, where teachers are assigned to departments, close ties with students are not maintained. The teachers, who are assigned to subject departments, have less contact with individual students. Special staff members counsel students and keep track of absentee students. One representative public school has two guidance counselors for each grade, nine family assistants, four social worker/investigators for attendance, three social workers, a dropout-prevention coordinator, a college counselor, a career counselor, a part-time psychologist, and a full-time physician in the health clinic.[27] Computerized attendance records, assistant principals, and counselors relieve teachers of guiding the students' development.[28] The difference in organization between Catholic and zoned public schools may be due to the difference in school size. The small Catholic schools have less need for a bureaucracy than the large public schools. There is also less need for central control because the schools are small enough for the principal to evaluate the performance of individual teachers.

Catholic schools may perform well in comparison with the zoned public schools because they demand much more from their students. Even honors students in the zoned schools spend less than one hour per night on homework. Ninth-grade English homework might be: "Write two sentences about a character in the book we are reading." The teachers effectively agree not to demand too much in exchange for the students' implicit promise not to cause trouble.

Also, the Catholic schools and their teachers have greater independence from central control than the zoned public schools and their teachers. The teachers in the zoned public schools have little discretion; restrictions by the Board of Education and by union contracts place severe constraints on their initiative. Public school systems depend on a combination of hierarchical controls and statistical measures of performance based on standardized tests. To improve the average scores of low-ranking schools, the central authority undertakes various measures, resulting in bureaucracy and lack of independence for teachers, which reduces their effectiveness. Teachers are not encouraged to assess individual students' problems and independently decide the content and level of their courses; they must conform to detailed regulations.

As we have seen, studies of the Catholic high schools ascribe their success to their emphasis on discipline. They also mention that the highly structured curriculum is academic and that they make greater demands on students than the zoned public schools. The studies do not emphasize two important characteristics of Catholic schools. The first is their policy of screening applicants for admission, and the second is that they are Catholic. The policy of selecting students who are likely to perform well enables them to insist on discipline and to make greater demands on students. According to Bryk, Lee, and Holland, most of the high schools require applicants to take either standardized achievement tests or school-constructed tests; they require an interview with prospective students and their parents, a letter of recommendation from the applicant's elementary school, and school records. Bryk, Lee, and Holland say that the Catholic high schools are not highly selective because the typical school accepts 88 percent of the students who apply.[29] However, the application process itself eliminates many children. The prospect of failing admission tests discourages elementary school graduates from applying.

The fact that the schools are part of the Catholic Church facilitates their enforcing discipline and demanding more from students than the zoned public schools. Most of the students come from Catholic families. Hill, Foster, and Gendler say that in one high school 65 percent of the students are from such families.[30] According to Bryk, Lee, and Holland, in 1983 the Catholic enrollment in Catholic secondary schools in the United States was 86 percent of the total.[31] These students and their parents are likely to accept the schools' values. Most of the teachers also are members of the church. Hill, Foster, and Gendler report that of the 34 teachers in one Catholic high school 22 were Catholic, and as children, most had attended a Catholic high school. One quarter of the teachers were brothers.[32]

The schools teach Catholic values. The basic curriculum, required of all students, includes four years of religion.[33] Among other subjects, the courses discuss peer pressure, obedience versus freedom, sexuality, moral behavior, and personal responsibility for making moral decisions. These courses support the teachers' demands on students. Moreover, occasionally the schools celebrate the Mass. Despite the fact that not all students are Catholics, religion is not an incidental aspect of the schools.

The special character of the Catholic schools makes it difficult to generalize from their experience. It may be difficult for other private schools to make similar demands on their students.

Proponents of school choice point to the superior performance of alternative schools within the New York City public-school system.[34] Because they are not Catholic schools, their experience may be more useful
for predicting the success of a school choice program. Students about to
graduate from elementary school who want to attend a particular school
apply for admission. There are now about 50 Educational Option High
Schools—the official name of the alternative high schools—in New York
city. The number of places in these schools is smaller than the number
of applicants; therefore, the entrants must be selected.

Deborah Meier, the founder of the first alternative school, undertook
to improve the education of children in East Harlem. This is one of the
poorest areas in the city, and its children's reading scores were among
the lowest in the city. Meier is the director of the Central Park East
Secondary School (CPESS), which is part of the alternative school program in East Harlem. The major difference between the alternative and
the zoned public schools by far is in class and school size. Meier stresses
the importance of small classes and a small school, which enable teachers
to know the students and their parents and to confer with one another
about individual students' problems.[35] In classes with only 14 or 15 students and with periods that are two hours long teachers can consider a
child's difficulty with math and console an adolescent suffering from a
family crisis.[36] The school as a whole has 400 students. Other alternative
schools are also small and have small classes. By contrast, average class
size in the zoned public schools is about 35. The maximum is set at 34
by the Board of Education's contract with the UFT, but the union com-
plains of many violations. As we saw earlier, the zoned public schools
have as many as 4,000 students. The alternative schools are in a better
position to give students individual attention.

There are other differences. The alternative schools encourage parents'
involvement by inviting their participation in the school's governance
through advisory boards and parent councils. Furthermore, according to
Meier, school choice fosters parental involvement because parents are
keen to cooperate with the teachers in a school that they have chosen.[37]

Another characteristic of the alternative schools is their greater independence of the Board of Education. According to Meier, teachers can
more easily solve problems when they have independent authority than
when they must conform to externally imposed regulations. Meier
spends much of her time building external sources of support to gain
some freedom from domination by the Board of Education. The alternative schools are not completely free of central regulation. To ensure
that the schools get a fair share of problem students, half of the students
admitted are selected at random from among the applicants, and the
other half are chosen based on the requirement that the distribution of
reading scores of admitted students must be similar to the distribution

of all New York City students.[38] Other regulations govern faculty employment and curriculum.[39] Nevertheless, the alternative schools have much more freedom than the zoned public schools.

CPESS assumes that the students who choose to enroll accept its goals.[40] Instead of requiring students to learn by rote, it prepares them to solve problems systematically. The students do independent reading in class and at home and much writing, and they are expected to master the course materials.

The alternative schools inspire students' efforts by engaging their interest. Dispensing with breadth of coverage, the teachers at CPESS encourage students to prepare papers requiring intensive study of a narrow subject. They try to excite the students and at the same time train them to think rigorously and to evaluate evidence by having them investigate narrow subjects rather than giving traditional survey courses that provide superficial knowledge of a broad field.[41] Some schools have offered courses on broad themes drawing on different disciplines. If the theme is water, students may be taught some biology as they study fish, chemistry in connection with pollution, and physics in connection with ocean currents. The theory is that students learn more by directing their own research.[42]

Many of the alternative schools specialize in a particular field. The names of some of the schools indicate their interests: Coalition School for Social Change, Economics and Finance, Environmental Studies, Museum School, Health Professions and Human Services, Jacqueline Kennedy Onassis/International Careers, Leadership and Public Service, School for the Physical City, Science Skills Center High School. Students at the Museum School surveyed the mammal collection at the American Museum of Natural History and wrote essays on the ethics of collecting specimens.

That the alternative schools in New York perform better than the zoned public schools is evident in the number of students in the 1994 class who graduated in the expected time—59.6 percent—compared to 48.6 percent of their peers in the zoned public schools.[43] According to Hill, Foster, and Gendler, the students in the Catholic and alternative schools are much more successful academically than those in the zoned public schools. Only about 5 percent of the zoned schools' graduates receive the Regents' Diploma, marking successful completion of a demanding college preparatory program, compared to over half the graduates of the alternative schools, and over two-thirds of those of Catholic schools. Less than one-third of the graduates of the zoned schools take the SATs, and fewer than one third of the test takers score better than the national average for all black students. Over half the alternative school graduates take the tests, and more than 40 percent score higher than the black student average.[44] These results may be compared to those for graduates of the Partnership Program in the Catholic schools, which pays the tuition fees of some black and Hispanic students. About 85 percent of these students take the SATs and over 60 percent score above the black students' average.

Critics of the studies favorable to the Catholic and alternative schools attribute the results to characteristics of the students' families and to the schools selecting superior applicants for admission. We look at differences in family background and in reading test scores. Nearly all students in the zoned public high schools in New York City are black or Hispanic, three-quarters are from welfare families or in poverty, and the parents of only 56 percent have completed high school. Between 65 percent and 75 percent of the students are admitted with reading scores below grade level.

While nearly all students in the alternative schools are black or Hispanic, only about 40 percent are from families on welfare or in poverty, and about 86 percent of the students have parents who have completed high school. On the whole, the parents are better off and better educated than the parents of students in zoned public schools. Moreover, the fact that they apply for admission to the alternative schools suggests that their parents are more involved.

Despite the requirement by the Board of Education that those admitted to the alternative schools have the same reading-score distribution as students in the public-school system as a whole, they have much better reading scores. Only between 25 and 40 percent are admitted with reading scores below grade level. The success of the alternative schools appears to be due in part to selecting potentially better students than those entering the zoned public schools. Furthermore, the students in alternative schools probably are more motivated to study than other students and therefore might have performed well in traditional schools. In short, this evidence on the performance of the alternative schools is not absolutely clear. What appears to be due to superior programs, dedication of teachers, small class size, and so on may be due in large part to the selection of superior students.

Nor is the evidence of the superiority of Catholic schools as conclusive as one would like. In the Catholic schools 74 percent of the students are black or Hispanic, 40 percent are on welfare or live in poverty, and 69 percent have parents who have completed high school. Like the children in the alternative schools those in the Catholic schools appear to be more fortunate in their parents than the children in the zoned public schools.

Moreover, as we have seen, the applicants for admission to Catholic schools are likely to be good students. Thus, those admitted are better readers than their peers entering the zoned public schools. Only 35 percent of the students are admitted with reading scores below grade level.[45]

Thus, the studies indicating that poor children benefit more from a

Catholic-school education than other children may reflect large differences in involvement among poor parents. The small difference in student performance between all-Catholic and all-public schools noted earlier may reflect the small difference in parental involvement between all-Catholic-school parents and all-public-school parents. But poor Catholic-school parents probably are much more involved than poor public-school parents. Parents who have to make great sacrifices to send their children to Catholic schools are extraordinary.

The differences in the performance of students in the three classes of schools may reflect family background, initial preparation, and motivation more than what the schools contribute. The alternative and Catholic schools may appear to perform well because they practice selectivity and favor potentially good students. For their part, the zoned public schools must take all comers.

However, while admission policies may explain part of the difference in performance of children between alternative and Catholic schools on the one hand and zoned public schools on the other, it cannot explain the improvement in the performance of children in East Harlem. In East Harlem all students are enrolled in alternative schools. In 1973, which was before the alternative schools were organized, only 16 percent of the students were reading at grade level and by 1985 the proportion had increased to about 53 percent. Slightly over half may appear to be a modest achievement, but if half a class reads at grade level, its performance matches that of the national average for that grade. East Harlem had caught up with the national average.

Other data also attest to a huge improvement. Dropout rates are estimated to be about 1 percent,[46] which is much lower than the dropout rate of 19 percent for New York City high-school students as a whole.[47] Before the alternative schools were organized East Harlem's dropout rate was no lower than in New York as a whole. The gain in East Harlem was not due to a relative gain in family background. There is other evidence indicating the influence of alternative schools. In 1985, 386 East Harlem students were accepted by competitive high schools in the city, compared to about 15 in 1973.[48] In addition, about half the high-school graduates from East Harlem enter college.

Moreover, it is difficult to dismiss as unimportant the emphasis by the Catholic and alternative schools on academic programs, their demands on students, the great involvement of the teachers with their students, and the better discipline. Hill, Foster, and Gendler's description of lack of discipline in the zoned public schools should also persuade skeptics that the Catholic and alternative schools do a better job. The peer pressures are less harmful than in the zoned schools, the teachers are in closer contact with the students, and they make greater demands. The parents might also be involved if their children attended the zoned schools, but their children would get lost among the many children whose parents do not share the same values. A parent's involvement is more effective when it is supported by the involvement of many other parents. And the schools take active measures to promote their involvement.

Opponents of school choice invoke equity considerations. They argue that choice will create a group of public schools that will carry the entire burden of teaching disorderly, problem children. The performance of these schools will worsen simply because of the changed composition of the student body, and the quality of education will deteriorate. As a result, the children in the alternative schools will get a good education, while those in the zoned public schools will suffer. Opponents of school choice believe that all should get the same quality of education.

My own position is that the children who can benefit from school choice should not be sacrificed for the sake of equity. The goal should be improvement in the quality of education even if the benefits are limited to some students.

Policy Recommendations

Without strong outside pressure, the public school systems will not make the necessary, radical reforms affecting masses of students. Reluctantly, the teachers and administrators in New York have acquiesced to the organization of a small number of alternative schools. They will strongly resist the organization of many more. And school reformers will have a hard time persuading the state and the city to support a larger and more expensive program.

Without large additional funds and without the pressure of competition from private schools, the necessary educational revolution will not take place. Even if the public school systems agree to sponsor choice programs, competition from private schools is needed. The success of the current program within the New York public school system testifies to the hard work and dedication of the small number of teachers involved in it. However, enthusiasm cannot be counted on if the programs expand to include many teachers. Without the pressure of outside competition, a large public-school choice program will be less effective than the current small program. The teachers will not be any more dedicated than the current teachers in public schools. Competition from alternative sources of education is needed to ensure that the public school systems provide good service. Their monopoly power must be destroyed. My basic recommendation is that the federal government give disadvantaged parents vouchers usable in private as well as public schools, as the Reagan and Bush administrations proposed. New private schools funded by such vouchers will provide the necessary competition. Under the

Bush proposal the value of the vouchers was to have been $2,500, the current equivalent of which is $3,000.

The opposition by the public school systems and their administrators and teachers defeated the Bush administration's proposal to fund school choice programs in which private schools were to be included. Administrators oppose school choice, because it is associated with small schools, in which teachers take over the functions now performed by assistant principals and social workers. The Council of Supervisors and Administrators, which is the principals' union, has opposed increasing the number of alternative schools.[49]

Even the limited choice now available in New York came only after a hard struggle. To organize an independent school whose teachers made the basic curriculum decisions and chose new teachers, Deborah Meier had to fight the Board of Education and the United Federation of Teachers (UFT). Choice on a large scale would threaten the jobs of many teachers who lose students. Most teachers are employed under collective bargaining agreements limiting school districts' rights to transfer teachers, change class size, and change assignments. Under earlier contracts alternative schools within the public school system were required to select teachers from among those employed in the system. A recent contract allows small schools to hire other teachers, but this concession did not come without a fight. Moreover, a vast overhaul of a public school system will require large expenditures, which in their current strapped conditions neither state nor local governments are prepared to make.

Opponents of vouchers doubt that private schools will admit a large number of disadvantaged children.[50] The AFT argues that private schools select students on the basis of grades and other qualifications. Thus, according to the AFT, 71 percent of Catholic high schools require an entrance exam, as do 43 percent of other religious schools and 66 percent of independent private schools. In addition, few private schools serve children with disabilities. In Milwaukee, where poor families receive vouchers for private schools, 40 percent of the children who sought to participate could not find a school that would take them.

Private schools, including Catholic schools, screen applicants for admission to prevent potentially troublesome children from entering. This practice tends to result in favorable ratings for private schools. Moreover, they may continue to screen applicants even under a school choice program. Nevertheless, vouchers will result in many more disadvantaged children entering private schools. One reason the private schools in Milwaukee did not accept more applicants for admission was the limitation on capacity. Under the rules of the Milwaukee school choice program, schools sponsored by religious organizations, including the Catholic Church, could not participate. Thus, a major part of the private-school capacity was excluded from the program. If vouchers are available and cover the costs of operating a school, more schools will enter, and allowing Catholic schools to participate will add greatly to the available private-school capacity.

To force the public school systems to improve their services, new schools must provide a large alternative supply. Vouchers alone will not ensure a quick, large increase in the number of schools, and for some time the capacity of the new schools may be insufficient to break the monopoly power of the public school system. New private schools will have to acquire equipment and finance the construction of buildings as well as hire teachers and administrators. Moreover, the vouchers plus tuition fees affordable to disadvantaged parents may not cover the total costs.

The necessary school capacity in disadvantaged areas will probably require black organizations to organize schools. They should make the effort, even if they cannot expect the alternative schools within the public school system and new private schools sponsored by themselves and by others to improve the education of the majority of disadvantaged students. A partial solution is better than none. Better to offer hope to some children than allow them to languish in the traditional schools.

The AFT says that vouchers would reduce accountability in education because private schools are exempt from almost all public regulations. And it rejects the market as a regulatory mechanism because busy parents will not get the information necessary to make good choices. Moreover, not all private schools will be honest, and parental satisfaction is not an adequate standard of accountability when taxpayers bear the cost. By contrast, public schools must show how they spend their money, follow regulations about discipline, safety, curriculum, and teacher credentials, publish information about student performance, and they are responsible to elected representatives.

True, not all parents will be informed and demand a high quality of education. But in disadvantaged areas the present system is working so badly that competition from private schools should improve the public schools. The AFT is demanding that proponents of vouchers guarantee perfection. Moreover, school choice will enhance the education of children whose parents take the trouble to be informed and insist on a good education. Not all children will benefit, but that should not stop reform. It is possible that crooks will exploit a voucher program and set up scam operations to swindle uninformed parents. However, state regulation may prevent such exploitation. States now require private schools to meet minimum standards in order to be accredited. To participate in a voucher program schools may be required to have state accreditation.

It may take some time for effective regulatory policies to be developed and implemented. Later paragraphs propose that the alternative schools with their small classes be the model for a school reform policy. For the policy to be effective, the vouchers will have to be generous enough to support a high teacher-student ratio in many schools. Entrepreneurs may seize the opportunity for high profits. While the funds may be adequate for small classes, they may organize schools with large classes. The regulatory authority may mandate classes of a maximum size. However, there may be other opportunities for exploiting the system by offering unsatisfactory services. Moreover, it will take time for schools to establish a good reputation. While they do so, parents will find it difficult to make good choices. Nevertheless, this problem should not be allowed to stand in the way of educational reform.

Although the programs offered by the alternative schools in New York appear to work, it may not be necessary for a choice program to adopt their educational techniques. Good arguments can be advanced for teaching a comprehensive chemistry course beginning with the fundamentals, rather than having children learn the elements as an incidental part of investigating pollution. As one who teaches economics, I know that courses that investigate economic policy in relation to poverty or other subjects are ineffective in teaching the principles of economics. Also, when such courses are not part of a sequence including a course in principles, they do not accomplish their immediate goal. The tradeoff is between stimulating interest at the cost of ignoring fundamental principles and teaching fundamentals of particular disciplines at the cost of boring students. I do not pretend to be able to deal with this issue in secondary-school education.

Part of the success of the alternative schools appears to be due to small classes and small school size. Meier insists that these characteristics have been important. And Mosteller's study, referred to earlier, supports Meier's judgment. On the other hand, the Catholic schools appear to have been successful without having the advantage of small classes. It may be that Catholic schools succeed despite the large size of their classes because their admission policy is more selective than that of the alternative schools who, as part of the public school system, must have a more open admission policy. Moreover, the requirement that students' families pay fees may have the incidental effect of restricting the disadvantaged students to those from families who are especially involved in their children's education. Another reason Catholic schools succeed may be their emphasis on discipline. As I also have suggested, their success may in part be due to their religious character.

Because the Catholic schools' success appears to be due to their special character, their experience cannot provide the basis for a policy to reform education for the disadvantaged. Thus, their good performance cannot be taken to signify that other schools can do as well with large classes. Nonreligious schools would have great difficulty making demands on their students, unless their classes were small. And should the Catholic schools expand to include many more students from non-Catholic families they are likely to perform less well. Moreover, many non-Catholic families may find it difficult to send their children to schools teaching Catholicism. They may want a good education for their children, but they may not agree to surrender their religious training to the Catholic Church. And, the Catholic schools will not give up their mission of teaching religion to gain more students.

The alternative schools provide a better model for educational reform. An educational policy based on their experience will be expensive. Currently the alternative schools may not spend much more per student than the zoned public schools because they have teachers providing the services performed by administrators, social workers, and psychologists in the zoned public schools. However, policymakers may have to be prepared to spend more in the future.

Finally, more funds should be appropriated for financial assistance to disadvantaged students in colleges, professional, and graduate schools. The funds should pay for both tuition and living expenses.

The NAACP, the National Urban League, and the National Rainbow Coalition should turn their efforts to gaining support in Congress for the necessary legislation. In the 1970s they fought for busing and school integration, which they believed held the secret to good education. They have done nothing since that time. Unless reforms are made along the lines proposed here, there is little hope for education in the disadvantaged areas.

EMPLOYMENT PROGRAM

The immediate objective of public policy must be to reduce unskilled unemployment substantially. With the demand for unskilled workers falling, the government must create new jobs. However, much of the unemployment reflects the turnover of workers in particular jobs. Some workers are laid off or fired even when employment is rising, and finding a new job takes time. This frictional part of unemployment is probably about half the total. The goal of public policy should be to reduce unskilled unemployment to the frictional level, which will require approximately two million jobs. Additional reductions in the demand for unskilled labor due to NAFTA, the elimination of the Multifiber Arrangement (MFA), other trade liberalization measures, and continued mechanization and increases in the number of skilled workers will require the creation of more unskilled jobs.

To meet the goal of an additional two million unskilled jobs would require the reversal of the trade liberalization policy and a public employment program. The country can afford these costs, and it is only right that we bear them. With per capita GDP in constant dollars 2.2

times as great as in 1950, employed skilled workers have benefited from the growth of productivity, the major source of the worsening condition of unskilled workers. The cost of implementing the proposals should be charged against the benefits reaped from this growth. Also, the costs will be offset at least partly by reductions in other costs. The federal government is spending over $10 billion annually to combat drugs, the criminal justice system costs the nation over $60 billion, and federal, state, and local governments spend over $200 billion on public aid. A large public employment program will reduce these costs.

The government can preserve existing unskilled jobs by reversing its trade liberalization policy. There are about 12 million production workers in manufacturing, and of these about 4 million are in industries that imports may shrink. The number of production workers employed in the apparel, textiles, footwear, and toy industries is about 1.5 million. Excluding imports of competitive products would probably add about 400,000 jobs. The costs to consumers of the protection of the apparel industry, discussed in Chapter 4, are not high compared to those incurred by the continuing destruction of displaced workers' families. Excluding these and other imports manufactured by unskilled labor will reduce the unemployment rate of unskilled workers by about one percentage point. True, inasmuch as the restoration of tariffs will reduce exports, the gains in unskilled employment of unskilled workers will come at the cost of some skilled jobs. However, limiting imports of manufactured goods from developing countries will not reduce total exports substantially. Most of the imports from developing countries still consist largely of primary products, and much of our exports are to advanced countries.

Unfortunately, the administration is strongly committed to trade liberalization, and it will be difficult to cancel agreements with other countries. American unskilled workers will be fortunate if the growth of manufactured imports from developing countries slows down. On the other hand, the government may recognize that imports have contributed to the disaster of the inner cities. It is also possible that the government will abandon the myth that displaced unskilled workers find new jobs after they are properly trained. Policymakers may realize that welfare reform and training programs will not deal effectively with poverty and the associated problems of drugs, crime, welfare, and homelessness. They may understand that the benefits of trade liberalization do not compensate for the costs of these ills to the victims and to society as a whole. The realization may persuade the government to increase the protection against imports manufactured by unskilled labor.

A public employment program will be needed to make a substantial additional reduction. The Federal Civil Works Administration (FCWA) of the New Deal, which paid wages to unemployed workers whom state and local governments put to work, is a useful precedent. These governments and the federal government can employ more workers in hospitals, parks, highway departments, schools, sanitation, sewage, and in the conservation of natural resources. Excluding teachers, these activities employ 3.4 million workers.[51] A new FCWA might make grants to the state and local governments which would enable them to raise the number of workers by 10 percent, and the federal government might increase its employment in similar activities by the same percentage. An increase of employment of close to 400,000 would reduce the unemployment rate by one percentage point. The 10 percent figure is arbitrary. But the governments may not be able to add significantly more people without incurring additional costs of administration and supervision, resulting in intolerable waste. Larger increases may be considered because the combination of more import protection and the proposed increase in public employment will not achieve the goal of increasing the employment of unskilled workers by two million.

To avoid drawing workers away from industries employing unskilled workers, the program should not pay its workers higher wages. The average hourly earnings of production workers in the apparel industry is about $7.00. The lowest wages earned in the industry may not be much above the federal minimum wage of $4.25. Without any allowance for materials or overhead, the cost of employing 400,000 workers at $5.00 per hour plus fringe benefits will come to $5.2 billion. Adding overhead and materials costs will raise it to about $7 billion.

The government might decide not to cut imports from developing countries and to rely entirely on a public employment program to provide jobs for the two million unskilled workers who are unemployed because of the fall in demand for their labor. In that case, the cost will be about $35 billion per year. Because there is no prospect of the number of unemployed unskilled workers declining in the near future, the program will have to continue indefinitely.

Unions representing public service employees have opposed programs that employ welfare recipients. There is a danger that local governments will take advantage of them to replace employees with low-wage workers. Implementing the proposal may require rules designed to protect public service employees.

I do not propose that the government undertake construction projects, which are expensive. The ratio of total expenditures to payroll for highway construction is about 5:1. Other types of construction, including bridges, water, sewer lines, and utility lines entail similar or higher ratios. Moreover, such projects not only would have to pay workers union wage rates, but also would require the employment of skilled workers. On a massive scale, such projects would raise the wages of skilled construction workers, and they would probably also inflate the prices of construction materials. The nation may need to improve its infrastructure, but public works projects of this type should not be undertaken for the purpose of employing unskilled labor.

CONCLUDING REMARKS

The long-term program must be directed at raising the number of disadvantaged youths graduating from college and entering skilled occupations. Toward this end Congress should appropriate funds for vouchers usable in private and in public schools, which would be given to disadvantaged parents. Such a measure may not be sufficient to provide the necessary alternative elementary- and secondary-school capacity to induce the necessary radical reform in the public-school system. Black organizations may have to build their own alternative schools.

Congress should also appropriate more funds for financial assistance to disadvantaged students in colleges, professional, and graduate schools. The funds should provide for both tuition and living expenses.

The government should add to the number of unskilled jobs by closing U.S. markets to the products of unskilled labor in developing countries. The federal government should fill the remaining gap in employment created by the decreasing demand for unskilled labor by funding a public employment program.

NOTES

1. John H. Bishop, "Signalling, Incentives, and School Organization," Center for Advanced Human Resource Studies, New York State School of Industrial and Labor Relations, Working Paper No. 94–25, Cornell University, Ithaca, N.Y., October 4, 1994, 2.

2. Ibid., 7–8.

3. John H. Bishop, "Incentives to Study and the Organization of Secondary Instruction," Center for Advanced Human Resource Studies, New York State School of Industrial and Labor Relations, Working Paper No. 93–08, Cornell University, Ithaca, N.Y., January 25, 1993, 4.

4. Ibid., 4.

5. Eric A. Hanushek, "Economics of Schooling: Production and Efficiency in the Public Schools," *Journal of Economic Literature*, 24 (September 1986): 1162–63.

6. James S. Coleman et al., *Equality of Educational Opportunity* (Washington, D.C.: U.S. Government Printing Office, 1966).

7. Hanushek, "The Economics of Schooling," 1159.

8. Ibid., 1161.

9. Ibid.

10. Frederick Mosteller, "The Tennessee Study of Class Size," *Journal of the Future of the Child*, 5 (Summer-Fall 1995): 113–27.

11. Jonathan Kozol, *Savage Inequalities: Children in America's Schools* (New York: HarperCollins, 1992), 118.

12. Robert J. Rubel, *The Unruly School: Disorders, Disruptions, and Crime* (Lexington, Mass.: Lexington Books, 1977), 60–66. Cited by Charles Murray, *Losing Ground: America's Social Policy 1950–1980* (New York: Basic Books, 1984), 173.

13. Estimate based on enrollments of alternative schools as reported in New York City Board of Education, *Directory of the Public High Schools 1994–95*, 58. Alternative schools designated as "Total Educational Option Schools."

14. The author conducted a survey of tuition fees by telephone. The estimate of enrollment is based on information supplied by Robert A. Annucci, Deputy Superintendent, Office of Catholic Education, Diocese of Brooklyn, New York.

15. John E. Chubb and Terry M. Moe, *Politics, Markets, and America's Schools* (Washington, D.C.: Brookings Institution, 1990), 32–33.

16. James S. Coleman, Thomas Hoffer, and S. B. Kilgore, *High School Achievement: Public, Catholic, and Private Schools Compared* (New York: Basic Books, 1982).

17. Paul T. Hill, Gail E. Foster, and Tamar Gendler, *High Schools with Character* (Santa Monica, Calif.: Rand Corporation, 1990), 17–18.

18. Anthony S. Bryk, Valerie E. Lee, and Peter B. Holland, *Catholic Schools and the Common Good* (Cambridge, Mass.: Harvard University Press, 1993), 304–5.

19. Hill, Foster, and Gendler, *High Schools with Character*, 17–18.

20. Andrew M. Greeley, *Catholic High Schools and Minority Students* (New Brunswick, N.J.: Transaction Books, 1982).

21. Karl L. Alexander, *Comparing Public and Private School Effectiveness: Evidence and Issues* (Baltimore, Md.: Johns Hopkins University Press, 1984), 8. Cited by Myron Lieberman, *Privatization and Educational Choice* (New York: St. Martin's Press, 1989), 203.

22. American Federation of Teachers, *Myths and Facts about Private School Choice* (Washington, D.C., Fall 1993), 9.

23. Robert A. Annucci, June 10, 1996.

24. Letter from Robert A. Annucci, February 7, 1995.

25. Based on *Directory of the Public High Schools 1994–95*.

26. Hill et al., *High Schools with Character*, 22.

27. Ibid., 23.

28. Ibid., 24–26.

29. Bryk et al., *Catholic Schools and the Common Good*, 128.

30. Hill et al., *High Schools With Character*, 15.

31. Bryk et al., *Catholic Schools for the Common Good*, 69.

32. Hill et al., *High Schools With Character*, 16.

33. Ibid., 19; Bryk et al., *Catholic Schools for the Common Good*, 111.

34. Chubb and Moe, *Politics, Markets, and America's Schools*, 212–15.

35. Deborah Meier, *The Power of Their Ideas* (Boston: Beacon Press, 1995), 53–55.

36. Sam Dillon and Joseph Berger, "New Schools Seeking Small Miracles," *New York Times*, May 22, 1995, B4.

37. Meier, *The Power of Their Ideas*, 91–104.

38. New York City Board of Education, *Directory of the Public High Schools, 1994–95*, 58.

39. Hill et al., *High Schools with Character*, 30.

40. Meier, *The Power of Their Ideas*, passim.

41. Ibid., 50–51.

42. Dillon and Berger, "New Schools Seeking Small Miracles," B4.

43. New York City Board of Education, "The Class of 1994: Longitudinal Report," 13.

44. Hill et al., *High Schools with Character*, 31–32.

45. Ibid., 9.

46. Richard F. Elmore, *Community School District 4, New York City: A Case of Choice*, Center for Policy Research in Education, Office of Educational Research and Improvement (Washington, D.C., December 1990), 21.

47. Board of Education, "The Class of 1994," 6.

48. Elmore, *Community School District 4*, 21.

49. Sam Dillon, "Friction Over Experimental Academies Rises Along with Change," *New York Times*, May 25, 1995, B6.

50. The following is largely based on American Federation of Teachers, *Myths and Facts About Private School Choice* (Washington D.C., Fall 1993).

51. *Statistical Abstract of the United States 1994 (SAUS 1994)*, table 494, p. 319.

Index

About the Author

DAVID SCHWARTZMAN is Professor of Economics at the New School for Social Research in New York City. Dr. Schwartzman has researched and written extensively in areas related to economic policy, and his publications include *The Decline of Service in Retail Trade, Oligopoly in the Farm Machinery Industry, Innovation in the Pharmaceutical Industry, Games of Chicken: Four Decades of U.S. Nuclear Policy* (Praeger, 1988), *Economic Policy: An Agenda for the Nineties* (Praeger, 1989), and *The Japanese Television Cartel: A Study Based on Matsushita v. Zenith.*

ISBN 0-313-30166-2

9 780313 301667

HARDCOVER BAR CODE